FOR THE LOVE OF THE GAME

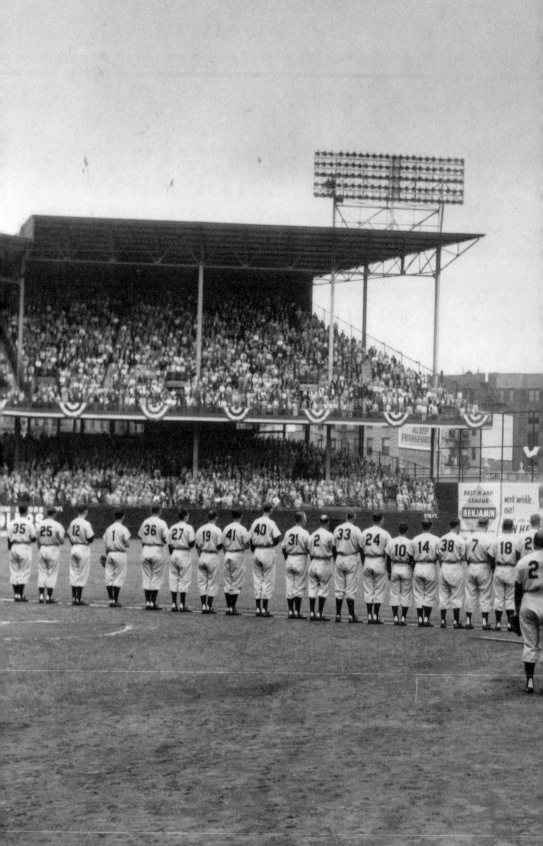

FOR THE LOVE OF THE GAME

Baseball Memories from the Men Who Were There

CYNTHIA J. WILBER

William Morrow and Company, Inc.
New York

Photographs on pages 34, 52, 61, 70, 79, 87, 106, 122, 130, 146, 156, 166, 175, 191, 208, 216, 224, 233, 246, 256, 262, 269, 277, 285, 291, 301, 309, 323, 331, 338, and 346 courtesy Cynthia J. Wilber.

It is the policy of William Morrow and Company, Inc., and its imprints and affiliates, recognizing the importance of preserving what has been written, to print the books we publish on acid-free paper, and we exert our best efforts to that end.

Library of Congress Cataloging-in-Publication Data

For the love of the game : baseball memories from the men who were
   there / [edited by] Cynthia J. Wilber.
      p.   cm.
   ISBN 0-688-10613-7
   1. Baseball—United States—History.   I. Wilber, Cynthia J.
GV863.A1F67   1992
796.357'0973—dc20   91-31089
                                                                       CIP

Printed in the United States of America

First Edition

1 2 3 4 5 6 7 8 9 10

BOOK DESIGN BY BERNARD SCHLEIFER

*This book is dedicated to
the ballplayers*

ACKNOWLEDGMENTS

THE WORK of this book included conversations over a two-year period of time with the ballplayers themselves, their wives and families, sportswriters, historians, baseball executives, scouts, coaches, managers, clubhouse men, groundskeepers, and a multitude of fans. This book could not have been written without the kindness and generosity of the men and women of major league baseball. Specifically, the project could never have been done without the help of my father, Del Wilber; Frank Slocum of the Baseball Assistance Team; and Joe Garagiola. They answered my endless questions, created open doors wherever I went, and provided two years of encouragement. This was indeed a team effort.

Special thanks are also due to Steve Geitschier at *The Sporting News* and Patricia Kelly and Thomas Heitz at the Baseball Hall of Fame for their help with the archival photos. My own photos could not exist without the expertise of George Young and Tony Coluzzi.

The tapes, transcripts, and photos produced during the course of this project will be donated to the Baseball Hall of Fame in Cooperstown, New York.

CONTENTS

Introduction   11
Joe Garagiola   15
Joe Black   27
Ted Williams   37
Chuck Connors   47
Birdie Tebbetts   55
Ben Chapman   63
Roger Craig   73
Frank Crosetti   81
Clem Labine   89
Al Rosen   97
Ralph Branca   109
Bobby Doerr   115
Jesse Flores   125
Jim Delsing   133
Johnny Vander Meer   141
Marty Marion   149
Monte Irvin   159
Norm Sherry   169
Tom Poholsky   177

9

Contents

Tommy Lasorda 185

Al Kaline 193

George Kell 201

Johnny Pesky 211

Terry Moore 219

Al Lopez 227

Del Wilber 235

Mel Parnell 249

Don Lenhardt 259

Bob Kennedy 265

Alex Grammas 271

Frank Robinson 279

Red Schoendienst 287

Preacher Roe 293

Robin Roberts 303

Bubba Church 311

Warren Spahn 317

Stan Musial 325

Harry Walker 333

Clyde King 341

Larry Doby 349

Sid Hudson 355

Yogi Berra 361

INTRODUCTION

Pursuing a dream is an act of faith. Achieving a dream is nothing short of miraculous. This book is about a select group of men who lived out their dreams: the ballplayers of the forties and fifties. Their stories tell us what it was like to live the dream.

THE BOOK BEGAN with my childhood in the major league ball parks of America. For myself, my brothers, and other baseball kids, the parks were our playgrounds, our home turf, and the adults in our lives were America's ballplayers. The sights and sounds of the ball park and the nagging smells of popcorn, hot dogs, beer, and sweat mingle together in our memories of the way it was.

In August 1989, I wandered the infield of Fenway Park with my youngest son and looked long and hard at home plate, my own childhood picture of where my father worked. I sat behind home plate in the old wooden seats, the same seats I had held on to learning to walk in 1952. My memories were of a baseball childhood as well as another time in American history when heroes were important and plentiful and America as a nation had dreams. I wondered as I sat there what it must have been like for those men, the ballplayers, to have reached for a dream and gotten it.

By September 1989, the idea had become a project and had taken on a life of its own. Between October 1989 and May 1991, I traveled more than seventy thousand miles to destinations that ranged from elegant hotels in Manhattan to rural Alabama, from West Plains, Missouri, to the Siskiyou National

11

Forest in Oregon. Everywhere, I was received with kindness, generosity, and the warmth of the extended baseball family. On more than one occasion, the door would open and I would hear, "Why, honey, you've grown!" These men and their families shared their memories, their photos, and their lives with a spirit of generosity that made this book possible.

As the book progressed, I realized that the history I was chasing was my own. It struck me how interwoven the baseball families were when I would walk into an unfamiliar living room in a town I had never before visited and find photos of myself and my brothers playing with other baseball kids, photos of birthday parties in ball parks to motels, photos of baseball barbecues and spring training, of kids and pets and packed station wagons. Photos of baseball families making do.

Writing *For the Love of the Game* had many unexpected bonuses, many friendships rediscovered and poignant memories that were little gifts of history. But the real bonus was spending time with my father and his friends and getting a glimpse of their experiences. The hours I spent sitting in the kitchens, dens, offices, and gardens, listening and talking of times past, of dreams come true, of joy and elation, and of loss are memories I cherish.

The men and their stories evoke memories of long train rides, twenty-one-day road trips, teams that felt like families, and ballplayers who played because of a passion for the game. It was a time before players had agents, before "lockouts," a time of real grass and wooden bats and chewing tobacco. America had just emerged victorious from World War II; democracy, family values, and an American way of life were dreams shared by millions. Baseball was the national pastime and ballplayers were heroes.

The questions I asked stemmed from my own questions about what makes baseball so important to this country. I asked these men why and how they pursued their dream of baseball; what it was like to have that dream become reality; what it was like to suddenly find themselves the heroes of a nation; and what happened when it was over.

Their answers are personal, introspective, and often funny. Their stories are their own, but together they begin to give form to the bigger questions of pursuing dreams and seeking out excellence and why it is that we love baseball.

Bart Giamatti wrote in *Take Time for Paradise:*

> Much of what we love later in a sport is what it recalls to us about ourselves at our earliest. And those memories, now smoothed and bending away from us in the interior of ourselves, are not simply of childhood or of a childhood game. They are memories of a time when all that would be better was before us, as a hope, and the hope was fastened to a game. One hoped not so much to be the best who ever played as simply to stay in the game and ride it wherever it would go, culling its rhythms and realizing its promises.

Perhaps the American love for baseball is about hope and simply staying in the game. It is also about chasing your dreams. Most important, baseball is about real people, young boys leaving small towns with nothing more than a glove and hope and finding themselves under the bright lights.

Let there be long slow summer games
on real grass and Georgia clay
with wooden bleachers and no damn DH

RICK WILBER

JOE GARAGIOLA

Joe Garagiola caught from 1946 to 1954 for the Cardinals, Pirates, Cubs, and Giants. His baseball life started on the streets of St. Louis with his boyhood pal Yogi Berra. After a successful playing career, Garagiola became a broadcaster and later the host of NBC's *Today* show. His book *Baseball Is a Funny Game* remains one of the best-selling baseball books of all times. In 1991 Joe Garagiola received the Ford Frick Award from the Baseball Hall of Fame for his contributions to broadcasting.

BASEBALL STARTED for me like it starts for anybody else. You start playing on the street. You dream that you're somebody. I dreamed that I was Joe Medwick. So did Yogi, who was not Yogi in those days, but Lawdy. Dizzy Dean was everybody's hero. But in the neighborhood I grew up in, soccer was our main sport. It was really an economic thing—one ball and twenty-two kids could play. We never played real baseball when we were growing up, it was always softball or a game called Indian Rubber which we could play in the street.

Yogi and I lived on the Hill, an Italian neighborhood in St. Louis. And the focal point of that neighborhood was the church. Everything was in Italian which was unfortunate because our mothers and fathers never really got to learn the English language. They would go to the grocery store and order in Italian. They went to church and the sermons were in Italian. In fact when I went to school I thought the other kids talked funny.

Yogi's brother Lefty was probably the best Berra player. Can you imagine a better hitter, a better clutch hitter, than Yogi? Well, his brother Lefty was a tremendous hitter. He was our

15

Stan Musial, Joe Garagiola, Yogi Berra, 1960

guy. Yogi's brother Mike was a third baseman, a lot of glove, who wasn't as good a hitter as either Lefty or Yogi. And they had this team and that was how we got to watch baseball. We got exposed to baseball by Yogi's brothers. We got our bats when those guys would crack them and then we would fix them up.

I believe that when you're born you're given two gift certificates by the Lord. One of them is for a dream and the other one is for ignorance, but the good kind of ignorance, where you don't know why you did it but you were too dumb to realize the situation so you went out and did it. My dream was to be a major league baseball player. Well, it's very naïve, very young, very immature, very dumb, to place your eggs all in that basket. I didn't say, "Well, what if I don't make it?" That was the furthest thing from my mind.

The way it happened, we were in a YMCA and Uncle Joe Causino would organize leagues and it would either be baseball in the summer or soccer in the winter. Yogi was always the best player.

Kids are the most honest people in the world and when we were growing up I had no problem with Yogi being the better player. How could I be jealous of Yogi? I mean from day one every time we chose up sides, the first words were always, "I'll take Lawdy." And if Yogi and I (or Lawdy and I) were on the same team, forget it. There was nobody in our neighborhood who could beat us. But we usually played against each other.

We both played in that league and we never had uniforms. We'd always hear the other teams, especially the ones with uniforms, say, "Watch out for the dago kids, they'll steal your bats." We were stereotyped even then. But that's how we started playing baseball.

During vacation time we'd always sit on my steps or at Yogi's house, but our real central meeting place was in front of Ben Pucci's house which had a lamppost; we'd always sit there at night. Anyhow, this particular day we were sitting on my front porch. There were about six or eight of us and we were trying to figure out what we were going to do for the day. A kid named Pete Fasani came by and said there was a league being started and some big-league players were going to give a speech. The only problem was that this was happening in Sherman Park, which was way in north St. Louis, and we didn't have any cars then. In fact, there were only two cars on the whole block.

Anyhow, Pete Fasani said, "Come on, hitchhike, or ride your bikes." What bikes? We only had two bikes. It's like the story of the fish and the loaves of bread—what're you gonna multiply the bikes or something? So we decided to hitchhike there so that we could get some autographs. We really wanted to see John Berardino, who was one of the players. And the other one was an infielder named John Lucadello. We went all the way out to Sherman Park and it was a long way. And this fellow who was talking to the kids before he introduced the two major leaguers said, "I've had these camps all over the place," and he was going on and on encouraging us, "and I look at this group and I think out of this group there'll be two of you who will some day be a big leaguer." And we thought, "Yeah sure, we'll be big leaguers. We'll be like Papa, we'll be working at the shoe factory."

They announced that you could sign up and play in this league and they were gonna have tryouts. The way they had tryouts was they gave you a piece of canvas with a number on it and you pinned it on your back. You took five swings and these men would be off to the side and they would pick their team. We thought, "What the heck have we got to lose—we're here." Well, of course Yogi hit and he got picked and I hit and I got picked.

At that time they had scouts, not like they have now with computers and all that, they had bird dogs. And there was a man who used to always sit in the stands who turned out to be a scout for the Cardinals, and his name was Dee Walsh. He was an old outfielder. Sometimes he would be the only guy in the stands. As a kid growing up, you heard about so-and-so being discovered by a scout and you always thought that a scout was a guy who drove up in a big Cadillac, who had a big, long cigar and a lot of money coming out of his pocket. Well, this guy just sat there; he was rather nondescript and he suggested that I become a catcher. He kinda talked me into it and one of the reasons he did was because I got to wear equipment. I thought it was really neat to be able to put on shin guards and all that. So I became a catcher and Dee Walsh would constantly be offering me suggestions.

One day he asked me if I wanted to make some extra money. He said, "Why don't you come over to Public School Stadium where they have a tryout camp and I'll introduce you to Walter Shannon and Gordon McGuire." My job at the tryout camp was to watch the bats when they went to lunch. And they gave me a couple dollars just to sit there. Well, that was tremendous. Then one day Dee said, "How would you like to work out at Sportsman's Park?" I thought that would be just great, because as far as I was concerned, Sportsman's Park was the Vatican. It was a dream place that I heard described on the radio.

In fact, being in the broadcast business I think one of the things that television takes away from us is our imagination. I used to sit there and listen to France Laux, the St. Louis radio announcer, talk about things like bulging biceps. I didn't even know what a bicep was. A bicep to me—what is that, a girl's bicycle? I didn't know. Finally someone told me what it was and I pictured these big arms on a strong guy.

We had a widow lady who lived next door to me, across from Yogi, and she was a big baseball fan. And she would take a couple of guys each week to the ball park. And what we did to earn that was to do errands for her. Her name was Dominica, and she would take us to Sportsman's Park and she would pay for us on the bus and we would ride it all the way to Grand Avenue. Then we would take the streetcar. And we'd always jockey to sit on top because that was the view. That was the first Yogi Berraism I heard. Yogi said, "I ain't goin' up there, ain't got no driver." Anyhow, we went and we would sit in left field. That was the closest we could get to our hero, Medwick. In those days when the game was over there was a gate between third base and the left field wall where the people could walk across the field and leave through right field. And the standard rule with the guys was when you walked across that field you scooped up a handful of dirt and you put it in your pocket. And then that night we'd sit by Pucci's lamppost and say, "Man, there it is—that's Sportsman's Park." It was like the Holy Grail, you know.

So when Dee Walsh asked me about working out at the ball park, I was ecstatic. He asked if I had any equipment, and I said that I did. Well, I didn't have beans. So I went back to the Hill that day and I said to the guys, "They're gonna let me work out at Sportsman's Park. But I've gotta get a catcher's glove and I gotta get shoes." In my neighborhood you couldn't ask your father for shoes that you couldn't wear to church, but we hustled around for some equipment. I got Bob Berra's shoes and they were so big that we stuffed cotton up in front so they'd fit. And Skinny Causani had a Walgreen's glove. I'll never forget, it was a light green, like a pukey green, and it was a terrible-looking glove. But I knew it was a catcher's mitt because it was big and different from a finger mitt. So I took that and

Lord knows I didn't know anything about sanitary socks or an athletic supporter or a cup or anything like that.

I took this little old brown bag and I met Mr. Joe Sugden. Joe Sugden was an old catcher and he sat up in the stands— he was in his seventies then, I guess—and he chewed tobacco. He had false teeth and when he chewed they clacked. He had these big, thick glasses on, and when I walked up the steps at Sportsman's Park, I was scared to death. This gruff voice said to me, "You Dee Walsh's kid?" And I thought, "Oh my God. What have I gotten myself into?" I said, "Yessir."

He turned out to be a beautiful man. Everybody loved Joe Sugden. And the first thing he did for me was to say, "Come on, let's go in the clubhouse." I was thinking this guy was a mean old goat and that I wasn't going to be able to do anything right for him.

When we went into the Cardinal clubhouse, I started almost trembling. I looked at those names like Terry Moore and Max Lanier. Sugden said, "Dress here, kid." It was a back anteroom. It was like a storeroom and there was a nail to hang your clothes on. In fact, when I played for the Cardinals I referred to that as the "donkey room" 'cause that's where they put the donkeys and when you tried out that's what you were, a donkey. I started to get dressed and I kept looking at the pants Sugden gave me to put on. They were Mickey Owen's pants and it was Bill Crouch's shirt. I put them on, and, man, I couldn't believe it! I didn't have high sanitary hose, I just had regular sweat socks and I put those on and then I put on the shoes that I brought—the ones that didn't fit. Well, when I came walking out, those front spikes were staring me in the face like little Dutch-boy shoes. Joe Sugden said to me, "Hey, kid, those shoes fit ya?" I said, "Yessir, they feel good." "You're a damn liar," he muttered. I thought, "Oh, this guy is awful." He told me to come with him and asked me what size I wore. Well, I didn't know, I really didn't. I always wore either my brother's or my uncle's shoes when I had to get dressed up. Sugden told me to take some shoes and they were Max Lanier's. They didn't fit me too well and I was terrified to be wearing Lanier's shoes. So we went over to Terry Moore's locker and I put Terry Moore's shoes on and they felt great—I mean, how could they not?

When I was all dressed, he said to me, "Come on, I want you to catch this guy that's out here. You think you can catch him?" I didn't know who the guy was and he started throwing and I didn't have a sponge for my catching hand. I didn't know about sponges at the time and I was catching with this little Walgreen glove. This guy was throwing hard and he hollered, "I flicked my glove. That means it's gonna be a curveball." I could at least expect it to go crooked instead of straight. I was catching this guy and I could feel my hand puffing up. But it really didn't hurt because I was in Sportsman's Park. I was warming up in front of the Cardinal dugout. I couldn't believe it. Now I didn't know if this fellow was getting upset or what, but he seemed to be picking up speed. He was really gunning it to me and I'd never seen curveballs break like that.

Finally when this fellow was about finished Joe Sugden said to me, "You know who that fellow is?" I thought he was another donkey like me. But Sugden said, "That's Jack Kramer of the Browns." I couldn't wait to go back and tell the guys. I had a terrible time getting the glove off my hand because it was so swollen. He let me hit some balls and I ran around the bases. I mean it was like Peter Pan. It was Joe Garagiola in Wonderland.

Next they sent me to Springfield, Missouri. This was 1941. And Yogi was playing American Legion ball. Mr. Rickey sent me down to Springfield, and my job was to catch batting practice and help the groundskeeper whose name was Bill Wolf.

Musial had a big year in Springfield in 1941 and part of my job as the assistant groundskeeper was to wash the sanitary hose. So it *is* the truth—I did wash Musial's socks to break in as a fifteen-year-old kid.

The president of the Springfield Cardinals was Al Eckert and at the end of the year he offered me a contract. There was a left-handed batter from Rochester named Hank Raymond and we all stayed in this boardinghouse. I was getting sixty dollars a month and when I told him, he said I ought to get a bonus. And what my brother and I decided to do was to ask for a bonus that was equal to the debt my father had on our house. So I signed that contract and Papa signed it and we got five hundred dollars.

I came back and I told Yogi I had signed this contract and

he was almost broken-hearted that he didn't get a contract. We couldn't understand it either because he was the best player and he should have gotten a contract. Yogi finally got his contract, but contrary to the story about the magnanimous Yankee offer, the guy who never got credit for it was a wonderful man named Leo Browne. Leo was an umpire, but he devoted the latter part of his life to American Legion baseball. He was involved with the Stockham Post American Legion team that Yogi was on. And when Yogi didn't get the contract, it was Leo Browne who said to his friend Johnny Schulte to sign Yogi. Johnny Schulte got a contract for Yogi on the strength of Leo Browne's recommendation.

But the Yankees did not give him "$500 like Joey got" as the papers wrote. They made it a contingency if he made the team. And Yogi's brothers and mother used to send him money with the warning, "Don't let your father find out because he'll make you come home." The Yankees were not that magnanimous.

There's that great Charlie Keller story about when Yogi met Keller in his sailor suit during World War II. Yogi and Charlie "King Kong" Keller were teammates on one of the great Yankee teams and Yogi once said to Keller, "I'll bet you don't remember the first time you saw me." And Keller said, "I really do. You were standing in the clubhouse—standing right in that doorway in the sailor suit." And Yogi said, "I bet you didn't think I was a ballplayer." And before Keller could say anything, the clubhouse guy said, "I saw you and I didn't think you were a sailor."

I go back to what I said originally—my dream was to be in the big leagues and there I was on my way, but I was supposed to be in school. I finally graduated and as a seventeen-year-old boy I played on the Columbus minor league team. Tommy Heath was the other catcher, and we had a lot of good players. Everyone on that team had either been to the major leagues or were on their way to the big leagues. Preacher Roe was on that staff; George Dockins, who went with the Dodgers; Jack "J.D." Creel, who came up with the Cardinals; Pep Young, who played with Pittsburgh; Emil Verban, who was our second baseman; Augie Bergamo, who went to the Cardinals. I could go on and on.

And I had a pretty good year. I hit .293 that year. I turned eighteen in February and the war was on. So I didn't know what was going to happen. The Cardinals decided to send me to Cairo, Illinois, where they were having spring training. I went to spring training, took batting practice, and hung around. Eventually they said I had to start the season, so I joined the Columbus team in Louisville, Kentucky, and played one game. I went back to the hotel and there was a telegram from my brother saying I'd just been drafted. So I went into the war.

That was April 1944 and I went to Fort Riley. I played baseball there which was a great experience for me. I played with guys like Peter Reiser and Lonny Frey, Harry Walker, Murry Dickson, and Al Brazle. Then I went to Fort Knox and then I went on to the Philippines. When the war was over they assigned me to what was like a USO group. Our job was to help entertain the real heros, the guys who came from fighting. They wanted to get home but there was always a lag in processing their papers. So we formed a baseball team and Dick Shawn was one of the entertainers. He was an infielder with the White Sox, and he was really funny even then. We called ourselves the Manila Dodgers and Kirby Higby was our manager. Higby only had two rules for the whole team. One of them was to never bunt—always hit—and the other one was not to hit a triple with him at first because he was gonna stop at second. He was great.

That's what we did to entertain. We'd play games in the morning, in the afternoon, then again at night. We were playing baseball all the time. Joey Ginsberg and I were very close. We were sitting in the mess hall one night listening to the Armed Forces Radio. This guy was doing commentary and he was talking about the Cardinals, saying they had no problems with their catching staff because they had this new young catcher and they were just waiting for him to get out of the Army.

According to this commentator, the new catcher had a rifle for an arm, he had the power of Superman, the speed of a bullet, and he was absolutely the greatest thing you'd ever heard of. I turned to Joey and I said, "Holy mackerel, if this guy is half as good as that big mouth is telling me, I'm gonna be in the minor leagues the rest of my life. I hope they trade

me." How could I have ever imagined that he was talking about me?

Well, the Cardinals ended up selling Walker Cooper to the Giants, and it left this big void. I was supposed to fill Walker Cooper's shoes. Well, that's wonderful, except nobody ever told me with what. On my best day I could never be Walker Cooper. But that's what people expected.

I finally got out on Mother's Day 1946. I worked out at Sportsman's Park about three days, and then I joined the team in Philadelphia. I remember walking into the Bellevue Stratford Hotel. I got there in the middle of the night and the guy at the desk said, "There's an empty bed in Marty Marion's room. Knock on his door and sleep in there." There was no way I was going to knock on Marty Marion's door at one or two in the morning. So I sat in the hallway until he woke up.

A couple of days later I finally played in my first big-league game and what I remember best was that I was so nervous a pop fly went up that was no higher than the ceiling and I really muffed it. An error. Then another pop fly went up back by the screen and there was no way I was not gonna catch that. I caught it and the momentum carried me right into the screen. My face hit it and with all the dirt and the dust, it looked like I had run into a waffle iron. My face was one continuous series of lines. And the rest of it, as they say, is history.

Joe Black, Jackie Robinson

JOE BLACK

Joe Black began his career in the Negro Leagues and pitched in the
major leagues from 1952 to 1957 for the Dodgers, Reds, and Senators.
He was Rookie of the Year in 1952 and pitched the opening game of
the World Series. Black's victory in the World Series was the first by a
black pitcher.

WITH THE BLACK PLAYERS you'll see that our ages will make
a difference when we talk about the dream. My dream was one
thing and Willie's was another; Campy's was another and if
you talked to Bob Gibson his would be another because soci-
ety changed during those years.

Back then we didn't know anything about civil rights—not
even human rights. That was just the way it was. When I was
a kid growing up in New Jersey, I lived with Italian families,
Jewish families, Irish families, and Polish families all around;
we were all poor folks. We were color-blind because we were
Americans. I'd go to a friend's house and spend the night, he'd
come to our house and spend the night. We had chitlins and
greens and when I'd go to their houses I'd eat pasta. We just
grew up that way.

Suddenly one day I found out about baseball. I was ten
years old, selling newspapers. Everyone was listening to the
radio, and I asked this man what everyone was listening to and
he said, "We're listening to the World Series." That was 1934.
I said, "World Series—what the heck is a World Series?" This
man told me that the Detroit Tigers were playing the Chicago
Cubs and the team that won was the champion of baseball.

I went home and I said, "Mom, when I get big I'm going

to be a baseball player." When she asked me why, I said, "They're big shots." I was ten years old then.

Then I started turning on the radio and listening to the baseball games. They'd broadcast from Philadelphia from Shibe Park and I'd hear Red Barber broadcasting from Ebbets Field, talking about the "catbird seat" and all the Dodgers. But my team was the Detroit Tigers and my hero was Hank Greenberg. I decided right then that I was going to be like Hank Greenberg. I'd go to the park and my friends and I would play ball.

We had sticks and balls and we played in the playgrounds. Baseball was my driving force. I'd go to school, make good grades and all because that made my mother happy, but I couldn't wait to play baseball.

I got into high school and went out for the baseball team. I wanted to play and the coach said they needed catchers. They put this mask on me, but I'd never caught before. So they'd throw the ball and I'd reach my hand up and catch it. I did this about three times and then the coach said, "Son, didn't you ever catch a baseball before? That is what the glove is for and when they throw it over to that side, then you move over and catch it with the glove." My hand was so sore.

By the time that I was a junior in high school I was big, five eleven and 180 pounds, and I was playing first base because that was what Hank Greenberg played. Senior year I was bigger yet, six one and 210 pounds, and I was hitting the heck out of the ball. The scouts came; they talked to all the other players and they didn't talk to me. So I went over and I asked one of them, "How come you didn't talk to me? I'm the captain of the team. I hit .400 and those guys didn't hit .400." The scout said, "Yeah, but you're colored, and colored guys don't play baseball." I said, "What are you crazy? I've *been* playing baseball," and he said, "They don't play in the big leagues." I was sure they did, so I ran home and looked at my scrapbooks. I had ten scrapbooks and when I saw that none of the players were colored, I tore up those scrapbooks. Except for Greenberg, I tore everybody up and I stopped talking to all of my white friends. I wouldn't play anymore. I heard a man on the radio who said that baseball is America's number one pastime and I thought, "I'm an American and they won't let me play."

My mother heard all of this and all she said was "Son, don't be talking that way." About a week later, she came home and I was just sitting on the porch. She sat down on the porch with me and said, "Son, I used to come home and you'd never be here, and every time I'd look you'd have on a different base-ball uniform. Now you don't do anything."

"I don't like baseball anymore, because it's not American," I said. She sat me down right there and she told me, "Son, your friends here didn't do this. It's the way it is in this coun-try. That's why we moved here from the South, 'cause you'd have a better chance. In the South it has always been colored and white and you just never knew it."

I sang "The Star-Spangled Banner" and said the Pledge of Allegiance to the flag and in 1941 Kate Smith sang "God Bless America" and I was singing it as loud as anybody. Then, all of a sudden, my dream was shattered.

Fortunately I was big, had decent grades, and I got a schol-arship to a black college in Baltimore. To get away from white people, I went to Morgan State College in Baltimore. It was known as the black Notre Dame of college football. There, my ignorance really showed. At the first assembly program they said, "Welcome to Morgan. Please stand and sing our national anthem." I was singing "Oh, say can you see . . ." and every-body else was singing "Let there be . . ." I had to ask, "What are you singing?" and this girl next to me said, " 'The Negro National Anthem,' " and I said, "There is no such thing." When the assembly was over, she said to me, "You must be one of those dumb niggers from the North."

She was right. She took me to the library and showed me some books. In the Jersey schools all I knew about blacks in books were pictures of black folks bent over and picking cot-ton or singing spirituals. I didn't know the contributions we had made. She showed me books; I started reading them and I began to feel proud of myself. I began to understand what my mother was saying. That I was somebody. My mother had told me that she was somebody but I didn't know what that meant. There at Morgan, I read and my head began to come up off my chest. I began to believe in myself. And baseball wasn't the only thing in the world. At that point I said that I was going to be a doctor, but my fingers would never let me be a surgeon, so then I said, "Well, I'll teach school."

That summer a friend of mine said, "Let's go to the ball game to see two teams of the Negro National League." I had to ask, "What's that?" and he said, "We got our own league because they don't let us play in white baseball." I went to Bugle Field, the ball park, and sure enough, they were out there. Like typical teenagers we were watching and saying things like "Look at that guy strike out, he can't hit." Finally, this fat man behind us leaned over and said, "Hey, where are you guys from?" We were so big and proud that we said, "We go to college." We told him that we went to Morgan. In the end he said to us, the big college boys, "If you're that good, why don't you try out for the team?"

I went for the tryout and I was hitting them and throwing them and they let me start that Friday. I could field well, but I struck out nine times in two days. They summed it all up by saying, "You couldn't hit a bull in the ass if it ran across home plate."

I got drafted into World War II and I pitched at Camp Crowder in Missouri. Tommy Bridges, the old Tiger pitcher, was coaching the team. I went to try out for it and he let me, but some of the players acted as though they didn't want me around, so I just said the heck with it and I left. The next day, two white sergeants came to my battalion and went to the officer and asked for Joe Black. He sent for me and they said, "Tommy wanted to know why you left." So I told them. They said to come back, that he wanted me to pitch. So I pitched for the camp team.

Tommy would say to me "Joe, it's too bad you're not white. You throw harder than most of the guys in the big leagues and you could be taught how to be a good pitcher."

I was pitching against major league ballplayers and I was getting them out, and then 1946 came and Mr. Rickey signed Jackie. In 1946 I was twenty-two, but when he signed Jackie I was ten years old again. Sitting there and thinking, "Hey, *he* can play in the big leagues." My dream came back to me and that was all I was thinking about. I worked hard in the Negro

League trying to learn the mechanics of the game. Jim Gilliam was my roommate and Felton Snow kept telling us, "You young guys got a chance because baseball is opening up now that Jackie is there."

When he was in the Negro League, Jackie wasn't even one of the top twenty players; he was way down the scale but he taught himself, and he had a lot of pride. And those guys kept telling Gill and me, "Take care of yourselves, stay clean, and learn the game." Man, we'd go into cities and we didn't get but two dollars of eating money and Gilliam would be saying, "Come on, let's go," and we'd go and see the ball game. We'd use our eating money to see the game and we'd watch the pitchers and the second baseman. That's all we did.

The dream was there but 1946 went by with nothing happening, and 1947 went by with nothing. Campy left, Newcombe left, Doby and Bankhead went, and finally, in 1949, Gilliam called me and said, "In February I am going to Florida. They just called me and told me that the Cubs bought me, and I'm going up." Then I was really devastated—my best friend! But halfway through the season, he was back with us and when I asked him what had happened, he said, "They told me that I couldn't adjust to integrated baseball 'cause I was a loner."

So 1950 came and that's when I went to Cuba for winter ball. Billy Herman was down there and he was pushing for me but I didn't know it until I got a telegram saying that my contract had been purchased. I called Gilliam in Puerto Rico and he said, "Me too!" Together we went to Montreal. Gilliam was starting at second base and I was the starting pitcher. I won the first three games, then lost two, won two, etc., when Dan Bankhead came and they sent me to St. Paul. My first year in organized ball in the minor leagues, I was 11 and 12, and Gilliam was Rookie of the Year.

Then the Korean War was on, Newcombe was drafted, and the Dodgers had a void to fill. I was in Cuba again and Andy High came to see me along with Buzzy Bavasi and Walter O'Malley. Billy Herman said to me, "This is it. They got the old man here and if he likes you you're going up to the Dodgers."

I pitched a two-hitter and sure enough I went to spring

training and Gilliam went back to Montreal. He was Rookie of the Year and they sent him back to the minor leagues and I went to the big leagues.

In the first exhibition game I was going to start against the Boston Red Sox in March 1952 in Miami. I was on the sideline warming up and I could hear people saying, "Is that that new guy? The guy to replace Newcombe?" So when I started warming up, I didn't pitch like Joe Black, I was pitching like Don Newcombe and people were saying, "Man, he throws hard like Newcombe," and the more they'd say that the more I would rock it.

Campy came by and he said to me, "You'd better save something for the game." And Pee Wee came over and said, "You gonna have anything left for the game?" I told him, "Pee Wee, I haven't even loosened up yet. I'm just rockin' and rolling." When the game finally started, I went out there and I got Pesky out. I walked Bobby Doerr and then Ted Williams came up. I threw the pitch and he followed the ball all the way. Then boom, I threw another one by him and I thought to myself, "Shoot, he can't hit." Then I let my best fastball go and he hit it so hard that it went over Furillo's head and hit the wall. And then Ted Williams had the nerve when he got to second base to say to me, "You're going to do okay, you've got a great fastball." I said, "Yeah, you just showed me." And he said, "Everybody doesn't hit like Ted Williams."

My dream was to be a ballplayer and it was based upon all of the concepts of this nation being a democracy, a melting pot for all creeds and colors to get along together. Job opportunities were supposed to based upon ability and not skin color. That's what I learned in my classes at Morgan, that's what I learned when I had to read the Constitution and the Bill of Rights, and that's what I learned when I sang "America the Beautiful"—because I loved that part where it said "And crown thy good with brotherhood/From sea to shining sea." That felt good in the classroom and to have a chance to play America's number one pastime, baseball, was just like putting the frosting on the cake.

Sometimes people try to equate it to their own experience. They say, "My parents came over as immigrants and we were very poor and so on . . ." but they had one common denominator, they were white. In this country, if you were white they gave you a chance and if you were a minority, black or yellow, they looked upon you as if you had a disease or something. And it hurts. It hurts because we say, "I haven't done anything to anybody. All I wanted to do was live a normal life." And when that is denied, you end up hating and the worst thing in the world is to hate. I knew what hate was when I told my mother that I didn't want to talk to any of my white friends anymore. They hadn't done anything to me, but they were white, and when you hate you lose your ability to think. Thank God for my mother because she started cooling me off from this hatred thing.

When the chance came to have my dream come true, man, it was exciting. My biggest thrill was October 1952 when that guy on the loudspeaker said, "And now, Miss Gladys Gooding will sing the National Anthem." It was the first game of the World Series. I was standing there and Gladys Gooding sang, ". . . the land of the free . . ." and I said to Jackie and Campy, "Thank God for the United States. At least we have a chance to make the dream come true."

I didn't care if I lost or not. Knowing that I was playing in the World Series, that was it. It was my dream and God was on my side and he let me win the game. But standing there were Charlie Dressen and Cookie Lavagetto, and there was Campanella, then there was Pee Wee, Snider, Hodges, Pafko, and then there was Jackie. And on the other side, there were no black faces. You could see the contrast, but you also could see the growth.

When your dream comes true you get new responsibilities. Some people don't understand that if you play something and if you win you have to take on the responsibilities of knowing how to act like a winner. You can't go around bragging. You've got to learn how to be humble, you've got to know how to be appreciative, and you've got to be willing to reach back and help somebody else come up. Even if you lose, losers have responsibilities. Losers have to know how to accept defeat. I didn't know how to accept defeat when I was seventeen. I hated it and that's what most people do when they lose, they hate and they are bitter. You have to learn to ask the question "Why did we lose?" Did we lose because they were that much better

or did we fail to perform in such and such a way? That's what this is all about, because when you dream and your dream comes true and you are content, there is no growth, because you're not passing the baton back to somebody else. It took me a while to learn those things and that part I learned from the civil rights movement.

When I read that Vince Coleman had never heard of Jackie Robinson, I sat down and wrote him a letter and that's why Mr. Coleman ducks me now. I wrote him a nice letter saying, "Mr. Coleman, you may think that you are on top of the world, but if it hadn't been for a man named Jackie Robinson, you wouldn't even be playing baseball. I'm not going to spend time telling you who Jackie Robinson was, but there's a man that sits on your bench every day named Red Schoendienst. Go ask him, 'Who was Jackie Robinson?'" And I said if you don't want to do that, go up to the front office and get the phone number of a man named Stan Musial. He'll tell you who Jackie Robinson was. What you should be doing, and what every black ballplayer should be doing, is saying, 'Thank God for Jackie Robinson.'"

I just feel so grateful that I had a chance to make my dream come true, because so many people have dreams and they just keep dreaming and they die and their dreams were never fulfilled. When you see it come true, it takes a long time for it to sink in. But then afterward, it changes you.

Joe DiMaggio, Ted Williams

TED
WILLIAMS

Ted Williams, the "Splendid Splinter," played the outfield for the Boston
Red Sox from 1939 to 1960. Williams was voted MVP in 1946 and in
1949 and led the league in hitting in 1941–42, 1947–48, and 1957–
58; in home runs in 1941–42, 1947, and 1949; and in RBIs in 1939,
1942, 1947, and 1949. He was an All-Star in 1940–42, 1946–51,
and 1954–60. Ted Williams was inducted into the Hall of Fame in
1966.

IT WAS NEVER really a dream for me to make it to the big
leagues, and it really wasn't a decision at any other time. It
was just something that I wanted to do and that I was happy
doing. I wanted to do it more than anything else and I had the
opportunity and, what the hell, that was it. Even when I started
to progress I didn't realize how I was progressing. Except that
I was getting older and I was getting watched. I felt good about
that. I heard that there were a couple of scouts at the high
school looking our team over. Finally a scout come up to me
when I was sixteen years old and he said, "We have a little
tryout camp and I'd like to have you go on up." This was in
Fullerton, California, and that was on a Monday that we were
going to try out. I weighed about 145 pounds and on the Sunday before the tryout I got hit right on the upper leg with a
fastball from a guy named Tex Rickart. He could throw hard,
jeez, could he throw hard, and he had a heavy ball, 'cause when
that ball hit me it felt like a sixteen-pound cannon hit me. It
went right to the bone and the next day I was supposed to
have my tryout! Well, of course, I couldn't run a lick and I
didn't hit particularly well that day and of course they passed
me right up.

It was a Cardinals camp and the first thing, the very first thing they did was put a big number on your back. There were about five hundred kids there and I was near four hundred someplace. I couldn't run, so it blocked me right out of the picture. It was just as well, because I still had another year in high school.

I played another year of high school ball, then I graduated in June and signed up with the San Diego team. The local team, I didn't sign with anybody else. Detroit was looking at me, the Cardinals were looking at me, and the Yankees were looking at me. They really didn't have a chance. The thing that discouraged my mother was that they said things like "He looks pretty good . . . He's got some good moves . . ." and this would be typical of scouts talking to anybody, whether they liked them or not. Then they would say, "He had some pretty good moves and he swings a bat pretty good, but he's so skinny that I think a year of playing baseball would kill him."

So you know that was that, and I signed with San Diego. That was when I started to eat like I never ate before, because the team had a little account and I could eat whatever I wanted. Then I started to put on some weight, maybe five, seven, eight pounds a year. Three or four years of that and you know I was a bit bigger size and stronger.

I remember reading about it, the ball scores, and it was all in the East, because at that time there was nothing west of St. Louis. New York seemed like it was the end of the world and Boston, God, I'd hardly ever heard of Boston. It's hard to imagine that I finally got signed by the Boston Red Sox.

What happened was Mr. Eddie Collins came out to California and he was going to pick up the options of Bobby Doerr and George Myatt. The Red Sox decided they didn't want George Myatt and they did want Bobby Doerr. While he was out there looking at those two guys, Eddie Collins saw me hitting batting practice. I wasn't even playing. He went to the owner and he said, "Who's that young kid in the outfield? The left-handed hitter?" The owner of the club didn't even know who in the hell he was talking about! He said, "Well, who do you mean?" and Collins answered, "That tall, thin, *skinny*, left-hander." Finally, he decided it was me and he told Mr. Collins, "Hell, he hasn't even played yet."

Mr. Collins told him right then in 1936, "I want first option on that kid." The next year he saw me again and he picked up that option right away. Then I belonged to the Boston Red Sox at the end of 1937. San Diego got a hell of a lot of players in those days for me. They got cash and they got players, outfielders and infielders, and it was a big deal for them. It turned out to be a big deal for me, too.

I was all set to go to spring training with the Red Sox in 1938 after being sold to Boston. But Los Angeles had the greatest storms it had ever had that year—all the bridges were down and everything else. I was supposed to go to Los Angeles to meet Bobby Doerr and we were going to go to spring training together. I couldn't even get to Los Angeles, much less to the East Coast.

I had to wait for about four or five days and finally I could get to Tucson, Arizona. And Bobby could get from Los Angeles to Tucson. We met there and went out to Florida together. I was only there for about two weeks and then I was sent to Minneapolis, which was a farm team for the Boston Red Sox. Boston had a great outfield. Hell, today that would be an All-Star outfield. It was Chapman, Kramer, and Boswick, and that's a great outfield any day. I didn't fit into that, so I went to Minneapolis and I started to develop into the hitter that I was going to become. I was nineteen years old and I was going to turn twenty in August of that year.

I had a big year in Minneapolis and then from there I went to the Red Sox and they had prepared for me because they sold one of their outfielders to make room. I went to Boston and that was it.

When I left San Diego, my family was getting more excited to think that here I was, starting to go. I know they were watching me closely and I was starting to make a little money and of course they didn't have any money. I had to keep in close contact with my mother because I was helping her out. The biggest contribution that I was making at that time was that I had a job—playing ball. My mother was all excited about it but they didn't realize how important it was going to be.

I was never aware of having really made it, I never ever had those feelings. I was a little awed to think that here I was in the big leagues, but I didn't have any dreams about breaking Ruth's record or anything like that. I just hoped that I could do it, that I could perform. I was forever worried about that. Even later in my career, when I shouldn't have had to worry about anything anymore, I never thought, "Hey, I'm in the big leagues now." Hell, I was worried every minute that I was there.

I talked cockier than I felt inwardly. Apparently, I gave the indication that I thought I had it made, but in reality I was worried as much as you could be.

I can't even say that I felt great to get there. I was just there and I was trying to do it and I was worried about what I was trying to do and interested in what was going on. But as far as worrying about my own self, whether I felt good or bad, that wasn't it. I had always had this inner feeling that I wanted to show the other guys how well I could hit. Word was getting out that "jeez, this guy can hit" and I was thinking, "If they think that I can hit now, just wait until they see me a little later." That's the kind of stuff I was thinking.

I don't believe in my heart that I was the greatest hitter, even today. I am one of them, but to say the best hitter, I am not sure of that at all. But the thing of it is, to be rated with, say, the top five or ten hitters of all time, why, I think that's pretty good.

I never realized one bit that I was some kind of hero; I never had those kinds of feelings. I realize now, thirty years out of the game, that there could be a stronger case in my own mind that this hero thing might be true. The thing of it is that I never worried about that. Not a bit. I've got to say that never have I ever refused autographs, unless it was absolutely impossible. I was always kind of flattered. It made me feel good that some guy wanted my autograph.

Why does baseball mean so much and why are ballplayers so important? I sure wish that I had the answer to that. That mystifies me a little bit. But it is a clean game. It's America's game. It's the oldest game in this country. It has such a grab on people that apparently it is pretty near unstoppable.

They have made a few different rules in the game that haven't been altogether good and I think that there are a few circumstances that haven't helped the game. An example of that is that they build ball parks that are absolutely unfair to the batter, and other ball parks where the pitcher has a hell of a time keeping it in the ball park. There should be a medium there that is fair to the hitter and fair to the pitcher. And when that happens, chances of having a good ball game are a lot better than if it is unfair from the start.

The players used to be closer to the fans in the old ball parks and I think that is very important. They have a park in Miami that they are trying to make a major league park out of. And the distance from home plate to the center field seats is something like five hundred feet. Jesus, who the hell wants to sit that far away to see a game? It is important for the fans to be able to see the game and to be able to see the players' faces. Then they might even be able to hear them swear or hear them say something.

When the war came along, I wasn't drafted, I was 3-A, but I was being badgered a lot because I was a ballplayer. The war was on, I wasn't in the service, and all of this and that. Finally, someone found out that there was such a backlog of aviation cadets that if I signed up for that I wouldn't get called for three or four months. It was the perfect thing because that gave me a little more time to play through the summer. It was a great thing to become a pilot, but what I really wanted was to finish out playing that year. I played that year and then, boom, I was in the service with Johnny Pesky.

I didn't get into combat. But it did take a long time. I enlisted in 1942; it took me a year and a half to go through my flight training, then I was made an instructor, and then I went to operational training and was on my way to the South Pacific when the war ended.

I came back in 1946. I was lucky. I was still a young guy and it didn't bother me too much really to get organized again. It took some fellows a long time and some never did come back properly. I think that there were some ballplayers who weren't the same after the war. There were a lot of them that lost three or four of their best years to the war. But I felt I was right at my peak, even though I had been gone. I wish I had had those three years though. I had everything going then, but it didn't turn out that way.

In 1952, I served again in the Korean War and still I felt that when I came back from Korea like, hell, everything was the same. It didn't hurt me then, even though I was older. So I was lucky in that regard.

The science of hitting is more than just strikes and fastballs and curveballs and hitting it here and hitting it there. I think the overall issue was the type of pitcher, and knowing because of his delivery whether he was more inclined to be high or low, or whether he was more inclined to be inside or outside. The overhand pitcher is more inclined to be high, the sidearm pitcher is more inclined to be inside, the sinkerball pitcher is always down, and the high, hard-throwing guy is mostly up.

Here's the thing: All of the fellows that play have ability, a lot of ability. But how does ability apply to it all? This is what I think, a Rod Carew could never hit like a Babe Ruth and a Babe Ruth could never hit like a Rod Carew. So the good coach that can apply this knowledge to a young hitter says this: "You hit according to your capabilities, and if your natural capabilities lean toward a particular type of hitter, then we will stretch that way."

Somebody may not appear to be a guy who can hit a home run, but in fact anybody can hit a home run. I mean unless you are the smallest guy in the league, or the weakest guy in the league, or the scaredest guy in the league. I never knew a hitter who got as much out of himself as he should have. Everybody can improve. To say that hitting can't be improved is a lot of baloney. All you've got to do is sit down and talk to somebody who knows about it.

For instance, Willie Mays doesn't know a lot of things about a lot of things, and when you talk hitting to him, he doesn't know *how* he did it, but he knew what he had to do to hit. When it came to baseball, Willie Mays was a genius. He had the natural instinct.

Even in the case of natural athletes, more can be taught. You can always take what you have and make it better. That is exactly what I am saying about a good hitting coach—he takes what is there and makes it better. He doesn't try to change it into something else. He works with what is there.

When I was playing, the players were closer together and we had a chance to talk baseball more. When you talk about the forties and fifties being the golden age of baseball, all you need to do is look at what percentage of the players during those years are in the Hall of Fame. There are more of them from that era than any other. There were more great players at that time than in any other single era. Now what it was, I don't know, and maybe it was just the next step of development from the twenties and thirties, but if that is true, why didn't it carry on?

There were several factors that hindered the quality of baseball. They expanded the leagues to pretty nearly twice as big, and some of the best athletes started switching over to other sports, like basketball and football. That took a few of the better athletes away from baseball. In addition, you know, there was a period in the early forties and late thirties when the salaries were so poor it was better to be in the minor leagues in some cases. Many good players would have preferred to stay home and play for a lesser salary rather than go to the big leagues and spend more money because they couldn't get by.

When the players stopped traveling together on trains and having roommates it didn't change the game, but it took away the intimacy of the game. You could talk more about it, with maybe the end result being that you would understand it more and devote more time to really and truly looking at how you played or how you hit. If you never talk about it, it is very hard to get inside a lot of stuff.

I didn't work in the off-season, ever, but I probably should have gotten a job the second or third year that I was in the big leagues. The first year at spring training, I had to borrow money to get there. I should have had a job, but I didn't. God only knows what would have happened if I had lost out playing baseball. I don't know what the hell I would have done.

I was encouraged not to get a job by some people. They said, "Don't do anything, don't think about anything except baseball." Well, that was a ridiculous thing to say because we've all got a lot of other things to think about. Baseball is really just a very small percentage of your life, and maybe less than you would like it to be. So you've got a lot of years to do other things and to worry about other things. You had better prepare yourself.

The hardest part of leaving baseball was that I was worried about what I was going to do. I had saved some money, but certainly not enough to live on for the rest of my life. My

last day came, and the very next day I got a telegram from the Sears Roebuck merchandising vice president, Mr. George Strouthers, saying, "I'd like to come to Boston, Saturday morning to talk to you."

I called him and I knew exactly what it was. They wanted me to go into their sports department, and that is exactly what I did for the next twenty years. I was with Sears Roebuck. It was a fortunate thing for me because I was making the same kind of money that I was making playing baseball and I was doing something I loved. Sears had a program where they were trying to upgrade everything that they had in sporting goods. So it all fell in line for me. It was another lucky break in my life.

Of course there are a lot of great memories. The memory of my first home run, the memory of home runs in important games, but the thing that is everlasting in my mind and that I think about more than any other single thing, and this is the truth, are the great people that I met in baseball. You never realize it until you are the hell out of there and you are away from them. And then you look back and you say, "Jeez, what a hell of a guy he was."

I look back and I say, boy, what a hell of a guy Vern Stephens was, and a great player. He didn't have quite a long enough career and I don't know why but, boy, I'll say to anyone, look at his statistics—they are pretty good. And then you say what a hell of a guy Del Wilber was, a good catcher and a guy everybody liked. Then I go back and say Johnny Pesky or Dom DiMaggio or Bobby Doerr or Zeke Zarillo or Leon Culberson—all of them were nice guys and good friends—and guys like Tex Hughson and Boo Ferriss and players like Woody Rich and Jim Tabor and Eddie Pellagrini. There were a lot of great guys, it could be a very long list, no question about it.

I don't really know what it is that makes America love baseball so much, but it is our national pastime and the oldest game. It has stayed strong in the minds of the fans—baseball has still got it.

Seventeen-year-old Chuck Connors with the Bay Ridge Celtics, Ebbetts Field, 1938

CHUCK CONNORS

Chuck Connors played first base from 1949 to 1951 for the Dodgers and Cubs. He also played professional basketball for the Boston Celtics after World War II. In 1952 Connors landed the part of a state trooper in a Tracy/Hepburn movie called *Pat and Mike* and began a successful acting career. Connors, who is best known as television's *The Rifleman,* gives credit to his baseball career for his Hollywood success.

IF A GUY GETS into the major leagues for one ball game he can always say he was in the major leagues and that happens to very few people. I was at a baseball card convention in Anaheim a couple of years ago and the fans could ask questions of all sorts and kinds concerning baseball. I would take the humorous ones and give Campanella the serious ones. Near the end of it someone said to me, "How many home runs did you hit in the major leagues?" I said two and everybody laughed, and I said, "That's two more than you hit."

The war took up three years of a lot of guy's careers, including mine. I was twenty-five. Nobody complained about that in those years, we figured it was our duty. I was a young and old teenager during the Depression. When I look back at it I can remember good times, but I also remember not eating and my folks scratching for food. While I was in grade school I played ball of some kind every day and the camaraderie within the group of boys made the hard times a lot easier. During the course of those eight or ten years I learned a lot about life and the fun life can be. Baseball surely provided that for me.

I was born in Brooklyn, New York, and I lived in the shadow of Ebbets Field. That's a bit of an exaggeration. I actually lived about twenty blocks from there. But the dream of every kid I knew that played baseball was to play for the Dodgers. And I did for a short, sweet moment. I remember sitting at the Bossert Hotel in Brooklyn in early April 1949 and I was one of the twenty-five guys on the Brooklyn roster. All I could do was sit there thinking to myself, "There are millions of people in the world but there are only twenty-five Dodgers and I'm one of them." A Dodger signed, sealed, and delivered.

You've got to be lucky but then if you are lucky you've got to be able to take advantage of the luck. That's where your talent comes in. I got a hold of a little bit of it, and for that I am very grateful.

I got started in real baseball when I was about thirteen years old. We had played on the streets of Brooklyn stickball and boxball but no organized baseball because we just didn't have the equipment. I was throwing a rubber ball against the wall one day and this kid came by me with a first baseman's mitt and a baseball and a bat, and he said, "Hey, why don't you come out and try out for our team?" I said, "What team?" And he said the Babe Ruth Celtics—that was the name of the ball club. I went down about eight blocks to this sandlot and I started working out with the team and eventually became a part of it.

The coach of that team was a guy named John Flynn and he and his wife could not have children. He was a bank teller at Chase Manhattan and he kept all of us together from 1934 until I left in 1939. He kept that team and our group of kids together in a lot of ways. He was a great disciplinarian. He was about five two, this man, and a dapper dresser. He knew everything theoretically about baseball, basketball, and football. We had a group of thirty-five kids in this club and most of us played all three sports. I got to be really involved with baseball through John Flynn. In 1937 a coach for a Brooklyn private high school, the Adelphi Academy, came out to watch us play a sandlot game and they gave me a scholarship to high school.

Because of baseball I got a good education. The coach we had at that high school was a former Southeastern Conference heavy-weight boxing champ, Hollis Botts. He was a first baseman playing semi-pro ball on the weekends and coaching our team, so I was in good hands both in sports and in schoolwork. After that I got a baseball scholarship to Seton Hall College, which was a great baseball school in those days.

I got signed by the Dodgers just before the war. I went away one year with the Dodgers but they forgot to pick me up on option from a Class D to a Class A, so the Yankees picked me up. When I came out of the service in 1946 I had to go to spring training with the Yankees. Actually, it was with the Newark Bears, which was the number one Yankee Triple A team and they wanted to option me to Beaumont, Texas.

In Triple A ball that one year, because of the war they had to waive you out of the league. That had never been true before and was never again true afterward. But in 1946 that was the way it was and on that waiver the Dodgers picked me up for their Montreal ball club. I went to Montreal for three weeks. At Newark, I had played against Jackie Robinson for a few weeks and then I went to Montreal and played with him. And then they optioned me out to Newport News and I had a good year and played with Gil Hodges and led that league in home runs.

The next year was 1947 and I played in Mobile, Alabama. We won that pennant and went to the Dixie Series and I played there with George "Shotgun" Shuba, and Cal Abrams. From 1948 to 1950 I played with the Montreal Royals. We won the Little World Series and then Brooklyn finally sold me to the Cubs and I went to spring training on Catalina Island. I had a great year in L.A. (.321) and in the middle of the season they sent me back to the Cubs, where I played out the season. That's how my career went. That was 1951.

I wanted to pursue baseball. Hell, I knew that three months after I went with that club in 1937. I mean it was all-consuming. My father never saw me play but my mother was supportive. She used to come out to the games and bring chicken and stuff. She'd walk right across the diamond and the game would stop and she'd give everybody cold chicken and iced tea. She was terrific. My mother saw me play and then she saw me act. She used to go to ball games at Dodger Stadium all the time. She died in 1971 at 6:30 in the morning in her little apartment in L.A. in the valley. She was having her cup of tea at that hour, reading the sports page, and she died. She died doing what she liked.

I remember the trains like it was yesterday. Even with the Cubs we took trains in the fifties. We played cards—hearts— by the hour while we were riding those trains. Clay Hopper was my manager in Montreal. He was from Greenwood, Mississippi, and he could play hearts better than anybody else. Everybody played hearts. Pinochle was for classy people. The Cardinals used to play pinochle; I guess they must have thought they were pretty classy.

I go to ball games every chance I get and when I'm here at the ranch I've got a satellite and I can get everything. That's all I do.

There're a lot of mistakes made by young ballplayers today. I don't think that 5 percent of the major leaguers today can bunt. How hard is it to bunt? Jesus. They take the bat and *shove* it at the ball. You're supposed to use the bat and catch the ball. And I can prove that 'cause I got film where I'm bunting a ball in 16 mm film on Catalina Island in 1951. Three, four bunts, perfect. These young guys if you dare to say anything to them like that, they say, "What do you know, you're an old-timer." Well, what I say is come here and I'll show you.

We had not only "make-up" doubleheaders, we had scheduled doubleheaders. There were twenty-five doubleheaders every year. Everybody played every game and I don't remember that many injuries. Today they've got these sports doctors, the great equipment, the great food, the exercise, these great trainers, the great locker rooms and facilities, the great ball parks, the easy traveling, the great hotels. They should be a lot better than we were. They should be, but, Christ, all I hear today is hamstring and rotator cuff. The most I ever made playing baseball was five thousand dollars but I was grateful, truthfully, to baseball for giving me the stage to move me into show business. It was a real springboard.

I didn't go directly from first base to film. But it was a matter of that old good fortune. I played with the Cubs and they discarded me to L.A., which was right. I should have been sold. I came out here and I had one of the greatest years I'd ever had (.321, 22 homers in 70 games). I was a real showboater and really wild. Now who goes to the games in L.A.? Producers, directors, writers, casting directors. So because of the good year (I couldn't have done that in a bad year) I became a kind of favorite of the show business people, unbeknownst to myself.

In 1951 in late September I got a phone call and the guy says, "Hello, this is Billy Grady, casting director for MGM." I said, "Yeah, you're full of shit." I thought it was a ballplayer playing a prank. He said, "No, Chuck, this *is* Billy Grady. We like your style and we'd like you to come over and test for a part in a movie." I still didn't believe him and I said, "Who the hell is this?" And I hung up. I didn't believe that.

He called me back and he convinced me to go and see him. I got out to MGM and had to take a hard look around at this completely different kind of world. And I was well aware of the fact that my career was getting close to the end with baseball. Anyway, I was in awe of it all. So I went to meet him and he was a very personable guy. He told me about this picture that they had going and said that I had to go and meet the producer.

Now you've got to remember that I was totally naïve about this form of business. Every time I had ever read a movie magazine, they always referred to the producer's office as "sumptuous". So when I went up to meet the producer, he was sitting up in his office, and I was sitting there looking around at this office and thinking, "Jesus Christ, it *is* sumptuous." Meanwhile, he was talking to Billy Grady and he walked around me—around the sofa. I heard his voice but I was not paying attention to him. And heard him say at the end, ". . . so I'd like you to test this young man, but I don't want a quick test. I want you to work him all day." So I jumped right in and said to him, "Mr. Weingard, you don't have to worry about that test. I'll do the picture." Not realizing that he was gonna qualify me. I really didn't know I had to pass a test. He just laughed.

Anyway, I did the test and I got the part. It was the part of a state trooper in a Tracy/Hepburn picture called *Pat and Mike.* The first actor I acted with was Spencer Tracy. As a rookie. And in the same scene right beside him, Katharine Hepburn. And right beside her, Charlie Bronson. It was only a seven-

page scene, but it was terrific. I couldn't believe that I was doing it, and starting with Spencer Tracy. I always tell people that my career went downhill from there on.

But I've been at this for thirty-eight and a half years, and it's all because of baseball. Baseball, if you make any kind of a name, can take you to a lot of places in the world. When I was hitting home runs in the sandlot in Brooklyn somewhere, nobody would have called me to MGM. But that's how I made the transition. Thank goodness that the Cubs had a team in L.A. If I had been playing in Boston, they'd have sent me to Louisville and they don't make movies in Louisville.

BIRDIE TEBBETTS

Birdie Tebbetts caught from 1936 to 1952 for the Tigers, Red Sox, and Indians. He was an All-Star in 1941–42 and 1948–49, and a major league manager for eleven seasons. A career baseball man, Tebbetts has worked in baseball all of his life and still scouts for the Baltimore Orioles.

I THINK THAT MY story can be told in a sentence. I was born into the game. I was born into a baseball family. We were poor but it was right at the height of the Depression, so we didn't know we were poor. I had no father; he died when I was two. My mother worked to take care of the three of us. That gave me much more free time than the average guy would have had. We had to seek out our own recreation and that was the best thing that ever happened to me.

At the time that I was growing up, I had an uncle who I thought was the heavyweight champion of the world. He was a baseball player, his name was Arthur Ryan, and he had played professionally. He had broken his leg before he went to the big leagues, but he became a minor league manager. A cousin of mine played as high up as Rochester. The only thing that I ever remember is baseball. I was brought up with baseball, and I always had a relative to play with.

We had to fend for ourselves. We would get a nickel rocket and tape it up and get a bat from the five-and-dime or a cracked one from a semi-professional team and tape that up. We learned how to tape bats, nail them, and do all of these things. We didn't need any outside help to form a team. I was out of the Irish neighborhood and there was a French neighborhood and a Greek neighborhood and a Polish/Lithuanian neighborhood. We would automatically meet at a certain place on a Saturday and we'd start playing with a five-cent baseball that we had cut open and stuffed with whatever rubber we could get and taped into the shape of a ball.

We lived in a factory city, Nashua, New Hampshire, and in those days the world depended upon the wool and the leather that came out of New England. That was before the unions came in and the wool mills moved to the South. I worked in the factories and I played ball for the factory teams.

The factories had team all throughout the New England area. On Sundays they would have games in what was called the Blackstone Valley. New England was full of wool mills and the owners of the mills were like generals in the army: They wanted the best team and they wanted to win.

One day I got a telephone call from a ball club that I played with in that valley. Hank Greenberg was playing in the valley and he said they wanted me to come down and catch the game Sunday. The guy that pitched the ballgame was Lefty Grove and he was the greatest pitcher in the world at that time. He got ten dollars a strikeout, and if a guy hit a home run they shot off a cannon in this big, open field. If somebody did something sensational they'd run around with a hat and everybody would throw in a nickel or a dime. That was the way that it was played.

I think maybe the biggest thrill that I ever had, and I didn't realize what a thrill it was until twenty years later, was when my high school had played a ball game in this little city of Nashua. Later that day a knock came at the door of our little apartment and there was a man there who asked if my mother were Mrs. Tebbetts. When she said yes, he introduced himself and said, "I am a scout for the New York Yankees and I'd like to talk about your son. My name is Paul Critchell."

The amazing thing to me was in a little tiny town where nobody ever left, a New York Yankee scout came to my door when I was sixteen and I didn't even know that he was the most famous of all scouts. When I finally found out who Paul Critchell was it was years later and that was when I got excited about that visit.

I knew I was going to play baseball, but I didn't know how

or where. However, I did not sign with New York. During my high school years I worked out with the Pittsburgh ball club and with the Boston Braves ball club. They worked out people to find out if they wanted to sign them.

I also worked out with the Detroit baseball team, and Bucky Harris was the manager of the team. He asked me if I would come back to Boston the next time they came into town and be prepared to stay over one night and to have my mother come with me. I was eighteen, maybe only seventeen at that time. I came down and I worked out with them, and as it turns out they had brought people in to watch me. So I signed an agreement to join the Detroit baseball club at the conclusion of my college career.

I wound up going to Providence College, which is fifty miles away from Holy Cross. I was very, very happy with my choice and I have been all of my life. During the summer this contract provided me with X number of dollars to play semi-professional baseball any place they put me. But they intended to put me into the big leagues with Detroit. When I graduated, I joined Detroit, but only to complete a road trip. Then I began my minor league career. It was still during the Depression, and I gave myself three years to get to the big leagues. I had this college degree and I didn't want to be a baseball bum—that's what they called guys who sort of drifted around in those days. But it all came true; I was with Detroit in three years and I didn't leave, except for the Army, for sixteen and a half years.

The first time that I walked on to the field there were five future Hall of Famers on that team in Detroit: Goose Goslin, Hank Greenberg, Charlie Gehringer, Mickey Cochrane, and Al Simmons. I hadn't actually come up to play baseball; I'd come to Detroit to get my tonsils taken out. I went into the clubhouse to work out and after the workout, Mickey Cochrane, who was the manager, asked me if I wanted to catch, and of course I said yes. I got showered and dressed and went out to take infield practice. It was the first time that I caught infield practice in the major leagues in my life, and they did it differently than they did in the Texas league. So I was reaching to catch a ball and the guy who was hitting infield yelled, "Look out!" I turned and the ball hit me right in the mouth. I

just picked it up and gave it to the guy, went into the bath-
room, cleaned out my mouth a little bit, and went ahead and
caught the ball game. I was swallowing the blood the whole
game. After the game they took seven stitches in my lip.

That was the first game I ever caught in the big leagues.
There was no nervousness at all—I was in pain! I kept hoping
no one would know I was hurt. I caught Eldon Auker, I got a
two-base hit, and as I remember, it won the game, but it wasn't
until after the game that I admitted I needed some help. My
teeth were loose and I was bleeding the whole game. You don't
forget a game like that.

Everybody has to go through this and I don't care who you
are—you can think all of the things that you want to think, but
once you get in that uniform and in that clubhouse, you turn
around and you wonder whether you should be there. It doesn't
make any difference what you say or how they write you up;
inside, you wonder, "Should I be here?" What you do answers
that question.

I don't know if that happens the last day that you play in
Triple A or the first day in the majors, I don't know when it
happens. I know that everybody that plays thinks they can make
it and they want to make it. But when they walk out on that
field, I don't care who they are, there is some doubt. You doubt
yourself for a while and then all of a sudden you know that
you are on firm ground and then you become a baseball player.
When you reach the end of your career, that's when part of
those doubts return.

Baseball followed me, sometimes I didn't follow baseball.
I enlisted in the Air Force and before I even had a uniform
they found out that I had arrived in camp, and the sergeant
came and said, "They want you to speak at such and such a
place about baseball." I gave my speech and after it was over
the colonel said to me, "I'd like to have a baseball team in the
camp. Would you put it together?" I told him quite honestly,
"Well, you just don't get five thousand boys and know that
you've got nine ballplayers, Colonel . . ." All he said was, "If
I can't have a good team, I don't want a team at all. It's bad for
morale."

About three weeks later I was sent to Detroit on a recruiting drive for the Air Force. I wasn't even a private. I don't

know what they called me but they gave me a temporary rank and off I went to Detroit. The colonel called me in before I left and said, "I want you to bring me back a baseball team."

So in our recruiting office the first thing I would ask a kid when he came in was, "Do you play baseball?" A lot of kids came in just to talk to me because of the fact that I was a Detroit Tiger catcher. We wound up with the best team in the area and probably one of the two or three best teams in the country. Then I had to do the same thing in the South Pacific.

Baseball life is tougher on the women than it is on the men. You know, it's the old, "See you later, take care of the kids." The price you pay by losing your kids is very high. You have to win your kids back later. They grow up and they go to school and they do all of these things and you don't know it. You're so deep into baseball that nothing in the world really makes any difference. Then one day you wake up.

It is a great life for the guy and if the girl is a baseball woman, it's a good, interesting, life too. You can take the kids to the ball park and buy peanuts and let the kids run around and get to travel some. The guy who marries his hometown sweetheart, that's the guy who is lucky. I don't mean hometown literally—I'm from New England and I married a girl from Vermont. She's hometown, she's not Hollywood, not Broadway. But if you get a "Baseball Annie"—and everyone knows what they are; they are around every ball park in the world— if you get tied up with one of those, it's not going to last too long and you are not going to have very much.

The ballplayers today have to have a seat between them when they travel and the ball club has to pay. That's stupid. I know some agents very well and I like them, but I never can get away from the feeling that the guy has ten ballplayers all making an average of three million dollars apiece. That comes up to a lot of money if he's getting 10 percent of it. That 10 percent that he's getting, he's taking *out* of baseball. It doesn't ever come back. I would rather have a groundskeeper have that extra money than some agent who causes the fans to dislike a kid who's a likable guy. It's just too bad that the money is going out of baseball. I don't care how much an umpire makes, and I don't care how much a baseball player makes, it is still baseball money and should stay inside baseball.

My career is distinguished in certain areas but it is an average career. I played in four All-Star games, but I never really
did anything. I want to be the guy who writes the book about
a guy who didn't do anything. I have a record that can never
be surpassed—it could be equaled but never surpassed. As a
World Series player, I didn't get a hit! I thought all of my life
that I had something else that no one knew about and that
maybe someday I could sneak that into this book that I am
going to write and say, "I am the only man in the history of
baseball who had exactly one thousand hits."

Now that's not very many hits, but at least it was my record.
Until one time I ran into a baseball maniac in Chicago in a
saloon and as we got acquainted he said, "Ask me any question in the world about baseball." I said "What did I hit in
1948?" and he said, "You played for the Boston Red Sox and
you had a batting average of .297." And I said, "What about
Bobby Doerr?" and he went through that. Then I said, "Who
is the only man in the world that got a thousand hits? He's a
friend of mine." He looked at me and said, "That's the first
time that I have been stumped for years."

The next time that I came into Chicago he came up, sat
down beside me, and said, "You're wrong. My son and I went
through the book, player by player, since the beginning of
baseball and there is a guy who played for you who got exactly
a thousand hits, and had you known it at the time you could
have put him up to pinch-hit any time you wanted to get that
extra hit. That was Dee Fondy."

I love baseball and baseball likes me. And that is why I am
still in it. I could retire. I live on a very lovely little island, I
belong to a great little club, all retired guys. They get up, they
play a little golf and they play a little gin rummy, and then
they have their social life. I don't believe I would live a year
doing that. I've reached a point now where I think I'd work
for nothing just so that I had the feel of the game with me.

I never did anything. I didn't hit a home run in a World
Series. My high is always just having been a major league
baseball player and the feeling that I am respected by other
baseball people. That's enough for me. Manager of the Year,
being picked over Bill Dickey and Yogi Berra to catch in an
All-Star game . . . so what did I do, play in this or that ball-

game? The high to me always has been that I am what I was. I don't want to be anything more.

The funniest thing that happens to me is when I am introduced to somebody who is a baseball fan and they say, *"Bernie,* I saw you catch so many times and you were so good!"I just say thank you very much. The guy probably never went to a baseball game that I caught in, didn't know my name—didn't quite get it right. I couldn't have really made too much of an impression . . . "Bernie Who?" that's what I call myself. I don't mind not being Birdie Tebbetts, sometimes I like being "Bernie Who?" I love to talk baseball and if anyone wants to listen, I'm ready.

BEN
CHAPMAN

Ben "Chappy" Chapman played major league baseball from 1930 to 1941 for the Yankees, Senators, Red Sox, Indians, White Sox, Dodgers, and Phillies. He managed the Phillies from 1944 to 1948. During the first All-Star game (Chicago, 1933) Chappy was the first batter for the American League on a team that included such all-time greats as Babe Ruth and Lou Gehrig.

WHEN I GOT STARTED, I was in high school here in Birmingham. My daddy had been a pro ballplayer for about eleven years but he never reached the majors. There was a fellow here in Birmingham named Fred Singleton. He was an all-American tackle at the University of Alabama and he could throw a fastball ninety miles an hour. We were playing a doubleheader and they asked me if I could get Fred to pitch for them. They told me, "If you can get Fred to pitch for us, we'll let you play." So I got Fred and one of the oddities of that game was that since I was playing shortstop, they moved their regular shortstop to right field, and that was Dixie Walker.

I wanted to play ball but my daddy didn't want me to because he never made it. I remember one time he told my mother when I was in high school that if I ever picked up a baseball bat to play pro he'd kill me. He was just kidding, because when I signed a contract he was the first one to sign with me. My whole family was supportive when it came down to it. I had two uncles who played ball also. I grew up in it but I really wasn't all that good; baseball was actually my worst sport. Football was my best sport. I could run a hundred yards in ten flat and that was pretty good.

It was about that time that the Yankees started watching me. They kept after me and that was during the Depression at a time when things were hard to get. My daddy was through with baseball and he was having to work out at the steel mill. So I signed a contract with the Yankees. That was 1928. I graduated one day and went to the Yankees the next. I was supposed to have been a shortstop so I went up to Asheville, North Carolina, and played shortstop, then I went to St. Paul, Minnesota, and played third base, and then to the Yankees and played third base.

I was such a horrible infielder that they finally put me in the outfield. That's true—that's a true story. [Joe McCarthy, the Yankee manager, moved Chapman to the outfield in 1931 because of his extraordinary throwing arm.] Even in the outfield I was a problem because I wore Gehrig out. I was very erratic with my throws.

I ended up my career pitching for Brooklyn after ten or eleven years as an outfielder. I had never pitched in a big-league game, but we ran out of pitchers, so I pitched one day and won. I think I won eight and lost five, something like that, and then Brooklyn traded me over to Philadelphia. They traded me to a man that I'd been on the Yankees with, Herb Pennock. [Pennock was the general manager of the Phillies from 1944 until his death in 1948.]

Durocher was clearly dropping a hint about something. Leo kept saying that I ought to go and that it would be the right decision and so on. So I went on over to Philadelphia and in two weeks time they made me manager. All the good hitters had come back from the war and I didn't have any intention of pitching to Musial and those kind of guys. They would have racked me up but good, so I took myself off of that pitching list. I stayed there four years, then I went into the life insurance business in 1948.

When I finished pro baseball, I finished, yes, ma'am. I came home to Birmingham and coached American Legion teams and stuff like that, but I had no ideas of going back and riding those buses anymore. I had a good job with the insurance company and it sounded like I could stay at home for a while. My wife and I had two boys and this house. So I was very content to leave baseball and live a normal life.

But the memories are still there. There were a lot of good times, a lot of thrills, and a lot of crazy times. I think back then that baseball was more entertaining. We did a lot of amazing things just to keep the fans happy.

I had a race one time with Bill Robinson, the tap dancer. They cooked up a race between me and three ballplayers and Bill Robinson in Yankee Stadium. Bill had already beaten Charlie Paddock, the Olympic champion. [Paddock at that time held the world record for 100 yards.]

They got us out there and started marking lines. Bill's starting line was some twenty-five yards up and I hollered to get him back to the start. They hollered back no, because he wasn't gonna run but seventy-five yards.

"Well," I said, "no wonder he beat Paddock." The officials all laughed like crazy and said, "Yeah, but he ran backward and he was fifty-two years old!"

I've still got the scrapbook here with the story. Robinson ran backward and he let me beat him. We were good friends and I could never have beaten him then. He could fly. He was slim and he could dance bojangles like nothing you've *ever* seen.

I knew that I could beat the other three ballplayers in the race, because I had already beaten them. But the funniest thing about it was when they shot the gun and I looked up and there was Robinson out in front of me and it looked like he was laughing right at me! He had those white teeth and white shoes and white trunks, and I was just trying to catch him. That was the silliest feeling I ever had and finally he let me beat him— I know that. That happened in Yankee Stadium in front of sixty thousand people. It was pregame entertainment. We used to do things like that all the time, have races and other crazy stunts, but that was one of the oddest things that ever happened to me in my whole life.

All those years playing with the greats in New York—it was quite a time, playing with Ruth and Gehrig, and I guess baseball meant a lot to people back then. I played in the World Series and in four All-Star games. I was very fortunate in the first All-Star Game in 1933. I remember to this day when Connie Mack told the ball club in Chicago that if the National League team pitched a right-hander that Averell would start and if they pitched a left-hander then I would start. I was lucky—they pitched Wild Bill Hallahan and I was the first batter ever for the American League in an All-Star game.

I was a major league ballplayer, and I don't know if we were heroes or anything, but back when we had Ruth and Gehrig and all of those people, it was really something. I could run, I could throw, and I could field. I hit over .300 for fifteen years. You don't see many ballplayers today doing that. Baseball was good to me and I was with the best.

I get a kick out this. There is one fellow who was voted into the Hall of Fame who was talking on and on about his record. A friend of mine who is a sportswriter sent me a copy of my record compared to this guy's and he beat me in only one thing, home runs. I drove in more runs, scored more runs, hit better than he did, and did everything else better.

We never made too much money, but it wasn't too bad. I bought a nice farm out here, forty acres out on the highway. I've got this nice home, and all of this came from baseball. And, of course, I was lucky I came under the pension. I was there when they started it in 1946. We were in St. Louis and Harry Walker was named our representative to go to the meeting. And the one thing we all insisted on was that he get us a pension. They got one organized and I think it was a hundred dollars a month at age sixty-five for a ten-year man and fifty a month for a five-year man.

But I almost didn't get into the pension. When we first started, you had to put money in and I gave 'em my check. [Every player that wanted to participate in the pension plan had to contribute $250 to start the fund.] I never will forget that after they accepted the pension plan, they wrote me a letter and told me that since I had not been an active player on the first day of the season I was no longer eligible for the pension. I had seventeen years in the big leagues and they said I couldn't get in.

That was a time when I blew my top. So I went down to Florida and saw Charlie Seger who was one of the instigators of the pension plan. Charlie said, "We're going to get you a pension." I said, "Charlie, I don't care if you get me a pension or not. I'm going to make my own pension in the insurance business." By that time I was really angry. Charlie said they were going to have a meeting in Miami in December to talk about four managers—Durocher, Southworth, Eddie Dyer, and myself. They were going to arrange it so that all of us would get our pensions. They went down there and they voted us in.

You know, I managed Harry Walker and I never will forget how he got the nickname the Hat. He'd take his hat off before every pitch. He was getting a little attention; Harry was always a little bit of an extrovert, and he took advantage of it. Pretty soon it got to where he was taking his hat off every chance he got. But the fans loved it and it was all part of the way that baseball was at that time.

When I joined Philadelphia, I picked Bubba Church up in the bowling alley out here in Birmingham. He told me he was a baseball player and I didn't believe him. I owned the bowling alley down here and he came in my office and introduced himself and he said, "I'm a baseball player," and I said, "Who said so?" and he answered me, "I did." That's how that monkey got in baseball. Of course the Phillies at that time couldn't even throw the ball around the infield. I had to draw diagrams to show those turkeys how to throw. But I took him to St. Petersburg with me and we signed him and we've been friends all these years since 1944.

I had fun playing ball, but I was a reprobate, a maverick. I haven't changed and I'm not going to change until they put me under. But baseball itself has changed. One of the reasons that baseball changed, at least partially why, is that we stopped riding trains. The companionship and friendships ceased when the trains were abandoned.

When we got on a train for a long trip nobody went straight to bed. We either went to the smoker or the dining car and played cards. I recall playing hearts with Ruth and Gehrig and we'd talk baseball all night long. Every time we'd go on a road trip we'd hit the train and Ruth would have the porter bring a card table and he'd set a fifth of whiskey right on the table. He could drink and the rest of us couldn't. We'd play hearts until midnight, that was McCarthy's deadline. I never will forget the Babe, he'd get so mad. We'd gang up on him, you know, give him the queens and he'd blow his top. You know, if you haven't played hearts, then you've never had any fun. Red Rolfe used to play pinochle. He was the only guy I remember who played anything but hearts, and he died early didn't he?

When you put in seventeen years, you cover a lot of people, but the one that I think I respected the most in all of those years was Herb Pennock—he was the number one man in my book. Herb was a Hall of Famer and a really nice gentleman. He lived in Kennett Square, Pennsylvania, out on a farm. Everybody respected him and that's why he got the job as general manager of the Phillies.

There were several writers that I respected a lot because they always told the truth. Frank Yeutter at the Philadelphia *Bulletin*, Frank Eck and Joe Reichler, AP/UPI writers, they were all good friends of mine.

I didn't run around, I didn't drink, and I don't know if that helped me or hurt me. I wouldn't go out and go to bars and sit around and drink. What I got in trouble for was speaking my mind and there are plenty of people around who would be glad to tell those stories.

The closest friend that I had was Dusty Cooke. Did you ever know the story on Dusty? Dusty and I had played in the minor leagues for the Yankees, and we were going to spring training together. Dusty was a left fielder, he got hurt, and they put me of all people in left field. I took his job. Then he went into the Navy and when he came out I saw him in Columbus, Ohio. I asked him, "Dusty, what can you do decent?" and he said he was a trainer. He'd never even gone to college, but he'd become a trainer in the Navy. So I said, "Okay, you are my trainer." He was a dandy too. I got Dusty in there and he was my closest friend, and then I made him a coach.

The greatest ballplayer I ever played with was Babe Ruth. There is no question about that. The Babe was wild, let's put it that way. They had no rules for the Babe. I'll tell you how good a team they were that won that pennant in 1932. The first five hitters in the lineup are in the Hall of Fame. You can't name another team all playing at the same time like that. It was Sewell, Combs, Ruth, Gehrig, and Dickey, every one of them in the Hall of Fame. And there's another fellow that should be, Lazzeri.

The biggest thrill for me as an individual player was in the 1932 World Series when they walked Bill Dickey to fill the bases with two outs. The score was tied in the sixth inning and

then they got to me and I said, "Dear Lord, please let him throw a fastball . . ." and he did and I got a base hit. That was the biggest thrill I ever had.

When I was with the Yankees I stole sixty-one bases in one year and those fans in New York had never seen that happen. Nobody had been stealing bases—I think twenty was about tops. The fans liked me for a while, then they got to where they didn't like me, but it was a good career. I enjoyed every minute of it. I have no regrets. I don't look back on it sadly. There were a lot of things I did that I should have done the other way, but at the time I did them my way.

I don't know what constitutes a good manager and I played under a bunch of them. Why, I played with one manager who drank whiskey every night. But maybe managing will drive you to drinking. A lot of players drank too. Lefty Grove and Lloyd Waner, who played for me his last year in Philadelphia, and who I played with in 1938 both kept a bottle of whiskey in their lockers. They always said, "Well, I can't play without it." Waner admitted that he couldn't hit unless he had a drink of whiskey, whereas Ruth did his drinking after the game.

Ruth was a good friend in the outfield, too. I'll never forget when I moved over to center field. All the Babe would do if they hit a fly ball is yell to me, "Come on, Chappy, come on, Chappy."

ROGER CRAIG

Roger Craig pitched in the major leagues from 1955 to 1966 for the Dodgers, Giants, Cardinals, Reds, Phillies, and Mets. Sitting in his office in the clubhouse of the San Francisco Giants, surrounded by the paraphernalia of baseball and pregame activity, Roger recalls his life in the world of baseball.

MY DREAM STARTED BACK in my hometown of Durham, North Carolina. Ever since I can remember, I used to be kind of the leader and go around and pick up kids to play ball. I started in elementary school then I played in junior high and high school. I was an infielder, then a shortstop. When I played American Legion ball, I started pitching, only because the pitcher got hurt and I had to pitch the game. Then I pitched in high school the last year. The reason the scouts even saw me was that we had a pitcher who was really outstanding named Julius "Doc" Moore. He's still one of my best friends. They'd come to see him pitch, but I'd be in the lineup instead and that's how I got scouted.

You know the movie *Bull Durham?* Well, that ball park is where I played my high school and American Legion baseball, right in that ball park.

I was one of ten kids. My dad never made more than thirty-five bucks a week in his life and raised ten kids. How he did it I don't know. In my world the major leagues were right there in my hometown of Durham. To me the Carolina League was the major league. I never really thought about the Dodgers or the Yankees or the big leagues.

73

We couldn't get in the ball games, so we'd go and stand outside and catch the foul balls that would come out of the ball park. If the ball was a really good one we'd keep it and not give it back. But they had a rule that if you'd bring a ball back to the gate then you could get in for free and that was how we got to see the ball games.

That's probably how my dream started, catching foul balls out there, just watching baseball and being around it. I used to try to be the batboy and stuff like that.

It's ironic, but in high school I was a lot better basketball player than I was a baseball player. I was offered a lot of scholarships to play basketball. I was big for back in those days and I ended up going to North Carolina State on a basketball scholarship. But when baseball season started my first year in college, I just got the itch—I wanted to play baseball. So I had a long talk with my dad. I wasn't doing too well in school; all I was interested in was sports. He said, "Well, my dad wouldn't let me play when I was growing up. I didn't get a chance to play, so I'm not going to stand in your way. If you want to go, go ahead." Since then, I've always said that going to college interfered with my education, so I stopped and signed a baseball contract.

I signed with the Brooklyn Dodgers who at that time had something like 450 minor league players and twenty-five farm clubs. Brooklyn was one of the great clubs at that time. People would say to me, "You're not going to make it to the major leagues." But I really never thought about that. Once I got down to spring training and started pitching and watching those other guys, I realized I was just as good as the guys who were there and I decided I could make it.

Back in those days, spring training included ten Class D clubs. It was really the rookie league, but some D clubs were better than others. I was on one D club to start with, and every time I pitched against another D club, if it was in a higher league, why, the next day I would be on that club. I'll never forget, there were so many players there, my first number was 231.

I don't think that I was ever a lazy person, but I just kept saying, "Do guys really get paid for doing this?" When I signed at that time, they had a rookie rule that if you got *more* than six thousand dollars then you'd stay on the big-league ball club. But I got six thousand even. That meant they thought something of me, but they could still send me down. So I started at the lowest level.

I started in Class D at Valdosta, Georgia. I led the league in strikeouts, bases on balls, and wild pitches. I played the next year at Newport News and then I was drafted and went into the Army for two years. I was fortunate that I was stationed at Fort Jackson in South Carolina, where we had a really good baseball team. A lot of guys had been drafted right out of the major leagues. I made that team and I got a chance to pitch to guys like Frank "Pig" House, Haywood Sullivan, and Ed Bailey. All three of those guys had already played in the major leagues and were great major league catchers. They were the ones that gave me the confidence. They convinced me that I could pitch in the major leagues. They were the ones that really got me over the hump and made me believe that I could be a major league ballplayer. That was 1952 and 1953.

In 1954 I came out of the service and I was playing basketball the last night before I was to go to spring training. I was intercepting a pass and a guy tripped me and I fell and broke my left arm.

My mother took me to the doctor that night and I told him, "I've got to go to spring training tomorrow, so just wrap my arm up and I'll have the doctor there check it out." The doctor didn't want to do that. He knew it was broken, but I talked him into it anyway. I went on to spring training and never told them a thing about it. I didn't tell anybody for two weeks. I was exercising and trying to pitch. I remember when the catcher would throw the ball back to me, if he threw it too hard I would let it go or I'd catch it bare-handed, and finally he asked me, "What's wrong with you?"

After about two weeks it got to where it hurt so bad that I had to tell them. I had a little fracture to start with and by then it was really big. Anyway, they set it for me and sent me back home. That was 1954, and I ended up going to three different clubs. I went to Elmira, New York; Pueblo, Colorado; and back to Newport News, where I really had a good year. I was 11 and 2 and I won three or four games in the playoffs. The next year I jumped from that Class D league all the way to Triple

A, which was hard to do. I was 10 and 2 in the middle of the year, got called up to Brooklyn, and Tommy Lasorda and I were on the same team.

I saw my first major league game in 1955 and I was the pitcher. I had never even seen a game! The first time I walked into a major league park it was Ebbets Field and I was the pitcher. I didn't have a chance to sit back and get scared. They just threw me right into the fire and I happened to pitch well. I pitched a three-hitter.

When I walked into that Brooklyn clubhouse there were guys like Duke Snider and Jackie Robinson and Pee Wee Reese and Roy Campanella. All of my idols and I couldn't believe it. I had to tell myself again and again, "I'm as good as these guys. I can play with them."

I'll never forget, I pitched a really good game and as the game was over Walter Alston, the manager, came up and asked, "Are you married?" and I told him, "My wife and baby are up in Montreal." Walter said, "Well, you won't be pitching for four or five days. If you want to fly up there, pick them up, and drive them back, then you can do that." I had to ask around how to get to the airport and Jackie Robinson said, "Come on, kid, I'll take you." He took me to the airport, and what a conversation we had! We talked about baseball and what it had taken for him to get to the major leagues. How tough it was and what I had to do off the field. I'll never forget that as long as I live. Jackie really gave me a break. I found out later that he lived in Connecticut and he went way out of his way to take me to the airport.

I had never been to New York before, never seen a subway, never seen a major league ball park. The only major league ballplayers I had ever seen were in spring training. I had never been with a major league club in spring training; I was always with the minor league club. So when I was called up, I was in awe. I had heard of these guys, but to be there with them, you are talking about a dream. Then we went on and won the World Series.

I won a game in the World Series and when I went home to Durham they paraded me through the town. I was sitting in the back of a black-and-white 1954 Buick riding down Main Street. My mother was in the car with me (my dad had passed away and didn't get a chance to see me pitch in the major leagues) and I was in my uniform because we had played an exhibition game that night. It was a big day, really something special. That was a real dream come true.

We were poor kids when I was growing up but I think we gained from it. My roots and my family are everything. The things I do now are the things that I learned from my mom and dad and I think those things are priceless. You can't even compare that with being rich.

One time my dad told me, when I was about fourteen years old, "Son, I want you to clean the garage today." So when I came home I cleaned the garage. He came home after work and asked me, "Did you clean the garage right?" He went out and looked at it, looked all around, took off his coat, took his tie off, rolled up his sleeves, and started working. He said, "I want to show you something." He started working and I jumped up and offered to help, but he said, "No, I just want you to sit over there and watch." Well, he cleaned that garage so clean, it was spick-and-span. Then he said, "I just want to tell you one thing. The hour and a half that it took you to clean this garage, you wasted that hour and a half. If you are going to do something, then do it the best way that it can be done, no shortcuts."

There he was, a guy who had worked all day long, had ten kids to feed, and he came home and took the time to teach me that. Many times I saw him come in after work and my mother would have supper ready. He'd come in and she'd shake her head no to him—really quietly—and he'd say, "Oh, I'm not hungry tonight, I just had a sandwich, I'm not going to eat tonight." Then he'd go out on the porch or something and he'd rock. Because there wasn't enough food for him. For our Sunday night suppers, and I never will forget this because I thought it was the greatest thing in the world, we had peanut butter and crackers and water. That was our meal. I used to look forward to it, I loved it. On the weekends we didn't have any lunch, but out behind our yard was a big orchard and my brothers and I would go out there and eat pears and apples. Those are the things that you take with you for the rest of your life.

My wife and I have been married forty years this year. We

got married when I was in the Army. I was getting paid eighty-eight dollars a month and we lived off of the post. How we did that I don't know to this day. We had our first child in the service and then after that I was playing ball. She raised four kids, taking them out of school, traveling across country, renting houses, and living the baseball life.

One time, in 1959, I still had a bad arm and we were sent to the minor leagues. We were in Vero Beach, Florida, and I got sent to Spokane, Washington. That's over three thousand miles away and my wife was seven and a half months pregnant. The manager told me, "You've got to take the train or the bus or whatever it takes to get there," and I said, "Listen, my wife is seven and a half months pregnant. I can't let her drive all the way up there by herself." He only said, "Well, you *are going* to pitch opening night." I said, "I'll be ready."

We drove straight through, and at the end of each day's driving I would stop on the side of the road and she'd drive the last five or six miles while I would run alongside the car—to stay in shape. Then we'd stop, eat dinner, get up early the next morning, and go. I was there to pitch opening night in Spokane.

Baseball is a simple game, but you can see something new every game. During the course of a game, nobody, including my players and coaches, walks in front of me because I don't want to miss anything. If you observe you can learn something every game.

It's a very demanding job and a very demanding life. I've been in baseball forty-one years. But it's still fun, otherwise I wouldn't be doing it. I know if I were retired or out of baseball I would be teaching young people, because I like it. Coaching and managing are the next best thing to playing.

My players are like my kids. It's tougher nowadays to manage; I've got twenty-five sons out there in the clubhouse and they are all different. Back in the old days a motivating speech was "Hey, kid, today you're going to pitch and if you don't pitch well we're going to send you to Double A!" That sure motivated me! If you tell kids that nowadays, they call their agent. Today you've got to stroke 'em and tell good things. They don't want to hear or read anything bad. I try to be *so positive* with them. No matter how bad a day they've had, I'll

find something positive to say to them about their performance. Then we can talk about what they might have to work on. I tell these young guys today, "You are the luckiest young people in the world, playing a game that you'd play just for the fun of it and becoming some of the wealthiest young people in the world."

But no matter what, this game has just got that magic about it. It is something special. When I was playing with the Mets, we didn't win very many ball games, but when we did win a game at the Polo Grounds, the fans would stand on the side of the street by the clubhouse and chant, "We want Hodges," or whoever until that guy came out and waved to them. It was unbelievable. We were the worst team in baseball and I'd ride in a cab somewhere, run up a tab of twenty or thirty dollars, and when I'd go to pay, the cabbie wouldn't charge. Sometimes I'd go to pay my bill in a restaurant and the waiter would say that someone else had paid my check. I'd ask who so I could at least thank them and the waiter would say, "They're already gone, they left."

I never dreamed growing up in Durham that this was what life could be like. My dad was a great baseball fan, but he never saw me get to the big leagues. Imagine if he had seen me play in the big leagues, or manage in a World Series.

FRANK CROSETTI

Frank Crosetti played shortstop and third base from 1932 to 1948 for the New York Yankees. He was an All-Star in 1936 and 1939. After seventeen years as a player, Crosetti was the Yankee third base coach for twenty years.

I WAS A SICK kid and the doctor told my parents, "You'd better take this kid to the country if you want him well." So they moved to Los Gatos, a few miles south of San Jose. The city of Los Gatos had a ten- or twelve-acre plot where the sewer plant was and they gave my dad the land for taking care of the sewer plant. My dad cleared the land; he cut the trees down and dynamited the stumps. Then he raised vegetables, corn and tomatoes and potatoes, and all of that stuff.

As kids, going to grammar school, my brother and I would have to irrigate. We would let the water go in four or five rows so it would take longer to get to the end and we would go over to an empty field and play one-a-cat.

One-a-cat is a game every kid knew. We'd have home plate and then so many feet off we'd put a rock for a base and that'd be first base. The fellow hitting the ball would hit one and the fielder would have to get that ball and come back to home plate before the batter got to the base and back to home plate. We played three outs that way. I'd hit until my brother could get me out three times and if he didn't get me that would be a run. We used the big end of the corncob as a ball. We had a bunch of corncobs and when they dried they'd get hard and we'd chop the big end off. For a bat we'd get a board and whittle it down on one end to make a handle.

81

Babe Ruth, Frank Crosetti, 1931

When I'd go to school, I'd be the first one there. I'd get there early with a ball and a bat and I'd be waiting for all of the other kids to come to school because I wanted to play. At lunchtime I'd have a sandwich in my left hand and I'd be trying to catch the ball with the other hand. After school I never wanted to go home. I'd be the last guy to leave the grounds. That's how much I wanted to play.

In the summertime we would pick prunes in the valley. It was full of prune orchards and miles of apricot trees. We'd pick prunes and have prune fights and we'd pick and cut apricots. The kids would all be around a big tray where you cut the apricots. The woman who leased the orchard was there at the apricot table one day and she was asking us what we wanted to be when we grew up. I was waiting for her to come to me, and as soon as she said, "Frank, what do you want to be?" I said, "A baseball player!" I was maybe nine or ten years of age, so you see it was in my mind even then to be a baseball player.

We moved back to San Francisco when I was in high school because my brother wanted to be a druggist and he went to the University of California to study. I went to Lowell High School and I played a little bit for the school team and started playing semi-pro. Those days in San Francisco there were a lot of leagues and a lot of teams.

There was this kid living on our block who was playing for a team called the Portola Natives and he asked me if I wanted to play with them. I was thirteen then. We went out to the Jackson Playground in San Francisco and he told the manager about me. They asked where I wanted to play and I said anywhere. I just wanted to be able to play. They put me in left field and I played for the Portola Natives that summer. By the time I was fourteen, I was playing for several teams in the area.

At fifteen, I was going to Lowell but I didn't want to study. I didn't want to go to school anymore at all, I just wanted to play ball. One time I cut school for two weeks. I used to go out and watch the San Francisco Seals (who were in the Pacific Coast League) during the day when I was supposed to be in school. Then I'd come home after the game. Finally they caught up with me and my mother got pretty upset.

I quit school and went to work down at the produce market. I had been there for about a week when this kid came along (I was sixteen years old then) and said, "Do you want to go to Montana and play ball with me?" and of course I said yes as quickly as I could. We were to get two hundred dollars a month and that was in 1927. The other guy's name was Joe Guerrero and he had been to Montana before.

My mother didn't want me to go. Montana Power was the big utility company up in Butte, Montana. There were three teams in Butte and one in Anaconda, and my mother absolutely didn't want me to go because in those days if you played any kind of sport you were a bum. So Joe Guerrero came over to our house to try and convince my mother to let me go to Butte. My dad was a big man, 240 pounds, and he was in the doorway taking it all in while they were talking. Finally I guess he'd had enough. He stepped into the room and he said, "Let him go," just like that. So I went to Butte when I was sixteen.

We were supposed to work for the power company, but we only worked about two weeks. They were building a big dam up there and Joe Guerrero and I cut pipe. We cut it all different lengths for about two weeks and that's the only work we did. We played twilight ball, so we'd begin at five or five-thirty during the week, and then we would play on Sundays. I stayed there until Labor Day and then we barnstormed home with a bunch of kids that lived in the area. Five of us came home in a car together and we played ball all the way down.

I was supposed to be in school still because I wasn't eighteen yet and I had to go to school part-time for a while. In the meantime, I got to play bush ball around town and then I'd go play at YMI, the Young Men's Institute. We played out at Recreation Park where the Seals played that winter.

I played as much as I could, and I would play for anybody. One kid would say, "Do you want to play in the two o'clock game in Washington Park in Alameda?" and then another kid would want me to play a ten o'clock game in South Side Playground and I would say yes to all of them. I'd go to South Side Playground and play the ten o'clock game as a third baseman. After that game was over, I put my shirt and my cords on, took my spikes off, and grabbed the trolley car. (In those days we bought a pair of spikes and we put them onto a regular pair of shoes.) Then I caught the ferry and then had to get a train to Washington Park in Alameda. I got there just in time for the two o'clock game to start, took off my cords (I had my uniform on underneath already), and in that game I played first base. Do you think any kids would do that today? Well, that's how much desire I had to play ball. I was in the winter league that year and that's when the Seals signed me.

They signed me up in 1927 when I was seventeen. My first year was 1928 and I played for the Seals for four years.

The Yankees bought me in 1930 and kept me out here for another year in 1931. When I was seventeen, the first year, I didn't play much. I was such a young kid that the Seals didn't want to farm me out. I was liable to get sick if they farmed me out to some Class D league in Mississippi or somewhere, so they kept me in San Francisco and I played a few games. They sort of nursed me along. The next year I played shortstop and I played most of the year.

One of those years, we had a catcher by the name of Alex Gaston. He said to me one day while we were working out, "You were born with a silver spoon in your mouth with regards to baseball." Back then I didn't know what he was talking about. But I think he meant that I was lucky to be a ballplayer, that everything was turning out right for me and everybody was taking care of me. I still think about that all of the time. Maybe it was just meant to be, me and baseball.

I was very lucky. I was lucky when I went to the Seals that they didn't farm me out and I was lucky that I went to the Yankees because we had winning clubs most of the time. I went to a wonderful organization and a wonderful manager. I think Joe McCarthy was the greatest manager that ever lived. Maybe if I had gone to somebody else it would have been different but Joe nursed me along too. Some other manager might have said, "Send him out." But not Joe McCarthy; he could tell, so he kept me around.

I didn't get too excited, but that was because I was bashful as a kid. I was too shy to worry about being in the big time. When I joined up with the Yankees, the Babe was still there, and I played with Babe Ruth for three years. The Babe was quite a person and I think he did more for baseball than anybody. It was an honor to play with him and to play with all of those guys. When I came up to the Yankees they were all very nice to me. Bill Dickey and Lou Gehrig were like big brothers to me and I looked up to them. Those were wonderful years.

In 1936, when I drove all the way to Florida with Joe DiMaggio and Tony Lazzeri, it seemed like nobody talked the whole way. Tony and I did all of the driving and when we finally got into Florida one of us said, "How about making the young dago drive?" We said to Joe, "Now you drive." He finally had to say something, but all he said was "I don't know how to drive." That's what he told us and we didn't know if he was kidding us or not, so we drove all of the way. The three of us were very, very quiet, but that's what happens if you put three shy, quiet people in a car together. It stays very, very quiet.

I was very lucky that I didn't get hurt or something because I didn't have anything to fall back on. Today I tell kids to get an education because if something happens to you, if you get a bad arm or a broken leg and you've got nothing to fall back on, you're in trouble. You'd better have something to fall back on.

I was fortunate that they kept me on as a coach and because of that I was in more World Series than anyone—twenty-three World Series, nine as a player and fourteen as a coach.

I've got World Series rings and pocket watches. Pocket watches were what we got originally. Ben Chapman is the one who started getting the rings for the World Series back in 1932 when we played the Cubs. After the fourth game Chapman came around to everybody and asked, "Don't you want a ring?" Chapman was really outspoken and direct. He came to me, and I was just a twenty-one-year-old kid, and he said, "Dago, don't you want a ring?" I didn't really know what to say, so I said, "Okay." Chapman talked to everyone like that, and then he went to McCarthy and told Joe we all wanted to get a ring. Joe said okay and they talked to the commissioner and that's how the World Series ring thing got started. They used to give us all kinds of things. I've got pocket watches and wristwatches and my wife's got a couple of wristwatches. I've got a sterling silver trophy and even some guns from the World Series. They didn't know what to give after a while.

We traveled on trains and I think we were more together

because we had private cars and also a private dining room. The other people on the train couldn't come into our car. We'd eat together and after the game we'd play cards, although McCarthy didn't let you play poker. No poker playing, absolutely. He said there is always a sharpie who might win a lot of money. If we were thinking about winning and losing money among ourselves, then we weren't thinking like a team and our minds certainly were not on the game. McCarthy was right to do that and in those days we weren't making much money anyway, so we played hearts—that he would allow.

There was this one time in St. Louis when we broke his rule and he even knew it. It had been raining for two or three days in a row and so naturally the guys were stir-crazy because they couldn't play ball. We stayed in the Chase Hotel in St. Louis, and some guys had the bellhop bring up a poker table and started playing poker. McCarthy knew about it that time, but he said, "What the hell, it's only one time and it's raining." I didn't play because I didn't gamble at all.

One of my favorite memories of all was winning the World Series in Chicago in 1932. We were going back to the hotel in the bus and we had to have an escort. Crowds of people were everywhere and we were weaving in and out of traffic through the streets of Chicago. As we were leaving Wrigley Field we were singing "On the Sidewalks of New York." "East Side, West Side, all around the town. . . ." McCarthy was in the back of the bus and he'd say, "Sing it again, boys," and with the police escort and all of the people in the streets, we would sing it again. That was my first year in the big leagues and probably the finest day of my life.

CLEM
LABINE

Clem Labine pitched from 1950 to 1962 for the Dodgers, Tigers, Pirates and Mets. Labine was an All-Star in 1956–57 and was renowned for his sinker.

IT'S DIFFICULT AT TIMES to fathom exactly what it is to have made it. In a way, it's sectionalized; there were so many things that happened in my career. There was the time when I believed I might make it and suddenly those hopes were dashed and then I believed I couldn't make it. I was lucky and my hopes all came back again.

In my time I suppose that the nation had taken baseball to its bosom. To go to a ball game on Sunday was like a picnic. It was apple pie and the whole bit and the ballplayers felt that way too; it was a family affair. The ballplayers felt that they were part of that atmosphere. Most of us were coal miners' sons, textile workers' sons, the very definite blue-collar workers' sons. So the faith of the fans was something that they were able to put into us for their own sake. Maybe we were living out their fantasy.

My father was a very hardworking man. He was not the type of father who could leave his job and come see me play. But he gave me the time to play. I am sure that when I was around sixteen it would have been easier to have had me working and bringing some money in. But he didn't do that. He said, "Go ahead and play. I know that's what you like to do, and that is what you want to do." As long as it was sports-oriented, they let me do it. For that I have to be very, very

thankful. As I grew up in the game, it became easier for him to take the day off and come visit, but up until that time it was an outside event for him. Looking into it, but not truly being there.

My father could not have taken me aside and said, "Well, son, here is how you are going to hit the ball and this is how you are going to throw the ball," because he didn't have that ability. At least he left it to the ability of the people who could help me and they did do it. And he gave me the time to try.

My mother was a loving mother. I can give you an example of what my mother was like. We owned a house, but we lived on the second floor and rented out the rest. It was a tenement house. We had an ice-skating pond right across the street—my brother and I were avid hockey fans and we would play even at night. We would come home for lunch or for dinner with our skates on, walking across the street, and my mother would put carpet and scatter rugs all over the place just so we could walk on those things and not take our skates off.

We used to have two radios, the one we had to turn off and another one under the bed that we turned on to listen to the ball games. She knew, but she let us do it.

I played from day one. I always wanted to be a pitcher, even though I played other positions. I played other sports too. I was a hockey player as well as a football and basketball player. But baseball was my sport. My real life. I had a high school coach, and if I had anyone who took an interest in me, a great interest, it was him. He sensed that I had extra talent as far as baseball was concerned, much more than other sports that I played for him. He went along with me through my education and everything else and he's the one who got me scouted.

In fact, my first real scouting took place in the parking lot at a racetrack, and I threw to a person who was a trainer and a scout for the Braves. His name was George Army. George liked what he saw, whatever you can see in a parking lot, and said that he was going to get me a tryout.

My tryout was to be with the Boston Braves, so my high school coach and I went up to Boston. He drove me up there and when we got there the Braves' gate was locked. We couldn't get in. We waited, hoping someone would open the gate for us, and finally someone came by and asked us what we were waiting for. We said we were waiting for a tryout. The guy said, "If you're waiting for a tryout, come on." So we went with him. His name was Charlie Dressen and he happened to be a coach with the Dodgers. I ended up getting a tryout with the Dodgers and not with the Braves. That very night, Branch Rickey, Jr., called my father and said he'd like us to come to New York so that they could speak to me. And that is how I got started. It wasn't a big deal. I got a five-hundred-dollar bonus. But that was right in line with everybody else at that time.

That was when I started getting into the real nitty-gritty. There was Yogi Berra in St. Louis who hadn't traveled anyplace, and Clem Labine in Rhode Island who hadn't traveled anyplace, and all of a sudden you're on a train by yourself traveling someplace. I was seventeen years old, very young. It was a shaky time and I did a lot of growing up in a hurry.

I went into the service right after that. I was young enough so that I didn't lose too much in those war years. I don't think it cost me that much. I went into the service at eighteen years of age and I came out at twenty. I think I grew up mentally and physically and that growing-up period was the best thing that ever happened to me. We were just teenagers and we were thrown in with grown men. There's a big difference between a teenager and a grown man, no matter what your aptitude is.

When I was seventeen I was in Newport News for a very short period of time because I was drafted. I came back in 1946 and again I went to Newport News. But by then things had changed immensely because all the athletes were back. They were older, but they were still pretty young guys and very stiff competition.

That was where I started to learn about life. What it was to be on my own, and what it was to have to relate to a team. To not allow myself to think as an individual or that I was better than the rest. Besides, they would let you know in a hurry that you weren't. And that's how it started. Most of us made our way through the minor leagues. We had to because that was the way it was.

I considered the minor leagues to be the best education that I ever got, and not only in terms of baseball. I got a lot of education in other things through individuals. I don't bleed Dodger blue but I believe in the Dodgers and I believe in their method of teaching. I think it is the best method ever. The people who work for the Dodgers love what they do and it's easy to understand why they want to belong to this group. I know that to have the opportunity at my age to be a part of this in any form, in any shape or manner, is a wonderful thing. Because it reminds me of what I was. It reminds me of being out here.

During that era the minor leagues were a better time and place. We had a close-knit group of young players and most of the time it was such that after a doubleheader on a Sunday we'd have a party. And at the party probably nine out of ten people didn't even drink because we were so young. Any of us that had children had very young children. To be really honest, I think I had a better time in the minor leagues than I ever had in my life. I wasn't so worried about someone taking my place because I was trying to take someone else's place.

Once I got to the major leagues, then the shoe was on the other foot and there was always someone back there who wanted to take my place. So I could never stumble.

We were all wanting to play, more than anything else. We would have played no matter what. The frosting on the cake started when we became professionals. Then there came responsibility, not only for ourselves but for the others that made up the team. All of a sudden it's not your high school team or your college team that you're playing with and it's not the local sportswriter. Now it is national playing and the world is interested.

That was when I had to ask myself some questions: Why am I here? What am I going to do after my career? About the middle of your career, when you know that there is a chance that it is going to start heading the other way, comes a time of a little panic. It is truly tough to bring yourself to the realization that the time is drawing very near.

My entire life changed when I went to Venezuela. The Dodgers sent me there in 1950 to play in the Winter Leagues because they were getting ready to bring me up. When I got down there, it was the first time that I had a chance to really do things by myself, without anybody standing behind me. I tried so many things, and that's where I learned to really come up with different pitches. I came up with the pitch that made my major league career. They call it a split-fingered fastball today. In my day we called it a sinker. From that time on, the difference in my facing batters was astounding. I was a much stronger pitcher after that.

When I went to spring training in Dodgertown [Vero Beach, Florida] I was so confident that I could hardly wait to get there. I didn't care how big they were anymore. It didn't bother me because my pitches were neutral pitches that were good against anyone.

I had a sense of confidence, but feeling like a member of the team, feeling like you belong, is another whole situation. The belonging only happens when the other ballplayers are your friends; then you know that you belong. I joined the ball club in the disastrous year of 1951. But toward the end of the year I was the better pitcher on the club. I had been so well accepted that I just knew that I was going to stay in the major leagues. And fortunately, I did stay. It's never the management really; they are the ones that keep you there, but it's your peers that tell you if you are going to be there.

When I walked into that clubhouse the first time I was nervous. We had a "rookie row," which was a place where you didn't get a stool, you had to stand up, and you had hangers on a pipe. You didn't have a stall. So you truly started to belong as you moved up on the pipe and finally you got to a stall. Then when you got deeper into the clubhouse that's when you were really accepted. I suppose it was building up seniority.

It was a very precarious time and it was a wonderful time. I think sometimes when you live with a little fear, it is better for you. It makes a better person out of you. I don't mean that kind of fear that drives you out of your mind. I mean a fear of not doing well that makes everything flow a little faster, and you end up a little stronger from the whole damn thing because you try harder.

I was an avid reader and I've always been a collector of books. I would never buy paperbacks, I would always buy first editions. Most ballplayers at that time were not regular readers and I had a lot of fellows who used to always come in and tear the last three pages out of my book. They figured that I was reading mystery novels or whatever. I'd never say a word to them and they'd end up saying, "He doesn't even read the book because he never says a word about the missing pages." One of the page tearers in particular was a fellow by the name of Ed Roebuck and finally I said, "Ed, I just want to let you know that they have libraries all over this country. All I have to do is go to the library and I can get the last three pages of the book any time that I want to."

John Podres was one of my roommates and we were great friends. I used to make John cash his check and I would take half of his money and send it home to his mother because otherwise he would have spent the whole damn thing. To this day Johnny says, "That was the greatest thing you ever did for me." I was a year or two older than John, and I knew the ropes a little bit more, so I helped him out.

Al Rosen, Ken Keltner

AL
ROSEN

Al Rosen played third base for the Cleveland Indians from 1947 to 1956. In 1953 Rosen led the American League in home runs (43) and RBIs (145) and was voted the American League's MVP. Rosen led the league in home runs in 1950 and 1953. He is currently the president and general manager of the San Francisco Giants.

I WAS AN ASTHMATIC as a child growing up in Miami, Florida, and one of the things that the doctors insisted upon was exercise. They didn't know all that much about it, but they said to my mother, "Just keep him outdoors." So she kept me outdoors and I gravitated toward balls and bats and things like that. In those days we could play any place. Whether we were playing in the park or playing in the streets, we devised all sorts of ways to play ball.

So I started playing. There was no little league, but in the summer there were park leagues. The kids would go and there was always a park supervisor and teams developed out of that. As we got a little bit older (twelve to fourteen) the teams would get sponsors. Some local guy would give us enough money to buy balls and bats and shirts and caps.

There were parks throughout the city and there was inter-park competition. That was all softball but there was also American Legion baseball. In Florida, we were playing ball of some kind all year-round.

I went to the playground at six-thirty or seven o'clock in the morning, then went home for lunch, played some more after that, and came home at five o'clock in the afternoon. I played all day. The days that we didn't have league games we would choose up teams by throwing up the bat and grabbing it, then we'd grab hands to the top and see who got first choice and that's the way it was.

In the evenings there were Church Leagues and one of the great things for me when I was young was to rush over there before games, when the men would let me go into the outfield and shag fly balls and stuff like that. Then I started playing in the Church Leagues as I got a little bit older. It was a gradual move from one league to another, but all along I had this love of the game and I wanted to play professional baseball in the worst way.

I knew that I wanted it. I can't tell you whether I was fourteen or fifteen or when it was, but I knew I was good. I never thought I was better than anybody else, but I played semi-pro even as a kid. I was just thirteen or fourteen, playing in the men's league and holding my own.

I met this golf pro who lived in St. Petersburg and he knew how interested I was in baseball, so he arranged a tryout over in Bradenton which is right across the bay from St. Pete. The Red Sox trained in Sarasota and had their minor league teams in Bradenton.

I went over to Bradenton one Saturday afternoon with my stuff. The Red Sox were expecting me and they let me work out. I remember that there was a fellow there, the farm director, by the name of Herb Pennock, and he suggested that I might want to join their minor league system.

I graduated from high school and I went to the University of Florida for one year. Then all of a sudden Pearl Harbor came. It was evident to me that I was going to go into the service and I still wanted to play professional baseball in the worst way.

So I worked out with the Cleveland Indians farm club and they offered me a contract for seventy-five dollars a month. I turned that down and I went to Suffolk, Virginia, and worked out with the Red Sox farm club.

The manager there, Elmer Yoder, said to me, "Son, you're never going to be a ballplayer. Go on home and get a lunch pail."

I was heartbroken, but there was a bird-dog scout in Suffolk who was the director of the YMCA, a fellow named Frank Stein.

I went to see him and he said, "A friend of mine down in Thomasville needs a third baseman because his third baseman broke his leg two nights ago."

So I got on a bus and I went down to Thomasville, North Carolina, home of the Thomasville Furniture Company. The whole town was just two blocks long and on the left by the railroad tracks was a big factory with this huge chair on top of it. That was the Thomasville Furniture Company.

I got off the bus and went to a café. I had been told that this was the place to go. It was a typical little town, and I was barely eighteen years old. I had my little bag and my glove was on the outside of the bag because I couldn't get it in with my shoes and stuff. I asked the fellow behind the counter, "Where can I find the manager of the baseball team?" He said, "You a ballplayer, son?" And I said, "Yes."

There was another fellow there, they called him Sailor. Sailor had been brain-damaged at birth or something but he still navigated pretty well. Sailor ran out of the door, came back within two minutes, and said, "Come on with me."

I followed him one block to the town's only gas station, where the manager of the baseball team was putting gas in his car prior to going out to the ball park. That was Jimmy Gruzdis and I signed a contract right then on the back of his glove compartment. We talked for a moment, he asked me what position I played, and I signed for ninety dollars a month. I had really come up in the world. That was the summer of 1942.

I went out to the ball park with him and I was absolutely ecstatic. I put on the uniform of a professional baseball player and played that same day. I got a base hit the first time up. I was off and running and that's how it all began.

But, the lunch pail—that never would have happened. He was wrong, I knew he was wrong, and the bird-dog scout knew he was wrong. He was just wrong. I guess maybe they were a little crueler in those days than they are today. Then it was "Go on home, son," and I'm sure I wasn't the first one who was told to get a lunch pail.

I played that season and then I went into the service. I played a little baseball in the service after I got my commission because they had developed so many ensigns they didn't know what to do with all of us. They sent us from Fort Pierce, an amphibious school, up to Camp Shelton in the Norfolk area and I played some ball there.

At Camp Shelton we had a very understanding captain, a four-striper by the name of Vail who loved baseball. We had professional players like Joe Beggs, an outstanding relief pitcher for Cincinnati; Mace Brown, who pitched for the Red Sox; Tony Rubella, who is now a scout, and a fellow by the name of Whitey Platt. I got a little bit of experience and I got to play against some other teams that had experienced players. That's where I first met Mickey Vernon.

Then I went aboard ship. I was a small-boat officer and went to the South Pacific. We didn't play any baseball, except when we had some time off on the atolls down there and we played another ship. I came back in 1946 and found out that my contract had been picked up by the Cleveland Indians (they had a working agreement with Thomasville). So I reported to camp along with all of the others.

There were so many of us that they put numbers on our backs. I think I was 247 or something like that. We started playing games in the morning and we played morning, afternoon, and night. I was assigned to a C league in Pittsfield, Massachusetts. I played there and found out at the end of the year that my contract had been purchased by Oklahoma City in the Texas League. Cleveland called me up at the end of the 1947 season.

In the spring of 1948 I went to spring training with the big team. When I walked into that big-league clubhouse the first time I felt in awe. Time passes and you can't remember exactly what your feelings were, but when people ask me what my greatest thrill in baseball was I always say it was the first time I put on a big-league suit.

That was the greatest thrill I ever had. I was in back of an awfully good third baseman by the name of Ken Keltner and that was frustrating. But it finally happened for me.

I didn't feel accepted. You can never be accepted when you are the heir apparent to a popular veteran. It is different today, but in those days Ken Keltner had been a sterling performer for Cleveland and very popular with his teammates, and I was not accepted because they knew why I was there. It had to happen; the writing was on the wall. Keltner was getting older and I led every league I was in in the minor leagues. I had had great years everywhere. Fortunately as time went on I became very friendly with a lot of the players, including Keltner and Bob Lemon.

I don't like to make too much out of the difficulties, yet one of the questions everybody asks is: "How tough was it to break in and did you experience any prejudice?" Well, if you can produce well on the field and handle yourself well off of the field, then that breaks down a lot of the problems that would come to someone who was obnoxious off of the field or who didn't produce on the field. So I think that helped me, but to say that I was accepted, no, not at first.

Two things really let you know when you were accepted in those days. One, when you got a lower berth and, two, when you were invited to sit in on the baseball confab in the men's rooms. That was a very big thing. Once you got into the men's room too, it was a very big thing when you got to sit on the banquette instead of standing up. When you were seated at the L-shaped banquette that was it—you had arrived.

When I first reported to Cleveland after the 1947 Oklahoma City season I joined the club in New York and I shared a locker with Ray Boone for two games. Then we went to Philadelphia and I shared a nail with Ray Boone. One nail and it was right by the door. We felt like we were almost out of there.

I don't think that it occurred to me that I was suddenly "there," but I remember the first home run that I hit. It was Opening Day in 1950 when I took over as the starting third baseman for Cleveland. That probably was the most significant event in my career because that won the fans and my teammates, who then realized that I could do something that was important to their success. In those days the higher that you finished the more money you made, and the extra money was very, very important. Even if you didn't win the pennant, you still got a cut of second or third place. I remember I was introduced and ran out to my position in front of fifty-five thousand people, and I can still hear them chanting, "We want Keltner." I hit the home run and the second day I hit another home run in the bottom of the eighth to tie up the game.

Probably more significant was when they moved me from second place in the batting order to cleanup—hitting fourth.

That really signified the approval of everybody, the players, the coaches, the manager, to move a rookie from batting second to fourth.

The friendships we developed during that time were very important. We were all very close. Ray Boone and I roomed together for years and when I found out that he was traded, my wife and I both cried we were so upset. That was the first time that anyone close to me had been traded.

We played every Tuesday and Wednesday night, Thursday afternoon, Friday night, Saturday afternoon, and Sunday afternoon. Monday was usually off and somebody always had potluck. The families got together and I was always included, even when I was single. The wives wanted to be sure that everyone was included; they were always cooking and having barbecues and I was always invited. Like Claire Kennedy, who took care of everybody. All of her little chicks had to come in. There was a great deal of caring and friendship; we knew everybody in our baseball world.

Bob Boone was the first baby I ever diapered. I went over to Ray's house after he was traded by Detroit. Patsy was cooking, Ray had to go out and get something, and Bobby started yelling. He was in his crib and I changed his diaper. Terry Kennedy was just a gleam in his dad's eye when I first knew Bob and Claire. Baseball was a family then. We saw each other's kids grow up and we shared all of that. Today, the players have their briefcases and they get on a plane and they sit there with their earphones. They're very much alone. I don't know how they do it. I don't know how a player goes into a hotel room and is alone all day.

That would drive me absolutely nuts. We needed that companionship. We went out to dinner together. There were always six or eight of us. We didn't have a lot of money but we knew all of the good restaurants and we were always with our teammates.

When we get together now in our twilight years we talk about it. We try to differentiate. We look out there and we see athletes with bigger, stronger, and faster bodies and we see great talent, and then we see other things going on. We have come to the conclusion that in those days, because of our conversations and time together, the knowledge of the game was greater. They just don't understand the game as well as we did. We were defensive specialists and we knew every hitter. We knew the pitchers and how they would pitch. We knew all of that.

I never had anybody tell me to move this way or that way, and I never had to look in and ask, "Should I guard the line?" I see that today with guys that have been in the big leagues a long time. They just don't know that much about the game. I'm not saying that it detracts from the game but the difference between the golden years of baseball and what I see today is a knowledge of the game—the gamesmanship. Everybody then didn't do the right thing all of the time, but by and large, we knew many things because we were together so much.

We were together for breakfast, we were together for lunch, we were together at the ball park, and we were together after the game.

We spent a lot more time in the minor leagues and we were very aware that someone else wanted our job. That's why we never got out of the lineup. The Wally Pipp story was much more prevalent in people's minds in those days than it is to-day. [Wally Pipp, an eleven-year Yankee veteran, left the lineup for one day in 1925 because of a headache and lost his position to an up-and-coming player named Lou Gehrig.] Every club had two or three Triple A clubs and Double A clubs. They had players who could really play, so you never wanted to get out of the lineup. If you did get out of the lineup, somebody could get in and get hot and you wouldn't get back.

One of the reasons, not the overriding reason, but one of the reasons that precipitated my early retirement was the fact that I knew they were going to trade me and I didn't want to wear another uniform. I had been in a Cleveland uniform since 1942. I didn't want to go to any other team to play. I knew that they had a deal worked out with the Red Sox because Hank Greenberg had told me. He tried to talk me into remaining in baseball so that they could trade me. He thought it would be good for me to go to the Red Sox, but I opted not to. I just couldn't see myself moving to another city. I felt so loyal to the team and to the city of Cleveland, I loved it. My children were born there, I was very much a part of the community. I was very active in civic affairs and in business. I just couldn't see myself in another place. The involvement in the community started when I was a player and I stayed in Cleveland during the off-season and went to work as a stockbroker. I was very much a part of, very much aware of my responsibilities to the community.

We have now become a very money-oriented profession and people are going to where the money is. You can't fault that; that's the system and you can't deny the system. If a player is with one club and he has a chance to make a great deal more money with another club, then he'll go. I have read where certain agents will say it's an inalienable right of an American to choose where he works and for whom and that's true. But it's not true and shouldn't be true in baseball, because you owe something to the community.

For the man who decides he wants to work for Boeing and gets a job in Seattle, Washington, as opposed to working for Hughes Aircraft in Texas, that is his choice. But no one gives a damn—he has no fans or public following. However, people do care about Will Clark and whether or not Will Clark is going to remain a San Francisco Giant.

The fans want very much to know that the player is as much involved with them as they are with the player. They want a little piece of the player. They want to be able to see the player, to be able to touch him, talk to him.

I still have people come up to me and say, "You know, I got your autograph when I was in high school, or junior high . . ." Baseball is so much a part of our way of life that people feel very strongly about things like that. That they talked with a major league player, or they were at a banquet with some player, or got the autograph of a favorite player, or their favorite player came out and did some kind of community work and they were there. That's very, very important.

I don't know what is so mysterious about it. There is an eeriness about the feeling that people have for baseball. Why? The only thing that I can think of is that many people think that they could be better than their best hero. If only they had wanted to, or if only their father had let them, or if only they had had a break to get in. They don't really fault anyone for not being that person, but they all feel that they could be better and they all feel that they would never fail in any circumstance. They would never strike out with the bases loaded, they would never miss a pop-up, they would never do any of the things that happen all of the time. They would be perfect. That gives them something, that gives them a feeling about themselves that nothing else can do. It has nothing to do with how much money they have. It has nothing to do with their status in life. It's just that they'd be the tops. That's what it is, they'd be the best.

Old-timers who sit and watch the game can only criticize because they remember themselves as better. Will Clark goes up and strikes out with the bases loaded and forty scouts; guys who have played are sitting up in the stands and they would never have struck out with the bases loaded. Never.

Or a pitcher throws a pitch and somebody hits it out of the park. Those forty guys are sitting there and they're saying, "I wouldn't have thrown that pitch." That's what baseball does to people. Baseball makes perfectionists out of all of us.

It allows the fan to become, for once in his life, top banana. It's part of owning the American Dream. Why do you think wealthy men, who become pillars of the community, very well thought of in their business careers, buy professional baseball teams? Because it gives them a piece of what they could never have. A man might be the top manufacturer of whatever, widgets, it doesn't make any difference, but when he owns a baseball team, then everyone knows who he is. Then he can be at the top. He can sit up and look at his players and criticize them. He's never been on a field, never played professionally, he's never been in a locker room, but he suddenly knows more about the game than they do.

People use the language of baseball to describe their own lives because there is a symmetry to it and there is a beauty to it. The language is beautiful. I am not at all amazed by the kinds of people who want to talk baseball. The President of the United States can talk to a guy who lives two blocks from the ghetto and works as a janitor seven days a week. They can sit down and talk about the same thing—they can talk about baseball. Everybody has played ball—they all know that you swing the bat, you hit the ball, you have to run this way. They aspired and had dreams, and maybe they revel a little in their heroes' dreams. People live and die with the Red Sox up in

New England and there's nothing like a Yankee fan or a Dodger fan. Every time that you do something well in baseball, other people feel like they did it with you. The fan sits there and when you hit a home run, that's what he would have done, and when you don't, it's not what he would have done.

There is a whole aura that has been built up and it all has to do with dreams, it has to do with wants, desires, and love. Think of the weddings that take place on home plate, the children who are named after heroes. Why? I don't know why, except what better thing is there to talk about? What common denominator do we have in this country that is better than baseball?

RALPH BRANCA

Ralph Branca pitched in the major leagues from 1944 to 1956 for the Dodgers, Tigers, and Yankees. He was an All-Star from 1947 to 1949. Branca is perhaps best remembered for pitching the "shot heard 'round the world" to Bobby Thomson in the play-off game in 1951.

IF YOU GREW UP as a boy in America during the Depression, baseball was the number one game and your hero was a baseball player. So, I wanted to be a baseball player. My oldest brother played. He was about fifteen years older and a sandlot hitter—and a very good player for sandlot ball. I believe that he had a chance to play minor league ball but he threw out his arm doing something stupid. He was together with a group of young guys and they were seeing how far they could throw and he ruined his arm. But he had that ability and he was like a second father to me.

I remember pitching to him when I was six years old in the driveway of our yard. Another brother John was a year and a half older and we were like twins we were so close. We had two more younger brothers also involved in baseball. John was a better pitcher than I was, and at one point in time I was a catcher because the Cooper brothers were in vogue at that time. That was probably 1939. I caught and John pitched. Then John was too old to play in the recreational league in Mount Vernon, New York, and I became the pitcher at twelve years of age.

When I went to high school, I was both the younger brother and the second pitcher because John was the better pitcher. In high school, John was number one and I was number two.

Then he graduated and I became the number one pitcher on the local high school team in Mount Vernon. For years I just sort of trailed along behind John to tryouts, but the hope was always there. The Dodgers liked me and had me come back when I was seventeen to throw batting practice. It was almost too much for me. I was just a seventeen-year-old kid and to go throw batting practice for the Dodgers when they were ready to open the season was overwhelming.

The ultimate goal was to play baseball, but then suddenly, because of the war, I was thrust into the big leagues. I had played minor league ball at seventeen, the next year I went to NYU and pitched, then I went to the Dodgers. (I had asked them to release me because I wanted to stay in school and they wouldn't. They knew that I was a prospect. At that point I figured that I might as well play pro ball and I was afraid that the word would get out that there was a pro playing in college.) So I worked out with the Dodgers and Branch Rickey sent me to Montreal, saying if I could pitch for Montreal I could pitch for the Dodgers.

I was eighteen years old and a skinny kid and I ended up playing for the Dodgers. That was very strange for me because my whole boyhood I was a Giants fan. I actually went to see a Memorial Day doubleheader at the Polo Grounds and saw the Giants play the Dodgers and I rooted for the Giants! A week later I was wearing a Dodger uniform. That was 1944. At eighteen, I had become a Dodger; I was in the big leagues and I still did not really know how good I was. I was filled with all of the doubts one has at that age.

I'll never forget the first game I sat on the bench. Hal Gregg was pitching for the Dodgers. He was a rawboned, broad-shouldered right-hander from California and he could throw very, very hard. I sat there on that bench and wondered, "What am I doing here?" (But you know realistically, when I finally became a man and I could throw hard, I could throw harder than Hal Gregg. Not to demean him, but his fastball was straight and mine had a lot of movement. I threw just as hard as Hal and probably a little faster. During that year, from eighteen to nineteen years old, I became a man and then I could really throw.)

Five days later I was in the bull pen, playing at the Polo

Grounds. That was something; I had been a Giants fan my whole life and there I was in the bull pen. I don't even remember who started for the Dodgers, but I came in during the second or third inning and pitched three and a third innings. The thing that really sticks out in my mind was the walk from the bull pen to the mound, which was 455 feet. The bullpen was right at the 455 sign. I felt like I was walking on a treadmill, and it seemed like I'd never ever get to the infield. Pitching my first game was almost euphoric. I couldn't really believe that I was in the big leagues.

Fortunately I pitched well those first three innings, but I was only eighteen and not mature at all. It was like the dream had arrived—there I was in the big leagues. And I kept thinking, "Is this going to last? Is the bubble going to burst?" It did last because the next year I went from throwing the ball in the mid-eighties to throwing the ball ninety miles an hour. I was a late developer and prior to that I was just a skinny kid. All of a sudden I became a man.

They sent me to St. Paul in 1944 when I was nineteen and I came back in the middle of that summer and pitched very effectively for the Dodgers. Of course, when you're young and you have a good fastball you can make a lot of mistakes and get away with it.

The next year I didn't do what I should have done because I got into Charlie Dressen's doghouse. I think he cost the Dodgers a pennant because he put me in the doghouse and I should have been one of his star pitchers. I had made the starting rotation in spring training and got hit in the arm and lost two weeks. I got into Charlie's doghouse because he asked me to throw batting practice and I told him I couldn't make any money throwing batting practice. Instead of him looking at me and saying something like, "Kid, I understand how you feel, just throw it," he took it as a personal affront and felt that I was going against him. It was an unfortunate thing for me and for the Dodgers because that was the year that we tied the Cardinals for the pennant and we ended up losing in the playoff game. He might have been mad at me, but I was good, and I was good enough to start the first playoff game in history. That's my vindication—that I was right and Charlie was wrong. Down the stretch I pitched two critical shutouts in September and kept the Dodgers in the race and then I was chosen to pitch against the Cards in the playoff game.

The next year I went to spring training and not only did I become the starting pitcher but I was the *star* pitcher for the Dodgers. I'm not saying it to have a big head, but I won 21 games and I was inexperienced. I lost a couple of 1–0 games and I lost a couple of games, 2–1 or 3–2. I could have won twenty-five games when I was twenty. I was ranked right with Warren Spahn and Ewell Blackwell the premier pitchers in the league. Spahn won twenty-one, Blackwell won twenty-two, and Larry Jansen won twenty-one. I had the third best ERA, was second in strikeouts, led the league in starts, and pitched 280 innings. Charlie Dressen was wrong; I think I could have pitched just as effectively the prior year.

The thing about it all was that it was during the war and I had an edge. The only ballplayers around were either too young or too old to be in the service. I learned fast how to be a major league ballplayer. I didn't go to the minor leagues, so my minor league training was really in the big leagues. I pitched half a year in 1944 and a half a year in 1945. When all of the players came back from the war, I was able to survive what I consider to be one of the toughest times in baseball, 1946 and 1947. We had a backlog of players who had played and developed while they were in the service. Yet I was able to stay on the club and survive. There were a lot of guys who didn't survive those years.

It was a dream that I got there at all. I was the only one out of the whole family who made it—the tallest in the family, the biggest in the family, and able to throw the ball ten miles an hour harder than my brothers could. I was blessed.

Both of my parents were immigrants. My mother's Hungarian and my father's Italian, and although they knew what baseball was about, it's hard to say if my parents ever really realized how important being a professional ballplayer was. I would think that they were very proud of me. But I don't think they knew the significance of being one out of four hundred big leaguers.

I came from a very large family, six boys and eight girls. Actually my mother and father had seventeen kids. Two died very young at the turn of the century of diphtheria, then one

died when I was an infant and my sister died when I was thirteen, so when I was playing there were thirteen kids in the
family. People knew that I took number 13 because it was the
number of kids in my family.

I played for ninety dollars a month. We all did, but there
was a carrot out in front. Everybody played for no money because the dream was to make it to the big leagues. Baseball
had a grip on the American people.

The thing about baseball in those days was that everybody
played it. Girls played softball; even punchball and kickball
were just variations of baseball. If you didn't have enough
players then you played one-a-cat which kids today have never
even heard of.

The Jackie Robinson story brought a lot of sociological
changes to our country. Because it was up front, a black guy
coming into a white man's sport. That changed America. The
heroes of those years were idolized by children all over this
country. It was a common bond, something that black and white
and rich and poor children all cared about.

When I grew up, I went out of the house every day after
breakfast, then rushed home and had a sandwich and a glass
of milk, and then right back out to play baseball. Now a kid's
life is programmed. The poor kid's got Boy Scouts on Monday
and Little League practice on Tuesday, and dance lessons and
tennis . . . everything is planned for him and he has no free
time to devise and scheme games. No time to enjoy the game
for the game itself.

Little League has its place but I think there is too much
emphasis on winning. The emphasis should be on learning how
to play the game and learning to enjoy it. My first reaction to
Little League was great—the kids are going to play baseball.
But then I went to a game and I heard a mother yelling at her
kid, "If you strike out don't come back." I looked at this poor
little tyke—he was ten years old—he had so much pressure on
him, and then his own mother said don't strike out.

I remember the first time that I had to go make a speech.
It was either a communion breakfast or a little sports award
dinner, and I was eighteen or nineteen years old and not used
to public speaking. I was as nervous then as the first time that
I pitched in the big leagues, but I did it. And I did it because

there was a responsibility. Ballplayers knew that fans bought the tickets and that's how they got paid. The thing that has happened now is that the main source of revenue is not from the fans coming to the game, it's television and the side revenue monies.

I think that guaranteed contracts have changed baseball. The ballplayers' attitude has changed because it's a seller's market; they're selling their abilities and getting paid an awful lot of money. They don't feel that they have any responsibility to act the part of the role model.

For us, baseball was family and there was an incentive to win because if you won the pennant you made extra money and if you won the World Series you made extra money. In 1947, the year the Dodgers won the pennant, I was making sixty-five hundred dollars and my World Series *losing* share was forty-seven hundred, and that was very significant. I think we all pulled for one another because that extra money was there and there was a pride in winning. Winning meant something.

Now, with the big money, there may not be that drive to win. If you're making three million, even if you win the World Series and get a hundred thousand, it's what, 3 percent of your money? I think we pulled together, we lived together, the wives depended on one another. I remember when my wife and I first got married the older wives had gatherings and Ann would go and they'd have showers for one another. There was a friendship there, a feeling that we could all rely upon one another.

Our friendships were very sincere. When we'd take the train from St. Louis to Boston, it was a thirty-two hour ride, so we got to know one another. We'd talk to the other guys. Now they get on a plane and just sit in the seat. They don't go up and down the aisles and talk to one another. They drive to the ball park and then jump in their cars and drive away.

But time and tide change everything. I hate to be an old-timer and say the game is not as good as it was when I played, because that sounds like sour grapes. But in my heart I really believe that the game is not quite as good because the players' attitudes have changed.

BOBBY DOERR

Bobby Doerr played second base for the Boston Red Sox from 1937 to 1951. After his playing career, Doerr coached for both the Red Sox and the Toronto Blue Jays and was elected to the Hall of Fame in 1986.

IT STARTED BACK WHEN I was just a kid growing up in Los Angeles during the Depression days in the late twenties. I was born in 1918. When I was nine or ten years old, I can remember, I'd take a rubber ball and bounce it off the steps on the front porch by the hours because it was fun doing it. As time went by (even when I was playing in the majors) I could see that that had quite a bearing on things because it gave me a rhythm and a feeling. As I look back, it was probably one of the reasons that I got to where I could field pretty well.

Things like bouncing that ball as a young kid are more important than anybody thinks. I talked to Joe Sewell about that one time at Cooperstown. He only struck out three times in a season going to bat over five hundred times, and he did that several different seasons. That's amazing and I asked him what the factor was for striking out so few times. He answered right off, "When I was a little kid going to school, I'd pick up rocks and swing at them with a broomstick as I went along. I'd do that constantly and I think I had excellent hand-to-eye coordination from all that practice as a kid."

We had a playground right near where I grew up and we were able to go over there to play just about every day of the year. There are not too many rainy days in Los Angeles. The professional players who played minor league baseball would

115

Ted Williams, Bobby Doerr

work out in that park during the winter and I'd go over there and shag balls. Baseball was all that I thought about.

My dad was so great about my interest in baseball. During the Depression he had a job with the telephone company. At his job they each took two or three days a week off to keep everybody working so that they wouldn't have to fire people. His income wasn't too much, but we did have food. A lot of kids would come to our place and it seemed like my mama was cooking breakfast for five or six kids all of the time. I look back now, and I realize that it was because a lot of them didn't have food at home. Pop would once in a while buy a kid a glove or a pair of baseball shoes. He was really great and very supportive. He'd always offer to take us to practice or anything like that. My parents would follow me all over to the different places where we played American Legion ball. He'd always be bringing other kids to the game. I have to say, it was a big factor in being able to go on and make it, because they encouraged me and when I got down and things weren't going well, my dad would always have some words of wisdom that would pick me up.

As a young kid I'd have to say that my fondest memory was in 1932 in American Legion baseball when we won the state championship. We went to Catalina Island and I was just fourteen years old. We won the championship on Catalina and we went to Ogden, Utah, for the regionals and won there. Then we went on to Omaha, Nebraska, but we lost the last game or we would have gone to Manchester, New Hampshire, to play in the Little World Series. I look back at that as a real accomplishment.

When I was sixteen I had already been working out with the Hollywood club. They gave me a chance to go out and field during batting practice and they liked what I did. In 1934, in June, we were just getting out for summer vacation and they came by and picked me up and wanted to know if I'd be interested in signing with the Hollywood team in the Pacific Coast League. They gave me a two-year contract, and it was ironclad that they wouldn't send me out. I thought that was pretty good and all Pop said was "Well, if you do this you are going to have to finish up your schooling during the winter months when you are through playing."

I went on and got my diploma that way. The fact was that I had already played with a lot of ex-professionals like Johnny Bassler, Fred Haney, Frank Shellenback, Cleo Carlyle, and Smead Jolley, so breaking in at such a young age wasn't as hard as it may seem.

It was a break that I got to come in that way. I played for Hollywood in 1934 and 1935 and then in 1936 they moved their franchise to San Diego. We were the first professional team to go to San Diego.

It was in 1936 that I found out about this part of Oregon [Rogue River] from the trainer of the ball club, Les Cook. He had been coming up here to Oregon for quite a few years in the off-season. In fact, several major league players were coming here at that time, guys like Del Baker, Bill "Raw Meat" Rodgers, Dazzy Vance. They all used to come up here and spend the winter hunting and fishing. Les Cook had all of these pictures of fishing and hunting on the wall of the training room and every day I'd go in and talk to him about it. I'd always thought that someday I'd like to live in the mountains and fish and hunt and when Les invited me to join him and his wife I accepted right off.

In those days there were no roads into this area and we had to take a boat to get up here. That's how my wife, Monica, and I got acquainted. She was from South Dakota and was teaching school up here at the time. Back in those days the CC camp was established here and they built this road through the mountain to give the kids something to do. Every Saturday night down at the CC camp in Agness they'd have something going on. They'd have a movie one week and a dance the next and that was the big entertainment for the week. And that's how we met. Our son was born in 1942, and he went to school in the little one-room school here.

I never did work in the off-season, and I never did play winter ball or anything else. I think it was good for me to get away after a full season.

That same year, in June 1936, I got to see Ted Williams come in for his tryout. Nobody knew who Ted Williams was or anything about him. Frank Shellenback was pitching batting practice, and this big skinny kid was standing by the batting cage. Finally Frank said, "Let the tall kid get in and hit a few." All of the older players around the batting cage were grumbling about this young kid who was going to take up their time. As I remember it, Ted got to hit about seven or eight balls, and he hit three of them out of the ball park! He hit them so hard that everybody noticed. Suddenly they were all saying, "Who is this kid?"

He had that good swing even then and we didn't have anybody on our club at that time who could hit a ball out of the ball park. Let alone hit three in one session of batting practice. I remember one fellow by the batting cage said, "Boy, this kid will be signed before the week's out," and sure enough, when we got ready to go to San Francisco, he had signed a contract over the weekend. I got to see Ted from the time that he broke in right on through. In those days Ted weighed about a 150 pounds and every night after the ball game we'd go get milk shakes together, to try to put some weight on. Ted always said even then, "I want to be one of the greatest hitters of all time." And I think he was.

In 1935 Eddie Collins came out to the Coast. He had heard about me and they [the Boston Red Sox] decided to take an option on buying George Myatt, the shortstop, and me, the second baseman. They decided to buy our contracts but to exercise the option in the summer of 1936. When Collins returned in 1936, he was the general manager of the Red Sox and he watched us play for a couple of games. Joe Cronin was still the Boston shortstop and since he was in his prime, they didn't need another shortstop and they didn't take Myatt. They bought my contract and while Collins was there, he saw Ted [Williams] taking batting practice. Collins liked his swing so much that he went to the owner of the ball club, Bill Lane, and he asked if he could buy Ted's contract. Lane said that they weren't ready to sell a contract, but they shook hands on the fact that the Red Sox would get the first chance to buy Ted's contract. And that's kind of how it all came about. Just good foresight on Collins's part to put the thing together at that time.

I'll always remember spring training in 1937. I was just eighteen, and there was Jimmy Foxx hitting balls out of the ball park like golf balls and Joe Cronin at shortstop and Lefty Grove pitching, and Pinky Higgins and Doc Cramer and the Ferrell brothers. My gosh, all of these guys—I had their pictures up on my wall as a kid. They were all my heroes and there they were, and I was with them.

I hoped that I could play well enough to make the club, but the breaks that I got were very important. When I broke in with Hollywood at a young age they needed a second baseman, so they played me. If they had had an established second baseman I would have been sitting around. Then when I broke in with Boston it was the same, they needed a second baseman. But if I had broken in with Detroit along with Charlie Gehringer, then I'd probably have sat around for four or five years and been optioned out. It would have been a different situation.

In those days, I don't think anyone ever got too compla-
cent. Even after I played ten years of ball, I still felt like I had
to play well or somebody might take my place. They had plenty
of players in the minor leagues who were good enough to come
up and take your job, and I think that kept us going all of the
time. I hustled and put that extra effort in all of the time.

I had a good spring training in 1937, and I made the club.
I started the season, but after a couple of weeks I got hit in the
head with a pitched ball by Ed Linke of the Washington club.
It didn't knock me out, but I was out of the lineup for a few
days and Eric McNair got back in. He was playing good ball,
so I didn't play too much that first couple of months. The last
month of the season I got back in and I played pretty well for
the rest of the year.

It was a big adjustment to come from California to Boston.
In those days we didn't have major league baseball out west.
I remember the first time that I walked into Yankee Stadium—
it was so big that I thought the whole thing was going to fall
down on top of us. I felt like a little dot out there. It was such
a huge thing to walk out there and look up into the stands and
then have the thrill of playing against Lou Gehrig.

Getting to play major league baseball was the biggest and
greatest thrill. I was apprehensive because I always wondered
if I belonged there.

My highest honor was being inducted into the Hall of Fame
in 1986. I'm sure my parents were proud of me. When I was
inducted into the Hall of Fame in 1986, my mother was still
alive. She was ninety-two years old and we all drove across
the country together. My mother, my sister, my sister-in-law
and my wife. We were all together and I was really happy that
she got to see that. I was only sorry that my dad wasn't there
to see it, or my brother. When you think of all of the players
that played and the fact that such a few make it into the Hall
of Fame, it was the finest honor I could ever have received.

In 1988 my number [1] was retired in Boston. And in 1990
it was the fifty-year anniversary for *Street and Smith* and they
picked their all-time team over fifty years and I was picked for
the second baseman. It was what they called their dream team.
That was another terrific honor. There have been so many hon-

ors, thrills, and memories that it's hard to imagine what my life might have been like without baseball.

I just lived for it. I suppose to succeed in anything you have to be that way. You can't go out and hate it and succeed. It was a great era of baseball that we all played in. When I broke in I got to see a lot of those great players who had played in the twenties, like Gehrig and Jimmy Foxx. I got to see Charlie Gehringer, who was my hero growing up, and he was every bit as good as I had ever thought that he was. Then there were the players in my era, 1937 through 1951, like the DiMaggios, Ted Williams, Bob Feller, George Kell, and a bunch of other great players. And as I was leaving I got to see others just breaking in, like Mickey Mantle and Whitey Ford. I even got to play against Willie Mays in an exhibition game at the end of my career. I saw three great eras.

Ted Williams did a lot of things that people never knew about—wonderful things. People would come to Ted almost every day with wheelchair kids or other kids back of the screen in Fenway and they'd ask, "Would you come and talk to these kids when the game is over?" He'd say, "When everybody is out of the ball park—and I don't want any press or anything— I'll talk to them," then he'd visit with them. Lots of times he'd go to hospitals. He just didn't want the press involved in it. That wasn't why he was doing it. Of course sometimes he just got so contrary that you'd like to wring his neck but that's the way he is.

Some people feel that there has been a big change in base-ball, but I've found that kids today work just as hard as we did when we played. I think they put in a lot of effort, but one thing that is different today is that they overcoach kids now. When we were playing we had to work out some of our prob-lems ourselves. I think we benefited by doing that. Now every time you turn around, you get somebody telling you what to do. Young players have got to make mistakes and they have got to work things out for themselves.

I think that kids need to be allowed to just do it on their own, and that repetition is very important in developing skills. Bart Giamatti wrote about this same subject in his book *Take Time for Paradise*. It's not a very big book, but on one page

there is a paragraph and a half that is so beautiful. I had to read this thing about five times and all it said really was that if you do a thing enough times, then you get good at it. I realized this is what I have been trying to say for fifty years, but I never did say it quite like that.

There is a lot of luck involved in baseball. When you're going good it seems like it's all good. And what is luck? Luck is really just a lot of practice, a lot of work. I think it goes back to bouncing the ball off some steps a jillion times and my God, pretty soon you have to get pretty good.

My generation grew up differently. We didn't quit at things, and that was just a way of life. It was survival of the fittest and we worked very hard. It comes down to working things out for yourself. Parents want to do things for their kids because they don't want their kids to have to go through what they went through. They don't want their kids to get blisters or to have to work hard. But hard work does some good things for you. Sometimes you have to work until you get the job done and that means you don't quit at 5:00.

I feel strongly about loyalty. Back then the Red Sox were the greatest thing on earth and I would have died if I had been traded from the club. I'd have had to think quite a bit before I'd have ever quit the Red Sox—that was a great town, a great park, and great people. We had a loyalty to our team, the owners, the town, and our fans.

JESSE FLORES

Jesse Flores, a right-handed pitcher, played in the major leagues from
1942 to 1950 for the Cubs, A's, and Indians. Known to many inside
baseball as Señor Flores, Jesse is a renowned scout.

I WAS EIGHT YEARS old when my family moved here to the
United States. My mother told us we'd go to the States for three
months but we never went back to Mexico. We moved to La
Habra, California, and I went to Washington High School here.
I worked in the fields with my family. I picked oranges and
lemons. All of La Habra used to be orchards, groves of oranges
and lemons. I think there were only about eleven hundred
people here when we came from Mexico.

When I first came, I used to see a lot of the American boys
playing softball and I kinda liked it. Then I went to school and
went looking for the softball game so I could play, and I enjoyed it. Then I started playing baseball, semi-pro, here in La
Habra. And I enjoyed that too. In 1938 I went to a tryout camp
in Los Angeles at Wrigley Field. I went as a third baseman
but I saw there were just too many, so I tried out as a pitcher.
From then on my life was playing baseball.

The tryout camp went pretty well and I signed with the
Angels. I lied to them about my age. I was twenty-four and I
knocked off three years so I could play, because I was sure
that they would think that I was too old. So I told them that I
was twenty-one. I guess they believed me.

They sent me to Bisbee, Arizona, and my mother couldn't
believe it. She didn't really like the idea. She used to go to

125

church and pray for me when I was pitching. She thought I was going to get hit in the head with the ball. I think she was a little worried about the people that I was with in baseball. She never went to a ball game, but she went to church a lot. And I never got hit by a ball, so maybe it was a good thing that she did go to church. Later on, I think my mother watched me on television. I thought so because I used to hear her talking to my sisters about how far I had gone. My mother never learned English, even after all of the years that she lived here. You know what my mother used to say to people coming into her house? "Hello." And you know what she used to say when they were leaving? "Hello." That was all she knew of English.

I had an outstanding year at Bisbee, where I won 26 and lost 6. From Bisbee I moved all the way to Los Angeles, to Triple A, and I was with the Angels for four years. Then I went to the Cubs in 1942 and they sent me back. At the end of 1942 I left the Pacific Coast League for the Philadelphia Athletics. I played five years for Connie Mack and we didn't have a very good ball club. We won forty-eight games the first year I was there, and I won twelve of those forty-eight.

I was sent to San Diego in 1948, and in 1949 Bucky Harris was the manager. They used to call him the Boy Wonder, and he said to me, "Jess, you're gonna win twenty-five games this year." Well, he didn't miss it by much because I won twenty-three. And I was sold to Cleveland after that. So in 1950 I went off to play for Cleveland.

When I came here from Mexico, most of the Mexican people wanted their kids to go to work. Hard labor. No school. Everybody was working just to get by and the kids didn't get a lot of chances for something better.

My mother never encouraged me because she didn't know what baseball was, but from semi-pro on, my dad was always there when I played. I was going to school and every Saturday and Sunday I worked to help the family. My brother used to catch me and he's the one who said, "Go on and play baseball, see if you can make it." Well, I got out and I tried it and I made it. I think without baseball I would have been just another worker.

My biggest thrill was when as a rookie I pitched the opening game in Philadelphia against the Red Sox. I got beat, 1–0, and I pitched a two-hitter. But I looked up and thought about how happy I was. I did a good job and it reminded me of all the times I had picked lemons and oranges. Right then I promised myself that I was going to do better and better.

My second game I pitched against Early Wynn in Washington, D.C., and we went 0 for 0 for fifteen innings. I beat him in the sixteenth inning. That pushed me a little more. You start thinking about where you have been and the tough times when the most you could make was two dollars a day, working ten hours.

I played six and a half years in the big leagues and seventeen years in all, the rest in the minors. When you have the dream and the desire to play baseball you still need to be willing to work and to struggle a little—especially if you are a pitcher. Early Wynn told me a story about when he was in the war and was trying to come back from Manila. He was knee-deep in the mud and he said, "What else can I do but fight? I *have* to fight." That's how Early used to pitch too. We always used to say if someone hits a home run off of Early Wynn, the next guy is going down! But there is a lesson in that too, because if you don't have the fight in you, then this world of baseball is just too hard.

When I quit playing I went to scouting. I bird-dogged for the Phillies in 1959, and the following year, 1960, I went to the Washington Senators (who became the Minnesota Twins in 1961).

Once, when I was with Philadelphia, I was staying in a hotel in South Chicago when I heard a knock on the door. It was about 1:30 in the afternoon, and I opened the door and in came Chico Carascal and Luis Aparicio, who was just a little skinny kid. We started talking in Spanish and we had a nice time together. Sometimes, the Spanish-speaking players got lonely with no one to talk to, and I think it was hard for Aparicio in the beginning. When the White Sox played the Dodgers in the World Series, I called him up at the hotel and I asked if I could have some tickets. Aparicio said, "My friend, you have the tickets. How many do you want?" and we went to see him play in the World Series.

Here in La Habra, way back, there was discrimination. I tried to buy a house behind La Habra Boulevard on First Street and when I went over to close the deal, they saw that my name was Flores and they said no deal. But in baseball, I never felt any discrimination against me. There were some jokes about me, but just jokes, and everybody gets those.

I had a car that I bought back East during the war. In 1943 we were training in West Palm Beach and the vice president of an automobile company was there. At that time you couldn't buy cars because of the war. So he made sure the Athletics could each get a car. I got one and I drove it all the way to La Habra. Then I went to San Diego, where one of my friends asked me, "Could I borrow your car?" I said yeah, and he said, "I got a date with this gal who sells tickets at the ball park." So I said first take me to Fifth Avenue, I'm gonna get a haircut. It was 1948, we had a bad ball club and I was having a bad year—I had lost already eighteen games.

I went to the barbershop (it was a Mexican barber) and I sat down to get a haircut and those guys in the barbershop were cutting me to pieces. They were going on and on about what a terrible pitcher that Jesse Flores was, all in Spanish of course. I just sat there watching the barber cutting my hair and listening. When I was done I got up and I asked how much I owed. As I was paying for my haircut, my friend who had borrowed my car walked in. He was looking all around for me and said, "Where is the guy who was sitting in the chair, you know, Jesse Flores?" The barber said, "That was Jesse Flores?" and his eyes went big and I didn't say anything. So my friend started talking to me in Spanish—"¿Buenas tardes, cómo está?" The barber felt terrible and apologized all over the place. He said he didn't know who I was and he never thought I was a Mexican. He thought I couldn't understand Spanish. That was the greatest kick I have ever had in my life.

I played a lot of years and I have done some good work as a scout. A scout is a very important part of this game and the people inside the game know that, but I'm not sure that the public knows what a scout does. I got a few guys into the game and I know there is one at least who is going into the Hall of Fame—Bert Blyleven. The other one who I think has a chance at getting into the Hall of Fame later on is Reggie Smith.

A lot of people ask me what it is that I look for in a young ballplayer. I always tell them exactly the truth. All you have to do is sit there and watch. When you are scouting you have to be there early to see if the guy can throw. You have to watch him warm up. If you want a guy who can throw, you've got to watch him.

I'll give you an example. I saw a guy pitch a doubleheader in American Legion ball and I knew I wanted to sign him. That was Jimmy Merritt and he was also a batboy for the Dodgers. The Dodgers were kind of hiding the guy. In other words he was almost signed and they didn't think anybody was going to pick him. During the draft I said I wanted to get Jimmy Merritt and we got him for four thousand dollars. The first year, he struck out 248. He was in three World Series. I was lucky— somehow the Dodgers didn't protect that guy or sign him, and I was watching. You always have to be watching.

Today there is too much money. I made eighty dollars a month my first year in baseball. Some guys today sign for one million or more. They have players on the bench now, in case somebody gets hurt, making three hundred thousand dollars a year. Just in case somebody gets hurt.

I used to scout in Mexico when I worked for the Minnesota Twins. It was hard getting some of those Mexican players to come here to play. They'd say, "No, we don't want to go; we still remember the Alamo." They were good ballplayers too. Now that they know that they can get the big money, they are coming over.

I think that baseball should do something for the old-timers. The guys who are running the pension plan now have got enough money in there to help the guys who started the pension plan. I think that they have enough money that they should thank the older ballplayers who started the whole deal. But, like the way we used to say in Mexico, *"El rico, que más tiene, más quiere."* [The rich man, the more he has, the more he wants.]

The greatest thrill for me as a scout was signing Tommy Hall. He's from Riverside, California. When I went to sign him, he weighed 131 pounds and his waist was twenty-six inches. He had these long arms; to be truthful he didn't look like much. The kid was skinny, but I decided I was going to sign him even if they fired me. So I did and the first time that he played in spring training they put him in to pitch with the bases loaded

and no one out. He struck out three guys in ten pitches. His ball used to just take off and sail.

You know what's my other big thrill as a scout? One day I went to a game when Minnesota was in town and I had eight players on that roster. Eight players that I had signed, just one more and there would've been a whole ball club!

I've been lucky in scouting in that the kids I signed had the desire to play baseball. Of course, I push them too; it is my job to push them. But you can get lucky and sometimes the kids are good.

As far as pursuing baseball today, I tell the kids that I believe that anybody can do it if they try. If you try hard then you have a chance to be successful. I tried it and I came from Mexico and I made it. Why not try it? The money is there if you want it. The money is saying, "Come and get me."

JIM DELSING

Jim Delsing, an outfielder, played in the major leagues from 1948 to 1960 for Chicago, New York, St. Louis, Detroit, and Kansas City. Delsing made trivia history when he was selected to run for a midget, Eddie Gaedel, in a promotional stunt that had been arranged by Bill Veeck, the owner of the St. Louis Browns, in 1951.

THE REASON I PURSUED baseball was this simple: I wanted to get off the farm. Making it to the major leagues was hard, maybe too hard, but it was something I had always dreamed of.

We all played baseball in all of our spare time. Every kid in the country played baseball. It was just what you did. I was sixteen years old when I first played pro ball and I didn't realize that it would make me ineligible to play for my high school during my senior year. I had made all of seventy-five dollars a month.

Boy, I was a real prospect! In those days, if you got the most hits you got to sleep on top of the luggage in the bus. I was sixteen years old, hitting .400, living in the YMCA, eating hot dogs, drinking malts, and sleeping on top of that luggage!

That first year I played at Green Bay, Wisconsin, which was the home of the Green Bay Packers. Our baseball coach was also the line coach for the Packers. We had our dressing room in the Packers' locker room and after every game we had a couple of cases of beer. I didn't drink beer then because I was just sixteen years old. One day after I had played a bad game, I was sitting in front of my locker with a soda. I was playing shortstop at the time, and everyone knew if I didn't kick the ball I was going to throw it away. Anyway, I was sitting there sipping that Coke and the coach, Red Smith, walked by. Well, he must have drop-kicked that soda fifty feet or so! He said, "You want to play a man's game, kid, you better drink a man's drink."

My dad was a farmer but he always encouraged me. He never got mad if I broke a window when I was playing ball, though he would have skinned me alive if I'd done it when I was supposed to be working.

I was scouted by Eddie Cotell. I went to a White Sox tryout camp and fared very, very badly. Eddie Cotell was the backfield coach for the Green Bay Packers and he was also a scout for the Cubs. So he signed me up. The first guy that scouted me hanged himself. No kidding, he looked at me for two days and went out and hanged himself. The thing about it was, I was waiting to hear from him to see how I'd done and when I went to talk to him I found out he had committed suicide! You *have* to love the game to keep playing after that.

I was called up to the Yankees in 1950 as a prospect—not a suspect, mind you, but a prospect. We went to spring training and had been there about three weeks when my wife, Roseanne, had a tubal pregnancy and had to go to the hospital. I had to leave with the ball club to go north and the doctor made her stay there for a while to recuperate. Then she had to drive by herself from Florida to New York. This was during the Korean War and people were very suspicious of any woman trying to check into a motel alone. They thought that you were trying to set up business, you know! One night she had to go to a police station to ask for help finding a place to stay. Finally, after driving from Florida to New York by herself, she got to where she could see the sign on the Belvedere Hotel where we were staying. But she couldn't get to it because they were all one-way streets. She circled for more than an hour and when she finally pulled up in front of the hotel, she just put her head on the steering wheel and sat there. The doorman at the hotel knew I was waiting for my wife. He came up to me and said, "Is your wife driving a green car? Well, I think you better come and get her." You know, it was a lot to go through.

June 14, 1950, the last day of trading, I was traded to the St. Louis Browns. We kept renting because we had no family in St. Louis but finally we thought it was ridiculous. We thought we should buy a house, even if it was a little one, just so we could have a place to live. I was on the road and Roseanne went out with Jo Sievers, Roy's wife. They were building these little houses and you could hold one for twenty-five dollars. Twenty-five dollars to hold a house! Anyway, Roseanne did it while I was on the road. Then she was scared to death—twenty-five dollars down on a house, and she was scared to death. What a commitment!

We moved in January 1952, before the streets were even paved and then we left for spring training which was in Burbank, California.

When we came back in March, the streets were paved. Then in August we were traded to Detroit! August 15, 1952—I'll never forget that Holy Day! You know what was funny, Roseanne was still getting the place settled and she was standing on top of the stove, trying to straighten up some cabinets. We didn't even have telephones in yet. She had the radio on, and they announced that Ned Garver and I were traded. She jumped down, holding the radio in her hands, as if to say, "Will you repeat that?" She couldn't believe it! She threw Kim, the baby, in the car and drove to a pay phone. It was an off day and I was in Cleveland, playing golf. All the guys were playing golf, including Marty Marion who was the manager. I played golf with him all that day and then after we got through he said, "You're traded to Detroit." I imagine he knew all day about the trade but didn't tell me. Roseanne knew before I did because she heard it on the radio, but we couldn't even talk to each other because of the phone situation. It makes it sound like the 1800s or something, what with no phones, no roads, etc. And imagine that we lived in that little house for thirty-six years after that! When you talk about things like that trade, you know that you played for the love of the game, because you certainly didn't play for the convenience that the job offered.

You should hear the story about the midget—August, I think it was, of 1951. Eddie Gaedel was the midget's name. They were having a fiftieth-anniversary celebration of something in between the first and second games of a doubleheader. Bill Veeck always had firecrackers and all kinds of things going on at the ball park. Well, that day they drove up with this big cake, brought it to home plate, and out of the cake popped Eddie Gaedel. That was really something.

I had played the first game of the doubleheader and I was kind of upset when my name wasn't in the lineup for the second game. I was surprised because I had gotten a couple of hits in the first game and that didn't happen every day, you know. When you're hot, you're hot. I wanted to play. I said something to Zack Taylor and he said, "Don't worry about it, just don't worry about it." I think that the only people that knew about it were Zack Taylor, Bill Veeck, Eddie Gaedel, and maybe the sportswriters like Bob Burns or Bob Broeg.

When this little guy came out of the cake, he walked over to the dugout and sat down. He had ⅛ as his number on the back of his little uniform and he was using one of those little autograph novelty bats that were twelve or fourteen inches long. That was what he was gonna use to bat! Well, Frank Saucier was leading off, playing right field, and he went out to right field to start the second game of the doubleheader. The year before, Saucier had led the Texas League in hitting. This was his first game in the big leagues and he was playing right field. When he came in he was taken out for a pinch hitter, which was the midget! You can imagine how he felt. So Gaedel went up to home plate, and as he got up there, after everyone laughed and played around for a while, the umpire, Ed Hurley, asked him to prove he was on the team. And the midget pulled a contract out of his back pocket. It was a legal contract because Bill Veeck knew they would ask him to prove he had one.

The funniest thing about it all was when Bob Swift, who was the catcher for Detroit, tried to give his pitcher, Bob Cain, a target. The first pitch they tried to throw in there was a ball. Gaedel only had about a three-inch strike zone, and they couldn't get close. So then Swift lay down and tried to give a target really low to the ground; the fans were going crazy by now, and they still couldn't throw a strike. Finally Bob Cain threw one underhand and he walked him. But I don't think anybody knew that before the game Bill Veeck had said to Eddie Gaedel, "I am up here in the stands and I've got a gun. If you swing at a pitch, I'll shoot you!" So anyhow, he was walked. Then Zack Taylor, who was the manager, said to me, "Delsing, go run for the midget!" So I'm the man who ran for the midget.

There is a story that goes with that. Frank Saucier was so mad that he never played again! He quit. Baseball was a game for him. It wasn't a joke.

Then, like I said, I was traded to Detroit in 1952 and we were there until 1956, when I was traded from there to the White Sox. The next year we went to spring training together and then Roseanne drove from spring training to Detroit with the kids to find a place to live. That year we were really lucky because we got the catcher Bob Swift's place. In turn, we rented our house out to Cardinals—Ken and Kathleen Boyer had it one year. You had to rent out your house, just so you could afford to rent one in the other city.

Those were our happiest years, in Detroit. The happiest days in baseball. Spike Briggs owned the ball club and he was great. They only had fourteen night games. It was wonderful. It was such a different life than, say, working a three-to-eleven shift, a swing shift, which is kind of what baseball is now. Spike Briggs and his wife had four or five little boys and he used to see us with the three little girls. He always used to say when he saw our girls, "You've got to come to my office. We're making a trade! But I want all three!" We always said, "Hell, you might as well, we've been traded for everything else! Now the kids are being traded." But it's true, those were the happiest of times.

When Jamie, our second child, was three weeks old, Roseanne drove to Detroit with a toddler and a new baby and the dog. She stayed in a hotel with the kids and the dog and a newspaper and looked for a place to live. She went out every day looking for places to live while I was on the road. Jamie, the baby, actually slept in a drawer. A real baseball baby.

When we were in the winter league in Santiago, Dominican Republic, we stayed at the Hotel Matum. We considered it our tomb. Anyway, that was where Kim fell from the balcony and broke her leg. That was 1958 and she was seven years old. We had a dreadful time there with that because they didn't even have a hospital. They had a little three-room clinic, no running water, no toilets or regular food or anything. She was in the clinic three days before we could move her.

Trujillo was still the dictator then, and we had trouble—like when we tried to have the St. Louis newspaper sent down to us, even if it would be late. When we'd get it, there would be all of these things cut out of it. It had all been censored. The newspapers you would get would have big holes in them. The first time we got one like that we couldn't figure out what the hell was going on. Well, it was a dictatorship.

The funny thing was that the hotel was owned by the brother of the Rosenbergs, the people who were convicted for espionage. To get there you had to fly into the capital in one of those little planes—we called them "knuckleballs." Then to get to Santiago you had to go 150 kilometers in an open-air German bus with wooden seats and no lights. All of this just to play baseball!

Anyway, back to the broken leg. When they decided they were going to do surgery—well, we didn't know they were going to do it right there. We thought they were going to do it in another hospital or something. They started wheeling in the oxygen as I walked in and the doctor had this stainless steel pan full of instruments. I said no. And they said, "*¿Qué pasa, por qué no?*" you know, Why not?

Then we got on the phone trying to get a hold of our doctor in the States, and the problems we had! Not just the time change, but the overseas call. You have to realize how many years ago this was. Then I had to be careful of what I said. It took hours because of the censoring. They bleeped every other word out. Finally the doctor called us back and said to put her in a body cast from the armpits down to the toes, and get her home as soon as we could.

We had to tie her to the floor of the airplane. We tied her to a canvas litter and then we tied that to the legs of the seats of the airplane. It was against every regulation. We could hardly get this seven-year-old in a body cast through the door of the airplane because we couldn't bend her! The season was almost over there and we were in the playoffs. I had had a pretty good year down there and they were wonderful and let me leave on that plane. They were fantastic, because they could have made me stay. I don't know that I would have, but they could have asked me to stay.

Finally we got home and the ambulance was there to meet

us and we got Kim all tucked in at the hospital. Then about 4:30 in the morning we got a call from the hospital that Kim had been trying to ring the little bell for the nurse. They didn't have those call buttons then. Anyway, she leaned over for the bell and rolled right out of bed on to the floor because they had forgotten to put the sides up on her bed! Then she had pulled herself down the hall with her elbows to the nurses' station. Can you imagine? Baseball kids really have all the fun.

I'm always amazed when I think back to my time with the Yankees. In spring training of 1950, these were some of the outfielders: Bauer, Mapes, Woodling, Lindell, Hendricks, Charlie Keller, DiMaggio, Jackie Jensen, Dick Wakefield, and myself. There were actually eleven of us. Eleven outfielders! But you knew that six were going to have to go someplace else. That was Billy Martin's first year too. Here's a funny thing. Billy had a girlfriend in Oakland and he wanted her to come to New York to visit. Her parents wouldn't let her. So he wrote a letter to her parents and said there was a very lovely married couple on the team who would chaperone her. This old married couple was Jim and Roseanne Delsing. We had only been married four months! We never saw them! Well, we went out with them one night but we never knew. Billy didn't even tell us until after she had left that we were supposed to be keeping our eyes on her.

When I played in the Pacific Coast League, I made the All-Star team each year and I was doing very well, hitting way over .300. Then, when I came to the Yankee organization, finally made to the big leagues, I had to take a cut in pay! That year everybody played for five thousand dollars and I had been making more in the minors.

We used to sit and wait for that contract to show up every year. Then we would write a letter back asking for an extra five hundred or whatever and mail it back. The organization would just send it all back to you. No letter or anything. Just the same contract. Take it or leave it. That was the way baseball was. So, I guess we really did play for the love of the game.

Johnny Vander Meer pitching his second consecutive no-hitter

JOHNNY VANDER MEER

Johnny Vander Meer, the Dutch Master, pitched from 1937 to 1951 for the Reds, Cubs, and Indians. He led the National League in strikeouts from 1941–1943 and was an All-Star in 1938–39 and in 1942–43. Vander Meer is the only pitcher in major league history to have pitched back-to-back no-hitters.

I STARTED LISTENING TO THE World Series when I was about eight or nine years old, and I started playing when I was ten or eleven. Back then there weren't many choices of things to do. Some kids wanted to be firemen, some kids wanted to be policemen, and I just wanted to play ball. So actually, it turned out to be a dream come true.

I grew up in Midland Park, New Jersey, which is about twenty miles north of New York City. I played grade school ball and I didn't play any high school ball at all. I took sick on the first day I was supposed to go to high school. I came up with peritonitis which you weren't supposed to live through in those days because there were no drugs. The peritonitis was caused by a ruptured appendix—it was thirty days before I was operated on and it had turned into peritonitis. I suppose it was the Lord's will that I was to survive. This is just a curious fact, but the day I got it, Tom Mix, the cowboy movie actor, got it too, and he was dead in three days!

I wasn't allowed to really participate in very much for a period of about two years. After that I had gotten so far behind I just stayed out of school. I didn't go to high school at all.

I cheated a little bit, just like any kid would and played anyway. My body had really developed. I was only about 110 pounds when I was fourteen years old, and by the time I was seventeen I was 175 pounds. I had that God-given arm. Nobody can teach you how to throw a ball hard. Nobody can teach you how to run fast.

I started playing semi-pro ball. This was during the worst part of the Depression and there was no Legion ball. So I started playing semi-pro ball just before I was sixteen years old. I played for a club in my hometown called the Rangers, and then I proceeded to heavier clubs. The last year, when I was seventeen, I was playing with really heavy ball clubs.

My parents were immigrants from the Netherlands and it was a ticklish situation with them. When they saw how much I wanted to play, they were willing to let me go. My parents didn't really understand baseball; work was their thing. The other problem was that I came from a very strict family and I never played any Sunday ball at all in my semi-pro career. My parents didn't permit it. The first Sunday ball that I played was in professional ball.

My dad was a foreman in a really large silk company, and the mill was everything to him. He thought the mill couldn't operate without him, and that's where he thought my brothers and I should go. But I wasn't meant to work inside. I'd have been a game warden before I'd have done that. I was meant to be outside.

I was raised in a very rural area and I had only pitched in about 7 good semi-pro ball games. I knew I was being scouted, and then I was picked as an "All-American Boy" who would be given the opportunity to play baseball through a promotion of the National League. The idea behind the promotion was that every kid in America has a chance to be a major league ballplayer. If you had the talent, you'd get your chance. So the Dodgers never even saw me play, but they signed me.

It turned out that I got my chance in four years, which was very quick at that time. They sent me first to Dayton, Ohio. That was Class D back then, and they took me to spring training in Miami, which was my bonus.

I was only making $125 a month in Dayton and I had been making more than that playing semi-pro ball. That was bad enough but then they couldn't meet the payroll and I was only getting paid $100 a month. Since I was an eighteen-year-old kid, I guess they thought they could rip me off. By the time the season was over, they owed me $200. The next year they sent me back to Dayton and I wouldn't play until they paid me the $200 that they owed me, because at that point I didn't know if I was ever going to get it.

Ducky Holmes was the owner and manager of the ball club in Dayton. He had been an old-time ballplayer for a few years, as well as an American League umpire, and he was a character. If my mother had known Ducky Holmes, I guarantee that I would have been home in fifteen minutes. He'd do things like get drunk and get kicked out of the ball park. He'd leave and go find a light pole to climb outside of the park. When he'd get up there he'd have a bottle in his back pocket and he'd give us signs from up on the light pole. Then after the game, the city would have to come with a ladder and take him down. He hit four umpires that year and the last time he got suspended for twenty days.

We went into Beckley, West Virginia, once and we drew the biggest crowd they ever had. They didn't come out to see us, they came out to see him. I was eighteen years old and I had sure never seen anything like that before.

One night we had Pants Powell, who later played with the Yankees, with us. He tagged up on third base on a play to win the ball game on a fly ball. Pants could really fly. He slid home and just beat the throw. Ducky took off from the coaching line and slid right behind him, stuck his spike in his back, and they had to put about eighteen stitches in Pants's back. Ducky did all kinds of things. One night in Beckley during a dull ball game, he suddenly appeared on a bicycle and rode around the bases! He made an amateur out of Bill Veeck.

He owed everybody money and payday would come and he'd say, "How much money do you need until next payday?" That's how he came to owe me two hundred bucks at the end of the season. He did it to me and to all of the other guys.

Ducky sold me to Scranton in the Eastern League, which was an A League. He did it without the consent of the Dodgers. He wanted to sell me to an Eastern League club where I would bring a lot more money and then split the money with the Dodgers. The Yankees tried to buy me and the Dodgers said that they couldn't because they owned me. All of a sudden everyone was saying, "How the hell did he get to Scranton?" I had to appear in front of Judge Landis in the fall of 1934 and he ordered me to the Scranton club. That decision took me away from the Dodgers.

Then I was sold to Boston, came up with a sore arm, and was traded to Nashville. Nashville sent me to Durham. Then I went to the major leagues from Durham. In fact, in 1936 I got the Minor League Player of the Year Award.

That's how the Reds bought me. When I walked into the Cincinnati clubhouse I wasn't scared because I'd been around for a couple of years and a clubhouse is a clubhouse, it's your work. But the biggest thrill of my life was when I got to the big leagues and I got my own locker and my own uniform with my name on it—the very thing that I was dreaming about. That was probably the happiest day of my life. I was very aware that my dream had come true.

I pitched my two no-hitters the following year, in 1938. That is what most everybody recognizes me for. It hasn't been accomplished since.

The first no-hitter was in Cincinnati, and it was a day game. The second no-hitter was in New York, in the first night game ever played in Ebbets Field, and it was packed. In fact, the fire department had to come and force a lot of people out of the ball park. It was pretty much a routine game all the way through until the ninth inning. I had been aware of the potential for a no-hitter in the first inning. There was a lot of pressure, but I think the thing that I had going for me was that in both ball games, I never *went* for the no-hitter until the ninth inning.

So I didn't go for it until the ninth, and I thought to myself, "I've got thirty good pumps left in me. I still have my good stuff, and, boy, they are going to have to hit the very best that I've got." So I reached out a little bit more than I probably had earlier. I got the first hitter out and then I walked three. (I led the league several times in walks, but I led it several times in strikeouts too.)

I was in trouble and there was a ground ball to third base with a force-out at the plate, and then Durocher popped out. In fact, I had Durocher struck out. When the game was over the umpire, Bill Stewart, came up and said to me, "John, I blew that two-strike pitch." I've often wondered if Leo had gotten a base hit if he would have run out there and said that then!

In my fifteen years in the majors, I always felt that somebody was trying to take my uniform away from me. It didn't take much to get you out of the big leagues. If things didn't go your way or you had injuries or you got cuffed around a little bit, they sent you out pretty quick. Today you can hit .200 in the big leagues as a catcher and stay in the big leagues. If you hit .200 when I was playing, I guarantee you that train would stop in Syracuse about three o'clock in the morning and you'd be getting off of it. [Syracuse was a farm team then.]

I had to work in the off-seasons. I did anything that I could do, all kinds of jobs. I worked with masons and plumbers, anything that I could make fifty cents an hour doing. I had to. I was never in debt in my life. I didn't have any money and I didn't have any way to get into debt. The minor leagues back then were rough. But that was what we wanted to do, what we ate, what we slept, and what we drank. We had that desire to stay hungry in order to accomplish what we wanted.

My parents were proud of me once I had made it. When you have parents who are immigrants, there isn't anything in this world but work, because they had to work and they didn't have a darn thing. They were way at the bottom of the barrel. My parents wanted everybody to work. It was a tough way of life, but it taught me a lot of good things.

I didn't get married until 1940, so I had already been in the big leagues for a couple of years and had been able to get on my feet. We trained here in Florida and my wife, Lois, had to drive all the way here by herself. Then, because we barnstormed back to Cincinnati with the team, she had to drive everything back to Cincinnati for the next five or six months too. She'd pack that car right to the ceiling and lay the kids in the back, and off they'd go. My wife was wonderful, and she did a damn good job.

When I quit playing I managed in the minors. In fact, the last club I had was right here in Tampa. I broke Pete Rose in right here. The players were getting someplace but I wasn't getting anyplace. Everybody on the club was making four or five times as much money as I was. I had been working in the

off-season for the Schlitz Brewery, traveling for them. I was very aware that there wasn't much security in the game then. Everyone said, "You were hired to be fired once you were a manager." The brewery kept after me, so I had a talk with them about being there all year-round and I decided to go with the brewery. I stayed with them for twenty years and that was the smartest move I ever made. I retired eleven years ago.

Baseball has a tremendous meaning for people. This country is a great sports country. Baseball is a great game now because you have everybody from every background playing it. I've always been a firm believer that the game has never belonged to the owners. It has never belonged to the ballplayers. It belongs to that guy who puts his money up on the window and says, "How much does it cost to sit in the bleachers?" That is who owns baseball. And it has got to be kept that way.

MARTY MARION

Marty Marion, considered by many to be the greatest fielding shortstop of all time, played for St. Louis from 1940 to 1953. Known as Mr. Shortstop and Slats, Marion was also one of the original organizers of the baseball pension plan. A Southern gentleman, Marion went up against Branch Rickey with a contract written out on a piece of scrap paper and won. His career in baseball included playing, managing, and even owning a ball club.

I CAN REMEMBER WHEN I first came here to St. Louis, baseball players couldn't rent a house, not any nice house. People kind of looked down on baseball players—they were a rough, rowdy group, like from the old Gashouse Gang days. When my grandfather, who was a preacher, heard I was going to be a professional baseball player, he went crazy. He said, "They're no good, they're all just a bunch of bums." So baseball wasn't the greatest thing to do back in those days. But now, oh my God, they're well respected. They're the cream of the crop. An athlete has the whole town at his feet. We had it pretty good though in the forties and it got better every year, until finally you were looked on as something kind of special. You were a hero.

A lot of things just happened to my career, they just happened along. I got started playing in high school. My school was called Tech High in Atlanta, Georgia. I was there four years and I didn't do anything my freshman year. The second year I went out for the team as a sophomore and the coach— I'll never forget him as long as I live—was old Gabe Talbot. He smoked cigars. High school baseball was not as sophisticated as it is today. We had a good team though, and we won the state championship two years in a row when I was there. I didn't get to play much that first year. I'd sit on the bench, next to the coach, all the time. All I did, it seemed to me, was run and get him cigars. I was his caddy! He'd say, "Marty, go get me a cigar," and I'd go and buy cigars for him. That was my first year in baseball. The next two years I guess I was what you'd call a high school star. I was hitting .500 and all that kind of stuff.

I went to a tryout camp with the Cardinals—and back in those days the Cardinals owned about every team in the minor leagues. Once they even had to release a lot of players because Branch Rickey had a monopoly on them. So I went to a tryout camp in Rome, Georgia. The scouts would get together all of the kids who could play ball and drive them up there. One day we were just finishing a squad game. I'd played two innings when a scout took me aside and said, "Hey, kid, how'd you like to play for St. Louis?"

That was 1935 and it was right at the end of the season. Matter of fact, we saw the Cubs cinch the pennant. I think that was when they won 21 straight games or something like that. Anyway, another boy from Atlanta and I were here for three days. Staying at the old Fairgrounds Hotel, we worked out with the team and they tried to sign us to a contract.

Well, I said, "No, I don't think so—we want to go home to think about this." All of a sudden we felt pretty important, just eighteen years old and the Cardinals thought we were good enough to sign a contract. So we didn't sign—we went back home to Atlanta. Just a short while later a guy named Frank Rickey, who was Branch's brother and a big scout for the Cardinals, drove up to our house in a big, old convertible Buick. Right up to the front door and came in and introduced himself.

He took us out to dinner, wined and dined us, and tried to get us to sign a contract with the Cardinals. But we were kind of hard to get. I worked out a deal where the other boy, whose name was Johnny Echols, and I would sign a four-year contract with a bonus of $500. I was playing pretty hard to get! Let me tell you something, $500 was a lot of money back in 1935. The first year we would make $150 a month, no matter where we went. The second year we would make $3,000 a year no matter where we played, and the third and fourth years we would make $5,000 a year no matter where we played.

The first year I played in Huntington, West Virginia. The second year I went to Rochester, New York, to Red Wing Stadium. I was there three years—1937 to 1939. I made $150 a week and I was the highest-paid guy on the team. We had a catcher who only made $50 a month. He lived in town though, so he got cheap rent. I got $3,000 a year and then in 1940 I came to the Cardinals and I was making $5,000 a year, which was a helluva lot of money then for a rookie. Most guys were making about $2,500.

To get back to Johnny Echols—Johnny was a good ballplayer and they sent him to Albany, Georgia. He progressed pretty well. Then all of a sudden, during his third year, they decided he wasn't going to make it, so they released him. I was at the Detroit Hotel in St. Petersburg, Florida, at spring training. Johnny came into the hotel one day and said, "Marty, the Cardinals released me," and I said, "They can't do that, we've got a four-year contract." We didn't really have a four-year contract written out in any kind of fashion, but we had an agreement. So he said, "Would you go to see Judge Landis with me?"

Judge Landis used to stay over at the BelAir Hotel in Clearwater, and he agreed to see us. So we drove over there one afternoon and we were sitting on the front porch with Judge Landis. Now the judge didn't like Mr. Rickey, 'cause Mr. Rickey had promised a lot of things to a lot of ballplayers and didn't fulfill his promises. So he said, "Tell me your story, boy." The only thing that I had to show Judge Landis was this scrap piece of paper. It wasn't a formal contract. So I showed him that and he said, "They promised you this, boy. And I promise you that they can't release you or Johnny Echols."

Mr. Rickey had heard about us having a talk with Judge Landis and he called me into his office and he said, "Son, let me tell you something—I can release Joe Medwick, I can release Dizzy Dean, I can release any player I want to any time I want to." I said, "Yeah, Mr. Rickey, you can, but you can't release me and Johnny Echols 'cause we have a four-year contract." That made him mad.

So Judge Landis called Mr. Rickey over to the BelAir and said, "You pay those boys." So they signed Johnny Echols back to the team and said he was making five thousand and they sent him all over the country. And every team they sent him to, they sent him on. Finally he ended up on the Cardinals. They didn't have any place to put him, so he got in a Cardinals uniform. I think he pitched batting practice, or whatever, and hung around here for about two months as part of the Cardinals ball club. They filed his release form after that and he went home to Atlanta. Johnny Echols was the nicest man. He was a good ballplayer, too, but he just didn't have that hard-working factor.

I came up in 1940, and the Cardinals never did ship me back down. I had a good baseball career. A few World Series, and I made a lot of friends. I think one of the hardest things a baseball player has to go through is when he retires. You're thirty-five or forty years old and you're though. You're a has-been! The first thing to go is your legs. You know you should get that ball or you know you should get to first base but your legs won't let you. Some of these guys today are remarkable, like this guy Ryan. They must be taking different vitamins.

The day that you retire is especially sad because you've dedicated your whole life to playing baseball, and you've just got to start over again—right then. Really, your life is just starting. You're pretty much spoiled by the time you get through playing baseball, 'cause everybody's been nice to you and you've been in a few World Series and this and that. Then all of a sudden you're nobody. But one helpful thing is the contacts you've made. If you're a baseball player, you can walk right into most any bank and say I'm Marty Marion or I'm Ozzie Smith, and they'll let you in. They'll talk to you. The door is open.

I've dealt a lot with bankers and they would always trust me. I never did borrow more than I could pay back, and they trusted me. I've had partners that were a lot better business-men that I ever was, but the banks would take my name before they would take my partners' names. They simply trusted me because of who I was.

I feel sorry for baseball players' wives. It's very hard life. Half the time they are not with their husbands. Those poor families. I've always been a real family man. I've gotten fired a couple of times because I didn't do what the owners said because I wanted to be home.

As close as we all were together, I hardly ever saw my teammates again after we quit playing ball. You know—they live way down there and you live way up here and you just don't get together. Even here in St. Louis, let's say Del Wilber. He was one of my best friends; now I hardly ever see him. I haven't seen Musial in three years. I haven't seen Red Schoendienst in three years. Now, when I owned the Stadium Club [a restaurant at Busch Stadium in St. Louis] I saw them all the time because I was in business.

But when I asked a lot of the players to come to the Stadium Club as my guest they wouldn't want to come to the ball park. They'd say the reason was because they would feel out of place. That's sad. But you know, I sold out three years ago and I haven't been back there since. Now I feel the same way—it's the same thing. I have no reason to do that and I'd feel out of place. All those years when you were working steadily you had a reason to be there. But if you just go down there as an onlooker you feel uncomfortable.

Every day the phone would ring like crazy when I was managing and when I was playing. But after I quit, that phone never rang. It never rings until somebody wants something. It hurts your feelings, so I can see how those fellows feel. They don't feel at home. We always call someone past their prime a "has-been," and I guess that's exactly what we are. It's kind of a cruel term, but you'd be surprised how cruel people are.

Now, my whole life is my grandkids. We have a family-night dinner every Sunday night, they all come over. We go to the farm every week. Everything is family because that's the only thing you've got. I feel sorry for the guy who is old and not married and doesn't have children around him. That's a lonesome life. I'm seventy-three now and if it weren't for my kids I don't know what the hell I'd do. They're your whole life.

Baseball is kind of a tradition. Baseball fans seem to keep records more than anybody else in the world. I care less about records than I do about winning or losing. I didn't care how many hits you got or any of that junk. As long as I played baseball, twenty something years in the big leagues, I've got one award that I kept. I don't have any old gloves, no old shoes, no bats, no autographed balls, none of that stuff. But I've got a plaque that I won in 1944 for being the Most Valuable Player in the National League, which was the first plaque they ever gave. I won it in the National League and it was during the war, so they didn't have any materials to even make it with. I think I had to wait until 1945 or 1946 before they even gave it to me. It's made out of gold and silver. It's called the Judge Landis Award. I think Hal Newhouser won it in the American League that year for Detroit and I won it here in this league. That is the only thing that I have in my home.

When you talk about the work ethic or hustling, well, I can't agree with that. I knew some guys who were awfully lazy ballplayers but who were great. It's possible they would have been better if they had worked harder, but it's possible they might not have been. When you think about a guy who drank, who was drunk on the field—I'm not going to name names—you always wonder if he would be any better sober. I'm thinking of this one particular guy who came through the dugout once and said to Dizzy Dean, "Dizzy, I had a bad night last night, don't throw at me," 'cause they used to throw at you all the time back when we played; that was part of the game. That particular guy only got four straight doubles off of Dean that day! Four straight doubles and he couldn't see well. He was a great hitter.

Stan Musial once told me, back when he was a kid and probably didn't even know what he was saying, that to be a good hitter and to have a good average you had to bear down every time you walked up to the plate. Every single time you try to get a base hit. I wasn't like that. I didn't think it was so important if we were ahead 10–0. But he bore down every time at the plate to try to get a base hit. He'd have done that even if they had been fifty runs ahead. I didn't have that same desire. I wanted to win, but I didn't think that it was very important to get a hit. Now when I went out to the field, I probably would have thought it was a crime if I'd made an error. I think I could have had a lot more hits if I had borne down every time and played like Stan suggested, but I didn't think that was too important.

My whole philosophy in baseball was just winning. That's what it's about. You know, I could have gone 0 for 4 and we won and I could have gone 4 for 4 and we lost—and that wouldn't have been so nice. I think the whole thing is winning. The whole attitude should be oriented toward the team.

There were a lot of great ballplayers, and I mean great, who never did get to a World Series and never were on a winning team. Once I kidded Ernie Banks about being the Most Valuable Player in the league one year when the Cubs finished eighth. He was the *best* player in the league, but he wasn't very valuable because they finished eighth. Everyone said, "Well, if they didn't have Ernie where would they have finished?" Ninth? There was no ninth. How can you be most valuable unless you help a team win something? Ernie may have been the best player in the league, but he wasn't very valuable to the Chicago Cubs. He didn't win many games for them, although he was a helluva player. Some people don't think like that; they think that just because you have a great year you should be the Most Valuable Player. To me, you've got to win something. How can you be valuable if you're on the eighth-place team? Why didn't this team win?

You can get into more arguments about baseball than just about anything else. Everybody knows what the score is. You go down and sit in the bleachers of Busch Stadium, and everybody is an authority on baseball. "He should have done this" or "He should have done that." That's what make sit so great. Everybody is an authority. Everybody gets his own second guess. Everybody thinks he owns a little bit of this thing called baseball.

I have a farm in mid-Illinois, about halfway between Chicago and St. Louis, and right about that area you are either a Cub fan or a Cardinal fan. The town is evenly divided, I'm telling you. And they fight like cats and dogs up there about baseball. They're farmers. But they love baseball. Never saw a baseball game, but they're experts! It is so funny to go down to the general store there and they'll say, "Hi, Marty, how's the game gonna come out today?" I'll say, "I don't know," and they'll say, "Who's gonna win?" and I'll say, "The team that gets the most runs, naturally." Well, they don't even talk to me anymore. They say, "He don't know."

I've done almost everything in baseball. I've gone from a player to a manager to a coach to an owner. I've done everything but umpire. And I do that a lot around here. Really, I don't think my grandkids know I was a famous ballplayer. Once, somebody came up and asked me for my autograph and the kids said, "What did you do?" Well, some of them know now, but when they were younger they didn't even know or care I played baseball.

I had a great time playing baseball, but I don't like to watch it. It makes me nervous. Like with the World Series, I saw a few innings and then I went to bed. I don't go to the games. I would hate the crowds, parking your car, then walking two miles to the thing and fighting your way to get in. Just to see a ball game? I think I've seen enough. Forty years of it and I've watched a few games—a lot of innings. But I have no regrets.

Most retired players are sad people. They're sad because they were such heroes. They were up on a pedestal in their day and now they have an entirely different life.

I had a dear friend, who was our trainer, Doctor Weaver, Harrison J. Weaver. He worked on my bad back so many times that I even roomed with him at night just so he could work on me. He had his hands cast in bronze and he said, "I've been working on you so long, you've got to have something to remember me by." Not only did he give me these casts of his hands, but he gave me his World Series ring. Isn't that amazing? These are the hands that kept me going. He rubbed my back so many times it was unbelievable. He was a great man. These are the hands that kept me in baseball.

Monte Irvin, Larry Doby

MONTE
IRVIN

Monte Irvin played in the major leagues from 1949 to 1956 for the
Giants and Cubs. From 1938 to 1948 Irvin played for the Newark Eagles in the Negro League and in 1941 he won the triple crown in Mexico. He was elected to the Hall of Fame by the Committee on Negro
Baseball Leagues in 1973.

MY FATHER WAS RAISED in the South and had a flair for athletics too. All of the farmers used to have free time on Saturday
and they'd get together and play baseball. Somehow they'd
make a bat and a ball. They'd get some wool and some cloth
and wrap it and tape it up and then they'd play. Sometimes
that was the only recreation.

So I guess I grew up with it. I had five brothers and four
sisters. In 1927 we left Alabama and moved to New Jersey when
I was only eight years old.

We were raised in the country, in Orange, New Jersey—
there was a lot of open space there at that time. So we could
just go out and learn how to do things. I got a strong arm by
skimming those flat rocks over a lake and I learned how to
swim at the dam. One day I just jumped in and started swim-
ming (I had told a couple of guys to stand by just in case).
Anyhow, athletics came naturally for me.

We enjoyed doing things together, particularly athletics. My
brother was a good baseball player, and he was a great pitcher.
He never played professionally, but he was as good as anybody ever wanted to be. You see, back in those days we didn't
think about becoming a professional anything. The door was
closed to the big leagues until Jackie Robinson opened it in

1947. So we just did it for the love of it. Baseball was very popular at that time—even more popular then than it is now.

In the next town, East Orange, there was a white professional team, and Negro League teams used to come to play in East Orange on Saturdays and in Newark on Sundays. They would play an exhibition game on a Saturday and have great crowds. When I say great crowds, I mean four or five thousand people, you understand.

We used to pay twenty-five cents to go and see them play. Seeing the Negro League teams further motivated me. I knew that I couldn't aspire to become a major leaguer because the door was closed and we never knew if it was going to open or not. But we used to follow the big leagues. At that time the Cardinals were very popular. And the A's had Grove and Foxx and Bishop and all those guys. They were my heroes and I used to root for them, but I knew I could never play. We rooted for them in spite of that fact because everybody, I mean everybody, was interested in the baseball.

When I was coming along, it was fashionable to play all sports. I participated first in soccer when I was in grade school, about eight or nine years old. Then baseball season came along and I was befriended by our coach—who may have gotten twenty-five or fifty dollars more a year by coaching soccer and baseball. Since I liked him so much, when baseball season came along, I started into baseball and then later on I got interested in football and track. So when I got to high school I participated in baseball, basketball, football, and track.

In those days you played what you were comfortable with, what you liked, and what you had a flair for. I just had a natural flair for athletics. I could run fast—faster than most of my contemporaries. I could throw farther, and I was rougher.

When I got into high school I became a real star and I made All-State in all four sports. I got a football scholarship to Lincoln University in Oxford, Pennsylvania, and I matriculated there in 1938. After a year and a half, I was tired of being broke and I didn't particularly like the coach, so I decided to leave.

I left and started to play with the local Negro League team called the Newark Eagles. I was eighteen years old and I was just a kid, but I could throw really well and run and most of all I could hit. I became a regular almost overnight and as time progressed I got better. When I first started I was making $100 a month and by the time that 1942 came along I was making $150. That wasn't that bad either because during those days the average salary was between $15 and $20 a week. We just didn't make much money.

I played for Newark from 1938 to 1948, for ten years—my best years. When Jackie signed, we weren't jealous of him, but we were envious. We wished we could get signed too. We were all hoping that maybe Jackie wouldn't be the only one. And sure enough, then they signed Satchel Paige, Larry Doby, Campanella, and Newcombe, and then I came along.

In 1942 I told the owner of our club in Newark [Mrs. Effa Manley] that I wanted to get married and I asked her if she could see fit to raise me to $175 a month and she said, "I can't do it, but you've got plenty of time, you are just getting started." I told her I had an offer to go to Mexico and that they were going to give me $500 a month, plus $200 a month for an apartment. She said there was no way that she could match that. The man from Mexico, Jorge Pasquel, is known as the father of Mexican baseball. He sent me two months' pay in advance and I played in Mexico in 1942. It was the best year I ever had in baseball. I had a new wife and a honeymoon, I led the league in hitting with a .398 average, and I was the RBI and home run leader. It was my *best* year.

I played for the Vera Cruz Blues, but we played in Mexico City because it was too hot to play in Vera Cruz. There were two teams in Mexico City, the Mexico City Reds and the Vera Cruz Blues. At that time, Mexico City had about three or four million people and it was a beautiful city. Everyone called it the Paris of the West and we had a great time. We used to play on Sunday and we'd start at ten o'clock in the morning so that at one we could get dressed and go to the bullfight. So everyone would see a baseball game, then go to the bullfight, and then go nightclubbing after the bullfight. It was just wonderful and even though it got warm during the day, every night it got nice and cool enough so the ladies could wear their furs.

I caught on with the Giants in July 1949. Before that I had

played with the Giants' farm club in Jersey City in the International League. I signed with the Giants at the age of thirty-one.

I started off slowly. I didn't hit much in 1949, but in 1950 I started to play regularly for the Giants and I started to come on. Then in 1951 I had a great year. I was most valuable player on the Giants. I led the National League in RBIs (121), I hit 24 homers, and I had a .312 batting average. By that time I was making $12,500, so I went in to talk to our owner, Horace Stoneham. He said to me, "Well, Monte, you had a good year, what about salary? What do you want for next year?"

I said, "Mr. Stoneham, I've never had any problems with salary—you and I have always gotten together on salary. Whatever you think is fair." So he said, "I suppose I'll double it." Just like that. I went from $12,500 to $25,000 and I was just delighted.

I felt like a million dollars. Finally I was making some decent money. I could possibly buy a new house, get a new car, put the kids through school, save for their educations, and so on. I could get my wife a fur coat and a diamond ring and so on, the whole thing. I went to spring training the next year and I was playing great again, and then in Denver I had a very unfortunate accident. I slid into third base and broke my right ankle. That was on April 2, 1952, and I was out until August 1 of that year. I came back and I played pretty well. In 1953 I worked hard and I had a lot of treatment for my ankle and a lot of exercise. My old high school coach used to come by and massage it for me—sometimes for a couple of hours. I came back pretty well and hit .329.

I made twenty-five thousand dollars from 1952 until 1955. I had four really good years and then in 1956 the Giants traded me to the Chicago Cubs, where I made only sixteen thousand. In 1957 the Cubs released me and I started to play in the Pacific Coast League. Out there I was making only thirteen thousand dollars playing with the Los Angeles Angels.

At that point I was thirty-eight years old and I had a degenerating disk in my back. I asked the doctor, Dr. Robert Kerlan, about it. He said that if I was out of baseball, my back probably wouldn't bother me and he wouldn't advise an operation. So I decided to quit rather than have an operation.

I feel fortunate, even though I would have loved to have played in the majors for twenty years; I knew I had the ability. I didn't get twenty years—I only got seven. But I am very grateful because some of the truly talented guys who used to play in the old Negro Leagues never got a chance at all. And Satchel Paige only played two or three years because he was a little old. At least I got a chance to earn a little money and a chance to play in the majors. I saw the best of two worlds and I feel very fortunate about that.

During those days, money was not that important. Of course we wanted to make some money, but we really enjoyed playing the game. Honestly, we loved to get out there every day and we liked to please the fans. We liked the adulation.

Most of the old guys that you talk to can remember almost every game that they ever played in because they loved it, and it was in their hearts. It was fun doing it day to day and trying to do it right, trying to get better, trying to beat the opposing team. I guess there are some players today who feel that way, but I don't think there are enough of them. We really enjoyed it—we treasured every moment.

I'm happy these guys today are making money, but they should play a little better and appreciate it more. Give a little bit more back to the fans and to the community. They don't know what hard times we had paving the way and how history was changing. Particularly the black guys—they should really appreciate it a little bit more. They should know how they got to where they are. In order to understand the future you *do* have to know all about the past. Jackie Robinson did a great job pioneering and so did the rest of us, but it wasn't easy then. It was hard work.

Young people should read and learn that part of our history so that they'll be able to tell it all to their kids as time goes by. We all need to keep in touch with history. When Jackie Robinson did what he did, when he succeeded, he helped athletically, culturally, financially—he helped the cause in every way. Before that it was tough for a black lady to go in and get a job as a secretary, or for a guy to work in an automobile plant. But when Jackie succeeded, then employers started to say, "What the heck, they're just like anybody else. They can do a job given a chance." Jackie helped bring all of this about. It still would have happened, but he caused it to happen that much faster. I was happy that I had a chance to make a contribution, too. I got some publicity and helped to contribute to the cause. I tried to do the right thing.

It's very important that we know our history, not just for the memories of the pain and difficulties, but because it gives us hope. It shows how quickly some things can change. And we can't live without hope. We must have hope.

It was a little scary the first time I walked into the Giants' clubhouse. I was a little apprehensive because I didn't know how my teammates would react, and I was also worried about just making the club. There was another black fellow too, named Hank Thompson, and we both reported at the same time. We were a little nervous, hoping that we could succeed and make a contribution. One thing that helped us was the fact that Leo Durocher, our manager, called a meeting and introduced Hank and me, and he said, "I want to say one thing, and that's all I want to say about it. If you can play ball I don't care what color you are, what color anybody is. You can be green and if you are a good ballplayer you can be on this team. That's enough and that's all I am going to say about this situation."

We had a lot of Southern guys on that team and they're some of my good friends now. We didn't have that much of a problem. But Jackie, you see, did have a problem because he was the first and the only one for quite a while. It was like a brand-new idea. One time I asked one of the baseball officials, "Do you realize that during the days when you had Babe Ruth and Lou Gehrig and Jimmy Foxx and Joe DiMaggio and all the rest of those great players that we had the equals of those guys in our league, too? What made you think that we couldn't make the majors?" His answer was "Maybe it was the era, but we just didn't think you guys could do it. We knew you could play pretty well among yourselves, but we just didn't think you could play major league ball." Can you even imagine that? That is the old plantation way of thinking, and it still exists today to a degree.

When any black person makes a contribution or succeeds in a public role, then it helps everybody in some fashion. Right now I'm just delighted to see Colin Powell make a contribution because it will help the whole world. We are all related in some way and by his succeeding it will make it better for other black soldiers to come along. Maybe one of these days he might run for president.

The one thing about this country is that despite what's wrong here, it is much better than the other countries. That's the first thing that you realize when you travel. It gives you hope that you can rise above in some way. Sports in particular have provided a way up for a lot of people in this country, and if you work really hard, you can get what you dream for. It takes a certain type of person to pursue that dream, a person who is willing to work harder to get something better.

I had the normal encouragement from my family. My mother wanted me to be a policeman. She thought that was a steady job and solid. My father said, "I can't help you to go to college, Monte, but if you get there I'll be able to send you a little money once in a while," and he told my mother, "Stop telling Monte not to play baseball." I appreciated his faith in me, and he was my biggest supporter. When I made the majors I used to take him to the ball park with me. One day the team stayed late after a big game, sitting in the clubhouse and drinking a few beers. When I came out he was signing autographs himself. He said, "Well, you took so long, I had to sign—my name, not yours!"

I hate to think about how it would have been different if I had my whole career in the big leagues, instead of spending ten years with the Eagles in the Negro Leagues—the record book would have been a little different. My statistics would have been much better. The reason I was inducted into the Hall of Fame is because they knew what I could have been if I had had the chance ten years earlier, along with what I did after I got the chance. So the special Hall of Fame Committee on Negro Leagues elected me to the Hall of Fame in 1973. When I made my speech, I said I just wished my father could have been there because he was the guiding force. He was the person behind the scenes. He encouraged me and stayed with me and advised me during all of those lean years.

I knew that I had truly made it as a major leaguer when I was playing in a tough game in 1950 and hit a bases-loaded home run off of Dutch Leonard. Dutch was a tough knuckle-ball pitcher and I homered to win the ball game. I said to my-

self, "If you can hit a home run off of this pitcher, then you have arrived." After that the confidence was there and I knew I could do it. I could do it all along but it was a matter of getting the confidence. It's like what comes first, the chicken or the egg? In order to get confidence you have to perform and once you start to perform well, the confidence builds and it all just keeps going.

My greatest memory was in 1951, the year that we came from behind to catch the Dodgers and in the last game Bobby Thomson hit that home run to beat the Dodgers. That year I led the charge and that's why the Giants voted me the MVP, even though Bobby hit the home run. That game, that triumph, taught me that the game is really not over until the last man is out. If you just keep going and keep going and do the best you can, then sometime later you will be rewarded. When Bobby Thomson hit that home run, it was for all of us, for playing so well and not giving up.

Baseball means so much to people that they can be either overjoyed or destroyed by the outcome of a game. There were two or three suicides after that game by people who were listening. People still come up to me and say, "I could kill you, because you guys beat the Dodgers." And I always say to them, "You should have been a Giants fan."

Larry and Norm Sherry, 1960

NORM SHERRY

Norm Sherry, a backup catcher, played for ten years in the minor leagues before making it to the big leagues in 1960. He played for the Dodgers and Mets. A career baseball man, Sherry has managed and coached since 1964.

I CAN RECALL THAT there was a creek that ran right in front of our house and I would stand out in the street and throw rocks to see if I could reach the other side. I think that's where I first started throwing. I had three brothers and we were always playing together, out there throwing those rocks or playing catch with any kind of a ball.

My parents moved to the West Hollywood area of Los Angeles. In grammar school I decided I wanted to be a ballplayer because we lived about five blocks from the Triple A ball park that was the home of the Hollywood Stars. My brothers and I would go down to the ball park all the time. We sold papers and picked up cushions after the game. We'd run outside in the seventh inning when they were ready to sell the papers and we'd hope the foul balls would come over the top of the stands so that we'd have balls to play with.

My life revolved around that ball park. When we'd come home after the game we'd start playing and pretend that we were the players that we had just watched. We emulated all of the guys that we saw playing. The Hollywood Stars of the Pacific Coast League—those guys were my idols. I didn't know big-league baseball. I didn't know that there *was* more baseball than the Pacific Coast League, because that's what I grew up with. I knew the big names like Joe DiMaggio, Babe Ruth,

Lou Gehrig, and people like that, but I really didn't know much about big-league ball until I was almost signing to play.

When I was in grammar school, I'll never forget when my second grade teacher, Mrs. Woods, asked every kid as they were walking out of the door, "What do you want to be when you grow up?" I said, "I'm going to be a baseball player."

I knew I was going to be a baseball player. I loved it. We played all day long. My mother used to threaten us—"I'm going to burn your bats, I'm going to throw away your gloves!"—because we would never come home. We lived three houses from the high school and we'd jump the fence and play ball in the field there. We wouldn't come home until it was pitch-black.

Both of my brothers signed and played professional ball. George only got to play one year and then he hurt his arm. But Larry had a great career; he really did a lot better than I did as a player.

I spent ten years playing in the minor leagues and two in the service before I got my chance to play in the major leagues, but I knew in my heart that I would get to do it. I got a lot of recognition in high school and the scouts were looking at me. The best thing that I could do was throw. I had a great arm. Probably from throwing all of those rocks. When I first signed I would take infield practice and the other team would come out and stand there to watch. I could really throw that baseball.

The first year that I went to spring training I was with the Dodgers in Vero Beach. It was my first trip to Florida and it was my first plane ride. Jack Lillis, whose brother Bob was a Dodger coach, and I were on the plane together. We started talking and he asked me what position I played. I said I was a catcher and then he asked me what it was that I could do well. I told him I had a good arm, and he said, "I want to tell you something: When you get to Vero Beach, you make sure that they all know that you have a good arm. You *fire* that ball as hard as you can, all the time. Make them understand. There are so many ballplayers that you'll only stand out if you let them see what's there."

I was sick as a dog for the first four or five days in Florida. I had left California with a T-shirt on and a little thin sports coat and we had waited for hours to change planes in Chicago.

It was freezing and snowing and I got sick. Then I came out and my first day out on the field we were taking infield practice. They had all of the catchers throwing the ball all around. I was the last guy because I hadn't been there and then they threw the ball in. They were finishing infield practice. So I yelled, "Hey, I didn't get a chance to throw," and the coach said, "All right, go ahead and throw one down to third."

I fired that ball and they ran everybody back out on to the field and took another two rounds of hitting just to see me throw. If I could have hit as well as I threw, I would have been something special. Hitting was something that took a long time for me to learn. I struggled in the minor leagues. I could always catch and throw, but hitting took me a long time to understand and to hit well enough that they would look at me as a big-league player.

Then when I got through playing, I started as a minor league manager and I knew, I felt, that I could get back to the majors as a coach, and I did. I've been coaching ever since. I coached two years with the Angels and then went back to coaching in the minor leagues. I had another two years with the Angels, four years with Montreal, and three years with San Diego. This is my sixth year here in San Francisco. So, all of these things that I had such a desire to do, that I actually believed were going to happen to me, did.

I went straight from high school to baseball. I signed with the Hollywood Stars in 1950. They gave me a Triple A contract, but they sent me to Class C which was the Cal State League in Santa Barbara.

The next year I started the season with Fort Worth. Like I said, I could catch it and throw it, but I couldn't hit it. I was hitting about .084 and they sent me to Newport News. That was where I first met and became friends with Roger Craig and Bob Lillis. We were all there.

After that year, I went into the service for two years and missed the seasons in 1952 and 1953. I played ball in the service in Frankfurt, Germany, and we won the championship. Our little team had some guys who were pretty good. We didn't have any real superstars but we had a couple of guys who had played minor league ball and we had some guys who just played Sunday ball.

I came back in 1954 and headed for Vero Beach again, and they didn't even know who I was. When I went in the service I weighed 160 pounds and when I came back I weighed 188. I got a lot bigger and I guess that helped my hitting later on too, because I could hit the ball a little harder.

I started out in Fort Worth and then I went back to Newport News. Roger [Craig] had just gotten out of the Army and he was there as well and we won the play-offs that year.

In 1955 I went to Fort Worth, ended up hurting my arm, and had to have elbow surgery. Then in the winter that year I had back surgery, disk problems. I had a miserable time in 1955, and that carried over to 1956 because when I went to spring training I could barely walk. I didn't get to play until the middle of the season and then they sent me out of the organization to Buffalo, New York, to play.

It was a good experience but I was still hurting, and in 1957 the Dodgers sent me to St. Paul. By that time my hitting had really come around and I was feeling pretty good about my ability. I was going to get married, and things were going pretty well.

Then in May, we were playing a game and, God, it was freezing out. The wind was blowing and the pitcher threw at me and busted my arm with the ball. I did get married a few days after that, but I was on the disabled list for most of that year.

Finally in 1959, I made the club and the second game of the season, I got a base hit and drove in 2 runs and won the game. That was on the road, in Chicago, and it was my first major league game. When we came back to L.A., they called me up and told me that they were sending me to Spokane again. I couldn't believe it. They did it because of paperwork. The other catcher was Pignatano and he didn't have any options out, so if they sent him out, they couldn't get him back. I had options, so they sent me out, saying they could always recall me.

In 1960 I made the ball club and I stayed until they sold me to the Mets in 1963. My last two years in the major leagues I didn't do very well. I had hurt my knees in 1962 and every time I would get down to catch, the cartilage would stick out and I had to push it back in with my hand.

I was backup catcher, but at least I did what I thought I was going to do. I did play. There was never a doubt and I knew it just had to happen. I don't know how you explain things like that. It was just the feeling I had for this game of baseball. I can't understand anybody who puts this uniform on and doesn't love it.

I did it because I loved it. It was my life. You don't want to put it in front of family and things like that, you really don't. But, I'll tell you, it is right up there.

My biggest thrill was hitting my first home run in the major leagues. We were in the eleventh inning and my brother Larry was pitching for us in relief. We were playing the Phillies and I think Ruben Gomez was pitching for them. He threw me a slider and I hit it over the fence in Los Angeles and won the game. My first major league homer made my brother the winning pitcher. I thought that was pretty good. A real family affair.

I was really thrilled when I finally walked into a major league clubhouse and put on that major league uniform. I remember my first at bat, I couldn't stop my legs from shaking. The first time I threw the ball to second, it went toward second base and then shooting on out to center field. I couldn't control the ball, it had so much stuff on it. Charlie Neal, who was playing second base, looked at me and slapped his face, like, "What is going on?"

I like to watch the movie *The Natural* now because that's the kind of thing I always dreamed of. You know, to get up and hit the ball out of the park and win the game. If you're a little guy like me that's what you think about.

When I got through playing, I came home to Los Angeles. A friend of mine had offered me a job working for J. P. Stevens and Company as a representative of the carpet division, going around to the major department stores talking to the carpet people. They offered me fifteen thousand dollars. I couldn't believe it because that was what I had been making as a ballplayer. Only J. P. Stevens was regular hours and I had an expense account. But I didn't want to give up baseball yet.

I went to the Dodgers, talked to Buzzy Bavasi, and he told me, "I can give you a job managing Santa Barbara, but I can only pay you six thousand dollars for the season." I took the job in Santa Barbara. I managed that team for three years and then I went with the Yankees as a scout because they offered me ten thousand.

When Roger [Craig] took the job as manager for San Francisco, he called me. Roger and I and Sparky Anderson go way back. We always told each other that if we had a major league job we would hire each other. So the first year that I got this coaching job in 1970 with the Angels, Lefty Phillips was the manager, and Sparky Anderson was going to be his third base coach. Sparky was offered the Cincinnati job right after that and off he went. Sparky asked me to be one of his coaches there, but what could I do? I couldn't leave Lefty too—then he'd have nobody. Sparky went on with his Big Red Machine for all of those years and when he went to Detroit he asked me again. I said no again because then I was with Dick Williams.

Roger and I had played together in 1951 and 1954, then played together in Spokane in 1959 and in the sixties in the major leagues. We were always good friends; his kids call me Uncle Norm and my kids called him Uncle Roger. Now I work for him. I've been here since 1986, and it's great for me to say, "I'm a coach for Roger Craig."

I started in baseball in 1950, so this is my forty-first year and I would do it all over again. I just wonder if my feelings would be the same if I were a kid today as they were when I started. Because the way that kids are brought up and the way that life is, isn't the same today. We had radio, no television, and we entertained ourselves playing baseball. That was the greatest thing that we could do.

When I was a kid during the summer I would get up at six o'clock in the morning and I'd beat on all of the neighbor kids' windows and yell, "Get up, let's go," and we'd go to the high school and play ball all day long. There is something about hitting a baseball, the feeling when you hit it well. You feel like everybody is looking at you. It makes you important for just that minute.

There are too many variables in baseball to call it a science. It's a game of emotions to me. It is a matter of how well a pitcher can handle his emotions in a tough spot, or how a hitter faces a tough pitcher. Some guys can't handle it and some guys can.

Controlling yourself—that's what is hard for everybody. That happens to all of the young guys coming up. They can't control the force that's in them that wants to make them good. They have got to learn to say, "I can control everything," and not let the situation control them.

Is it a science to throw a baseball? No, it's mechanics. I don't know how much science plays in it. There are certain ways that you have to use your body to throw a ball right so that it doesn't hurt your arm and so you can get the best out of yourself. But everybody is a little bit different and some guys do it differently than the next guy. And hitting? Who is going to claim that hitting is a science? How about Gil McDougald? He had a stance that was crazy and yet he could hit.

There *is* some technique as far as trying to have the bat strike the ball on the downward plane, hitting through the ball and then having the bat come up. And when you throw a ball your arm should go down and across and work in that manner. But just remember this when you talk about the science of it— some guys can do it all wrong and still do it better than everybody else.

TOM POHOLSKY

Tom Poholsky, a strong right-hander, pitched for the Cardinals in 1950–51 and 1954–57. In 1950 he was named the International League's MVP. Poholsky pitched and won a twenty-two inning game for Rochester against Jersey City in 1951.

I GREW UP IN Detroit during the Depression in the thirties and then in the early forties the war started. I was peddling papers all through the war years and I didn't get to play many sports because of my paper route. School would finish and I would have to go to work. I had played sandlot baseball and that was about all. Of course, in those days, to put a ball game together you'd just get your friends from the neighborhood and go out and play ball. There were a couple of fields around where that's exactly what we did.

Somehow, I was able to join the team my senior year, so I pitched my last year of high school in the spring. I had no visions of being a ballplayer but I followed the Detroit Tigers religiously. I still remember all those players from the thirties and the war years.

During that period of time, schools would double-promote kids and I moved ahead a couple of years along with a very close friend of mine. We got good grades and because they double-promoted us I ended up graduating at fifteen. There was a bird-dog scout there in Detroit and he wanted to sign me but he had to get permission from my parents to allow me to sign any kind of contract. They had to approve it because I was so young. That was also the case with two other boys on the same team, the second baseman and the catcher.

177

All of our parents agreed that they wanted us to go ahead and play baseball. Now when I talk with my mother about why she let me go at that tender age (I was the oldest in the family, the number one son, etc.) she just says, "Well, your dad and I thought that you enjoyed baseball and this was an opportunity in your life." To them it was that was plain and simple.

We graduated in early June and the very next day the three of us went to Durham, North Carolina, a Red Sox farm club. I was just fifteen years old and my travels prior to that consisted of around Detroit and out into the country. So for me to go to Durham was incredible. I could have been going to Singapore or Paris and it would have seemed just as strange and new because I had no concept of distance at that point in my life. I packed my trunk, tied a belt around it, got on the train, and waved good-bye to the family. Off I went to play ball.

When I think back, I wasn't scared, I really wasn't. It was a big adventure. The war was going on, so there was a lot of adventure in the newspapers with the battles and the heroes. I always read about the fighter pilots and the naval battles going on in the Pacific. I was just a few steps away from being part of that and since I'd been a newsboy I read the paper every day.

If I hadn't made it in baseball I probably would have ended up in an auto plant. But I had this desire to go to college. Maybe it came from reading about the war, or who knows what. I went away to play ball, and the contract that I signed gave me $125 a month for June, July, and August. One of the things that I did was save some of that money and in the fall of 1945 I started engineering school at the University of Detroit.

When the movie *Bull Durham* came out, I went to see it and that ball park is the same park that I first played in. The park itself, the stands, the hill in the outfield before the fence, all of that was exactly the same place that I saw when I got off the train in Durham.

The trains weren't air-conditioned in those days and they were still coal-fired. Somewhere along the way we went through a tunnel and I had my window open. As we went through the tunnel all of the soot came in the window; I looked down and everything was just black. I was off to a good start. I learned very quickly about some things you do and don't do.

I got to Durham in the early evening and they were playing a game. I took a cab from the station to the ball park. I had never taken a cab before. I walked in, the lights were on, and it was the first time that I had ever seen a night game. Watching the game, I thought to myself, "My God, those guys are incredible, they throw the ball harder and are running faster than anything that I have ever seen." The fellow who was pitching became my roommate that year, but when I saw him throw the ball that first night, I thought, "Oh God, I'll never throw the ball that hard!"

With my salary and rent and everything, I still managed to save some money. Taxes were lower—I don't think we even had any social security. Out of $125 we ended up with $118 or $120 as a net salary. We lived in a rooming house and we traveled by car. The team had three or four cars; we didn't even have a bus. The farthest town that we played was only eighty miles away, Nortonsville, Virginia.

Usually we'd drive to the game and then drive home after the game. Those were long days. The drive was slow, and they were all two-lane roads then. But we didn't care, we enjoyed ourselves.

So I played ball in the summer. I knew I'd be finished around Labor Day and that was when school started. Then I'd go back to school through January, stop to play ball, and go back to school again in the fall. I did that for thirteen years and finally got my degree in engineering. It took that long, but I never doubted I'd finish. Where I grew up, college was the last thing that people thought about. But I was sure I wanted to go. I went after several dreams, and I always knew I would get them. The first couple of years I didn't get the best grades, but it was a real change of pace to go from my life as a minor league ballplayer and switch over to school. It was hard, but I learned to do what had to be done.

I found out afterward from my mother that the team would write my parents and tell them how I was progressing, that I was behaving myself, that type of thing. They maintained contact with my parents because I was underage and they were liable for me. The team really did watch to see that I stayed out of trouble.

In 1945, there were a lot of older ballplayers on the team who were exempt from fighting. One player in particular, who was from Durham, was like a father figure to me. He took me under his wing. He was married and had a nice wife, and he watched over me.

The war ended in 1945 and in the spring of 1946 there were baseball players all over the place. A lot of the guys who were in the war came back hoping to play. In spring training in Durham in 1946 I think we must have had ninety guys in the camp. At that time, Durham was in a Class C league, which was one jump above the bottom. I think most of the minor league teams had similar circumstances with a lot of ballplayers in 1946.

They sent me to a Class D team in Millford, Delaware, that was in the Eastern Shore League. That was another eye-opener for me to see the Atlantic Ocean. I never knew what the ocean looked like before that.

Millford was a small town, maybe three thousand people, and we just played that peninsula on the east side of the Chesapeake Bay.

We rode by bus. We went to a town and played and came back home. I was fortunate enough to live with a family who took me in and treated me like a son. They'd feed me breakfast and dinner out of their own pockets. I paid only two or three dollars a week.

Our entertainment in Millford was to go over to Rehoboth Beach and enjoy the ocean. One vivid memory from that summer was a luncheon for the ball club. On the menu it was either oysters or clams—but whichever, I had never been exposed to anything like that. I looked hard at those things and then I managed to swallow them.

In the winter of 1946 there was a draft—each level or class had a minor league draft. I was reading *The Sporting News* in the middle of the winter and I saw that Columbus, Georgia, had drafted me. I didn't know what that meant because I had no concept of the business end of baseball. The Red Sox had put me on the Lynchburg, Virginia, roster in Class B, and Columbus, Georgia, which was a Class A Cardinal farm club in the South Atlantic League, had drafted me. I had heard stories in the minor leagues about what it was like to be on a Cardinal

farm club, about how they didn't pay anything, that they had
five hundred guys in the organization, and guys sat down in
the minor leagues for years.

I had heard all of these things in just the couple of years
that I had been in minor league ball and I didn't want to go to
Columbus. I wrote to the head scout for the Red Sox at that
time, a fellow by the name of George "Specs" Toporcer. I wrote
him and pleaded, "I don't want to go to Columbus. What can
you do to keep me from going to Columbus?" He wrote me a
nice letter back and said that that was the way that baseball in
the minor leagues worked and advised me to go.

Several issues of *The Sporting News* later, I was reading
again and it said that Columbus, Georgia, would hold spring
training with Columbus, Ohio, and the Rochester Red Wings
in Daytona Beach, Florida. All of a sudden this wasn't going
to be so bad after all. Now I was going to Florida. I was seventeen years old and practically a world traveler.

I liked that. I was from Detroit and there I was taking the
train to Florida for spring training. I think they sent me a contract for $250 a month. So I doubled my salary.

Daytona Beach was a sleepy little town on Florida's east
coast then. It was fantastic. I was on the beach every day and
having a good time. There were three ball clubs there and there
were a lot of baseball players around.

I went to Columbus and it was a fair-sized community. We
played in Columbus, Macon, Savannah, Charleston, and places
like that. We traveled by bus but we would play a whole series, so we stayed in hotels. I didn't pitch for a month and I
didn't understand why. Later on I found out that they couldn't
send me down because then the club they had drafted me from
could have had me back.

The manager was an ex-Yankee pitcher by the name of Kemp
Wicker. He had been with the Yankees for a short period of
time and he'd been up and down a few times. He sort of fa-
thered me along, he let me build my confidence, and I got in
a couple of games. I'd go in to pitch some relief and we'd come
back and win the game, and I started the second game of a
doubleheader now and then. That's the year that I first stayed
in a hotel that had air-conditioning. It was in Columbia, South
Carolina, and who knows, it may still be there. It was the Wade

Hampton Hotel and I think they kept it about seventy degrees. It would be ninety-eight degrees outside and you'd walk into that hotel and it would be like an icebox. I guess that was another giant leap away from Detroit!

I pitched a twenty-two-inning game in the International League in 1950 and Del Wilber caught all twenty-two innings. It was a Sunday and we had only one game. The game was in Rochester and against Jersey City. It was a beautiful day and everybody was thinking, "Oh great, only one game and we'll get off early for a change on Sunday!"

We started playing and it was 2–2 after the second inning. Then the innings just started going by. The fellow pitching for Jersey City was Andy Tomasic. He had good control and I had good control and a lot of outs were being made on the first or second pitch. All of a sudden we're into the tenth inning and then the thirteenth and then the sixteenth. As I recall there really weren't any great opportunities, like the bases loaded with nobody out or anything like that. The game just went right along. I felt fine. I don't know about Del—he was the one who was up and down for twenty-two innings.

By the twentieth inning, everybody was saying, "Hell, we'll just keep playing until it's done." I was in super shape. In those years I ran a lot and my legs were strong. As a pitcher, if your legs are out of shape, you're going to have problems. Finally, in the bottom of the twenty-second inning, one of our guys, the shortstop (Dick Cole) got a base hit. I think it was with one out, then the other pitcher balked, and Don Richmond, our third baseman, came up. He was hitting about .340, and he led the league that year. He just happened to hit a ball right onto the first base bag and it bounced over Norm Schup's head into the right field corner. Scoring was easy and we won it, 3–2. I was the MVP that year for the International League and that game seemed the culmination of it all.

Johnny Keene, our manager, went over and congratulated the opposing pitcher, which was a nice gesture. I can imagine how I would have felt to lose it after all those innings. Tomasic pitched as good a game as I did—but someone had to win it.

After Rochester, I came to St. Louis. The first day that I stood on the field with the Cardinals was really something. The Cardinals had Stan Musial, Enos Slaughter, and Terry

Moore. They had a wealth of young outfielders down in the minors who were very good, but there was no opening for them with those three.

When I came up to the major leagues and got on the roster, I was the first young pitcher that had come up after the war because they had Howie Pollet, Harry Brecheen, Max Lanier, George Munger, Ted Wilks, and Gerry Staley. Then Harvey Haddix was the next one who broke into that staff. It was a dream come true to go to spring training in 1950 with St. Louis, but the next thing was to perform and stay there. We never let little aches and pains or anything keep us out of that lineup because we could be replaced very easily.

I pitched Opening Day as a rookie in 1951 and that had never happened before in the Cardinal organization. We played on the road in Pittsburgh and it was twenty-nine degrees and snowing. That was the reason that they had me pitch. We played in the snow and I pitched against Murry Dickson.

I pitched against the great Dodger teams a lot. I didn't beat them often, but when I did it was eventful. One year I pitched against them three times and lost, 2–1 and 2–1 and 1–0, all against Preacher Roe.

I hurt my arm in 1959 and was sent to Houston. That was the year that Marty Marion bought the club. It was still a minor league team, but he envisioned a major league team in Houston. We had all of the old-timers in baseball on that club. We were a bunch of derelicts. I think we lost something like 104 games. At that time it was the American Association, combined with parts of the Pacific Coast League, which consisted of Houston, Omaha, Charleston, Dallas-Fort Worth, Tulsa/ Oklahoma City, Minneapolis/St. Paul, Indianapolis, and Louisville. We had a Mexican pilot who flew us around in an old DC-3 Miami Airlines charter aircraft. We had a great time, but we were a terrible team. I had been hoping to make a comeback, but my arm was so bad that I quit after that year.

Some things you never forget. I got the chance to play against some of the fellows from the early forties that I had heard about on the radio. I never even thought that something like that could be possible. I was in the right place at the right time. It was wonderful. Fate, or whatever you call it, plays a big part in our lives—or it might just be luck.

TOMMY LASORDA

> Tommy Lasorda, the man whose heart is said to bleed Dodger blue, pitched for the Dodgers from 1954 to 1956. Although his playing career was short, Lasorda is the ultimate Dodger. After scouting, minor league managing, and major league coaching, Lasorda became the manager of the Los Angeles Dodgers in 1976.

I THINK WHEN I was ten or twelve years old I started to dream about playing in the major leagues. Baseball was my really great love. All I ever wanted to be was a baseball player. We didn't have the Little League, we didn't have the Babe Ruth League, we didn't have the Stan Musial League . . . nothing like that.

What we did was play pickup baseball. Our neighborhood had a team and we would go to the one and only park in our town, Norristown, Pennsylvania, and if there were two teams playing when we got there we would play the winner. We'd wait around until their game was over and whoever won stayed on the field and the other team got on. It went like that as long as there were teams present. We played all day long, no umpires, no rules or anything like that; we just played.

All of our dreams were to be major league baseball players. I used to actually go to bed and dream that I was pitching in Yankee Stadium. The Yankees were my team. I knew all their middle names, I even knew their batting averages, I knew everything about them. I had absolutely no ambition to be anything else except a baseball player and that's what I concentrated on.

Then one day, there I was with the Brooklyn Dodgers and we were playing in Yankee Stadium, playing the Yankees in

what they used to call the City Series. When I was summoned in to pitch from the bull pen in left field, I walked in, looked around, and I thought, "I've been here many times in my dreams," but that was the first time that I was ever really there. That dream became a reality and it's positive proof that we must live our life with dreams, hopes, and prayers, because if you dream hard enough and you work hard enough, dreams do come true.

When I was sixteen years old I signed my first baseball contract and I've been in baseball ever since. I'm sixty-four years old, so my entire life I've been in baseball. I struggled a lot of years, but I never wanted to quit. I always wanted to remain, because I was doing exactly what I really and truly wanted to do. I never reached the plateaus that I had dreamed of, I never became the baseball player that I had hoped, but I did get to the major leagues.

When you look at where I came from, it was quite a feat. I was the third-string pitcher on the Norristown baseball team and the son of an Italian immigrant. When you're a third-string pitcher on the high school team, you're worthless. You don't get in the games. When we would play the other schools I had to carry the bats. But I told that coach one day, "You see those two pitchers, that Buddy Rider and Red Hennig? You put those guys in the game and you never put me in a game. One day you and those two guys are going to have to buy a ticket to see me play in the big leagues." He laughed, but in 1954 they did come to see me play with the Brooklyn Dodgers in Philadelphia.

So it's the "Lasorda proof" that if you want something badly enough in life, you have to work awfully hard, you have to have self-confidence, and you've got to believe. I did reach the major leagues. It wasn't a great or successful career, but it was exciting and I was doing exactly what I loved to do. Then, all of a sudden my career came to an end and the Dodgers asked me to become a scout.

I started scouting and I covered six states—Pennsylvania, Delaware, Washington, Maryland, Virginia, and West Virginia. I did that in 1961 and all of 1962. Then in 1963 the Dodgers moved to California. We had just settled into a new house and were living in my hometown, where my brothers were. But I wanted to move out to the West Coast because I felt that when you are out of sight you are out of mind. I thought if we were three thousand miles away and I didn't make this move, I would probably be a scout for the rest of my life. My wife, who is the greatest that God ever put on earth, said to me, "Wherever you go, wherever you're happy, we're happy, and wherever you go and you're miserable, we're miserable. You do what you want to do and we'll go with you."

We gave up a nice house back in Pennsylvania and we moved out to California. I started scouting and then they asked me to be the manager of the rookie league team. I did that for four years and then they moved me to Triple A. It was quite a jump from the rookie league to Triple A. I managed in Ogden, Utah, and then I managed in Spokane, Washington, and Albuquerque, New Mexico. Then they brought me up to the major league as a coach and I did that for four years and then I became the manager of the Dodgers.

So here I am starting my sixteenth year as a manager and my forty-third year in the Dodger organization, and it's been a very wonderful career, simply because I did exactly what I wanted to do. I love what I'm doing; there isn't anybody in this world that loves their job more than I love mine. I'm the happiest guy in the world.

I've said this many times: There are four things in my lifetime that I've never regretted: I've never regretted one day of the love that I have for God, I have never regretted one day of the family that God gave me, I've never regretted one day of living in the greatest country in the world, the land of opportunity, and I've never regretted my forty-three years with the Dodgers. I'd say it would be in that order. You're talking to the most grateful, most appreciative man in the world.

My father knew nothing about baseball and my mother knew *absolutely* nothing about baseball. My father was born in Italy—the only thing he knew was boccie—my mother was born in America, and they did not want me to play baseball. They wanted me to go to school. They wanted to prepare me for life, they wanted me to get an education, and they wanted me to go to college. But eventually my mother and father were very proud of me. When they learned about the game, they knew how important it was and what it meant in this country. They were happy for me.

It was a thrill and an honor to put on that major league uniform the first time. It was what I had dreamed of when I was ten and twelve years old. Suddenly there it was. Right there. I had worked hard for it and had my sad moments. I had tough times when I didn't make much money and struggled. But the love for the game was so strong that it made me continue—I just wanted to be in baseball. I loved it. I still love it.

When we played, it was a different ball game, very different. The players didn't make very much money. They had to work in the off-season. They had families to provide for and they never knew when the end was coming to their careers. They struggled; they had great days and not so great days. There were twenty-six farm teams; now there are five. The game has changed.

There was a greater sense of community in those days because everybody rode the trains and we had time to be together. There was more unity, more togetherness. In spring training we would eat, drink, and sleep baseball. We used to live in barracks with no heat. Freeze at night, no television. We weren't allowed to bring our cars down. Today we have color TV in each room, heaters, the rooms are beautiful, the beds are great—the times have changed.

All of the advantages are in favor of the players today. When we played, the owners had more control of the players. If you didn't want to take the salary that they wanted to give you, they told you to stay home. You had a family, you had to play to survive, so you had to take it. Now the pendulum is swinging the other way and the players have all of the control.

But it is still the best game in town! And I'll tell you why. You don't have to be big to play baseball. Everybody can play baseball and everybody does play baseball at some time or another. That's what makes our game so great. The little guys have been successful in our game. It's a game that is played by everyone, even your grandmother probably played baseball, and it's the best buy in town.

Take a man who works hard, trying to raise a family and earn a living. He needs an escape with his family. He has to be able to go somewhere, whether it is to an amusement park or to picnic grounds or the mountains or the lakes. So what greater place can someone go with a family of five than to beautiful Dodger Stadium and buy five general-admission tickets for about twenty dollars? Try to buy five tickets to a National Football League game for twenty dollars. Try to buy five tickets to an NBA game for twenty dollars. It's impossible. You can hardly fill your gas tank up for twenty dollars. Baseball is still the best buy in town.

I think the thing that I try to impress upon the guys playing for me today is they must be role models because youngsters look up to them. Idolatry is great. I idolized big-league ballplayers; I thought they were the greatest thing that God ever put on earth. Joe DiMaggio or Babe Ruth or Lou Gehrig—they could have put a hand on my head and said, "Son, don't ever do anything wrong," and I believe I'd have gone to the seminary to become a priest because they were my heroes.

Major league players must spend more time talking to the youth of this country and telling them how important it is for them to get a good education. An education opens many doors to success. If they spent more time trying to impress the youth of this country about how important it is for them to stay away from illegal drugs, those youngsters would listen to those major league players quicker than they would to their own parents.

Major league players can play a very vital role in this country being role models. They are put on a pedestal by the youngsters who try to emulate them. They try to bat like them, walk like them, dress like them, throw like them—so if they see that these guys are involved in drugs they will emulate that also: "If it's good enough for my heroes, it's good enough for me."

In the forties and the fifties, the players were proud of the game. They were proud to be a part of it and they did everything in their power to maintain the integrity of the game of baseball.

You look in the papers today, almost every day somebody is being arrested for rape, somebody has been arrested for selling illegal drugs, somebody has been arrested for taking illegal drugs. You never saw that in the papers before because no one did that. We were proud of what we represented. The whole

world has changed. When we were playing ball, if somebody had offered us an illegal drug, we'd have killed him.

Money has made such a big difference too. I once heard a preacher say that money is the root of all evil and then I heard another one say that no money is the root of all evil. I don't know whether it is best to have it or not. They make a lot more money today than we ever did, they drive beautiful cars and stuff like that, but the pride that we possessed was second to none. We clearly weren't playing just for the money; the money wasn't that good.

In baseball, if you fail seven times out of ten times you are a success. If you go to bat ten times and you get three base hits and strike out seven times you're a .300 hitter and you are a success. If you were a doctor and you operated on ten people and seven of them died you'd be in trouble.

There is a lot of strategy and instinct to our game. You've got to have instinct, good eyes, quick hands—there are so many things that you have to have.

It's like a motor of a car: You can take the carburetor out of the car and the car won't start. Put the carburetor back in and take the pistons out and it won't start. Put the pistons back in and take the plugs out and it won't start. It's the same thing with baseball. You can have a quick bat and you can have good balance, but if you have bad eyes, you can't see the ball. Everything has to work together, like the motor of a car.

AL KALINE

Al Kaline, Mr. Tiger, played the outfield for the Detroit Tigers from 1953 to 1974. Kaline was an All-Star from 1955 to 1967 and again in 1971 and 1974. He was awarded the Gold Glove ten times and was inducted into the Hall of Fame in 1980. Currently Kaline broadcasts for the Detroit Tigers.

I GREW UP IN Baltimore, Maryland, and there was a big power plant next to where I lived. The workers used to come out and play softball on their lunch break. I was always hanging around and once in a while, when they were a man short, they'd ask me to play. It got to the point where I was pretty good because they were always asking me to stick around the next day. I guess that's where it all started. I was about ten years old, playing with grown men. It wasn't like a do-or-die kind of thing, it was a slow-pitch game. But I could catch the ball and run and hit. From then on I was playing a lot of baseball. Playing as much as I possibly could.

I played on three different teams. I'd play one game, get in the car, and be driven by my dad to another game. I'd change uniforms in the car going to the next game. So I played a lot of baseball growing up, from the age of fourteen through high school and right into the big leagues.

My dad drove me every place. I was raised almost in the middle of the city and there were no ball fields close by. So every place I had to go I either had to walk or get a ride. And most of the places that I had to go my parents didn't want me to walk because I had to go through some pretty tough neighborhoods. I was really quiet and a very shy kid and my dad

193

used to take me over to the Police Athletic League at night so that I could play basketball and work out. He used to sit in the car and wait for me and then he'd drive me back home. He didn't push me, but he wanted me to play sports instead of just sitting home all of the time.

I played American Legion ball, but I got most of my experience playing four years of semi-pro ball. I wasn't paid but I played with guys who were former professional players. Back in those days, companies would pay these guys some extra money to play on their company baseball teams. So that's where I got most of my experience, against older guys who had played professionally. For some reason or other, possibly because they couldn't make enough money in baseball, they had come back and gotten regular jobs.

I never got paid any money, so that left me eligible to still play in high school. I enjoyed playing at different levels just to see how far my talent would take me.

I was scouted all the way through high school. I was aware that there were scouts there but they couldn't talk to me until I graduated. The one scout who signed me, Ed Katalinas, became the head scout for the Tigers. He came to watch us because he wanted to sign our shortstop, a guy named Charlie Johnson. Charlie told Katalinas, "The guy that you should want to sign is the center fielder," and that was me. Pretty soon, Katalinas made a point every time I was playing to be at the game. He knew he couldn't talk to me but he made very good friends with my dad.

It was a couple of days after graduation that I actually did sign with the Tigers. I signed with them, but I couldn't let my semi-pro team down. We were in the state finals and I told the Tigers I had an obligation to this team to play, and that I thought that I should play in the finals. They gave me permission to do it, but they told me please not to get hurt because at that time I had already signed a contract. That was 1953, and I went straight from being a high school ballplayer into the clubhouse of a major league team.

I joined the team in Philadelphia. I had to take the train up and I got to the hotel just as the bus was pulling out. I never had a chance even to check into my room. I put my bag in with the bellhop and I walked on the bus. I was never so scared in my life. I was eighteen years old, skinny as a rail, pimples all over my face, and everybody was sitting there looking at me.

I didn't know where to sit, so finally a guy named Ted Graves said, "Sit down here." He was the player rep, and I sat next to him and he went over what I was supposed to do and so on and so forth. Like tipping the clubhouse man, how to dress on the road—things of that nature. He really helped me a great deal. I was in complete awe when I had to put on a professional uniform and go out on that field.

My favorite memory, no question about it, was putting on a major league uniform that first time. It was too big for me. I was a little kid and I had to wear the batboy's uniform. They finally got me a number. I was number 25, but my pants were size thirty and the batboy was the only one who wore a size thirty. I still remember walking in that clubhouse, someone telling me where my locker was, and sitting down to put my uniform on. I had spent my life until then dreaming of being a professional ballplayer. Never even thinking about the major leagues, but just to sign a professional contract. Then all of a sudden, to walk into a major league clubhouse and put on my own uniform with my own number, was just an awesome feeling.

I had my own locker when I first arrived. I was right next to the crapper. In Chicago I had a nail, that was my locker. They always gave the youngest guy or the newest guy the locker next to the john and that was where I was. I didn't think anything of it. I knew that they weren't picking on me, that was just the way things were back then. We all had to earn our stripes and that only came with experience. It didn't bother me.

It was just unbelievable. The season had already started, and back in those days there were very few young players on the teams. Most of the guys had spent four or five years in the minor leagues.

But the players liked me and I got along great with them. They really did like me because I was quiet and enjoyed going out to the ball park and working. I enjoyed shagging for the older players, doing little things for the other guys. They all took me under their wing and helped me as much as they could.

That was really very nice considering that I was taking an older player's job. You know, there I was, a kid right out of high school. I never went to the minor leagues at all and one player on that team had to leave.

I was in complete awe of the whole situation but once I got on the field I was okay because I was in my element. I got in as a pinch hitter that first day in the eighth inning. I hit the first pitch to center field but I don't remember much about it because I was scared to death.

I used to read about these ballplayers all of the time. My idols were Williams and Musial and I got a chance to play against them.

I realized when I went out on the field and started shagging fly balls that I could run, I could catch, and I could throw with those guys. I'm not taking anything away from the players on our team at that time, but they were a last-place team and I felt sure that I could play with them in the outfield. That eased my mind right there knowing that at least I was on the level of major league outfielders. Hitting was different because no one can go from high school and expect to hit big-league baseball pitchers.

I didn't get a chance to play very much. I got in as a pinch hitter once in a while and as a defensive outfielder in 1953. In 1954, my first full year, I came to spring training with a really good attitude and had a good spring and made the starting lineup.

I was nineteen years old and I was starting to grow up. I was beginning to learn the ways of life of a major league ballplayer. I knew I had an awful lot to learn but I was willing. I was a person who could listen and learn and put those kinds of instructions into play. The older guys, like Johnny Pesky and Steve Souchock, really helped me and told me what I should try to do in different situations.

When I first put on that uniform, I knew that there were only a few people that ever got to the big leagues. Especially then, with the minor league system so big, there were so many teams in each system that a lot of players were just looked over because they were in the wrong place at the wrong time. I happened to be at the right place at the right time and I got a chance to play with a really bad ball club. I got a chance to play and to my credit I was able to produce when I was called on. So I stayed in the big leagues.

I worked every day of the off-season; even in my final year twenty-two years later, I was still working. My first couple of years I worked in a sporting goods store as a salesman in Baltimore. Then I moved to Detroit. I had just won the batting title in 1955 and I figured my chances of staying in one town were pretty good so we bought a house and moved to Detroit. I got a job as manufacturer's rep calling on the automotive companies. So I did that until I got the broadcasting job with the Tigers. We didn't have the luxury of the modern-day players who can work out and have gyms in their basements or private trainers. We had to get a job. I had kids and I wanted to be able to send them to college.

When we played, being a professional athlete involved the whole family. It wasn't easy to pull the kids out of school and travel, but we all did it. My wife drove back from spring training every year by herself with the kids and the packed car. Now I see players who ship their cars back while their families fly first-class. We used to talk about it all the time and it was scary. What if they had broken down on the road someplace? No gas stations, two kids screaming. But we all did it. We had to.

I quit playing baseball because my son was getting ready to go to college and I had never spent any time with him. I wanted to spend one summer with him before he went to college.

I think baseball was so special during that time because people were looking for heroes. Times were tough for everybody and the game gave them a release. It gave them something to cheer about and forget about their own problems. They knew that players, particularly in the forties, loved doing what they were doing and it showed. The fans appreciated that. I don't know what made ballplayers so special in the eyes of other people but families encouraged their kids to get involved in baseball. It's not a sport where you go out there and try to kill somebody or hurt somebody, and people can relate to that.

I always say that I've probably been the luckiest person that ever lived to play baseball. Because ever since I was twelve years old I wanted to be a professional ballplayer and I did exactly that. Very few people can say that they've done exactly with their life what they wanted to, and I did. My only thoughts through school were to become a professional baseball player. I was able to accomplish that and I certainly went further than I ever imagined possible when I was sixteen or seventeen years old.

To go into the Hall of Fame and still now to have a super job in baseball. I am a very, very lucky man.

To my parents' credit, they were the ones who really encouraged me. They'd say to me, "You'll have to work the rest of your life so go out and play now while you can." They told me over and over again that I would have the opportunity to work the rest of my life, so I should enjoy my childhood. I did and I made something of it.

I reached for a dream even though I never thought there was really any way that I could reach that high. I took one step at a time and went further than I ever dared to dream. It has just been an amazing go-around for me.

GEORGE KELL

George Kell played third base from 1943 to 1957 for the A's, Tigers, Red Sox, White Sox, and Orioles. Kell led the league in batting in 1949, was an All-Star from 1947 to 1954 and in 1956–1957, and was inducted into the Hall of Fame in 1983. He was born, raised, and still lives in Swifton, Arkansas, where for years there was a sign on the highway that read SWIFTON, ARKANSAS, HOME OF GEORGE KELL.

THE FORTIES AND FIFTIES were the best times in baseball—I am convinced of that. Baseball always had a hold on America, but it really took off after World War II. It was very competitive and when the great ballplayers like DiMaggio and Williams and Musial came back out of the service, America was starving for something like baseball and was waiting for them. I'm just proud that I was part of that era.

I played baseball every day of my life; I can't remember when I didn't. When I was in high school I would tell everybody that I was going to be a major league baseball player. I thought it was as simple as that. You just proclaimed whatever you wanted to be—a doctor, a lawyer, a businessman, or a major league baseball player. I never said just a baseball player, I always said a major league baseball player.

I was in love with the Cardinals. I lived about 225 miles south of St. Louis and the Cardinal broadcasts boomed into Swifton, Arkansas, every day. I listened to them and I proclaimed that I was going to be a ballplayer. It was a very naïve thing to do, since only about 1 percent of those who want to play ever make it to the major leagues.

My father encouraged me. He had three boys, and I said in my speech in Cooperstown that my father raised the three of us convinced that we would all become major league baseball players if not all Hall of Famers. Two of us did play in the major leagues but my other brother was killed in World War II. Otherwise my father might have had his three ballplayers in the major leagues.

My father was a very, very good semi-pro baseball player. In the thirties, baseball was the only game really. He would hire out to other teams on weekends or holidays and pick up a hundred or two hundred dollars pitching and playing for them.

I'd go along with him. My mother was also very supportive of our playing, but in her own way. I remember one time we went to a game—Swifton was playing the town next door, Tuckerman—on the Fourth of July and it was the biggest event in our part of the country at that time. There was a large crowd and I was only twelve years old. We were way ahead in the ninth inning, something like 10–2, and my father put me in to play at shortstop.

After the game, on the way home, my mother was fussing at my father, and of course I was sitting in the backseat as proud as punch. She said over and over, "He could have gotten killed! What if somebody had hit the ball at him?" And my daddy said, "He'd have caught it, that's what would have happened." I was very proud that my father had such confidence in me.

I played American Legion baseball at Newport, Arkansas, which is about twenty miles south of Swifton. In those days every little town had a minor league team, and Newport had a Class D team. I would play my American Legion game and then stay and work out with the minor league team and hitchhike home. That team was owned by the Dodgers, so the Dodger scouts were there and they kept looking at me.

The next year I went off to college and the following summer when I came back I was too old to play American Legion ball. The Newport team was looking for me and when somebody said I lived up in Swifton they decided to come up and get me. I signed with Newport for just about nothing in June 1940. I wasn't going to be eighteen until August. Even though I was just a kid, I'd been working out with them for a couple

of years and I felt like I was one of them. My father dressed
me up and got me all ready to go down there and I played
there that year and all of the next year.

They sent me to Durham in 1942 for spring training and
released me outright. *They released me outright.* I got to Durham and they had about sixty ballplayers trying to make the
Durham club. The Dodgers and the Cardinals had every ballplayer in the country in those days—it was the most extensive
farm system ever. Illegal too. They finally caught up with them
and they were ordered to release a bunch of players. But they
did release me outright.

I was so far away from home, I was nineteen years old, I
didn't have any money, and in those days there was certainly
no players union. So when they released you all they'd say
was "Hey, that's all, boy, go on home."

I didn't have a penny in my pocket. The ballplayers had
been staying in this hotel in Durham and we could eat there
and sign meal checks. So I didn't leave. I didn't have anywhere to go. They kept saying, "We released you, you've got
to go," and I kept telling them, "I'm going home as soon as
my mother sends me some money."

I stayed on for three or four days, not too long, and the
Lancaster, Pennsylvania, team came in for the weekend. Right
away one of the Dodger officials asked them if they needed a
ballplayer. He said to them, "This kid has got a chance and we
had to release him." I signed with them and two years later I
was in the major leagues.

Lancaster had a working agreement with the Philadelphia
A's, which belonged to Mr. Connie Mack. He also owned the
Wilmington club in the same league. It was totally illegal to
have an affiliation with two clubs in one league. You couldn't
do that today. The Philadelphia A's had the right at the end of
each season to buy two or three ballplayers at a certain figure.
This was established in return for certain aid that Philadelphia
might give to them during the season. So the second year that
I was in Lancaster, 1943, I hit .396 and led all of the minor
leagues in hitting. And of course, I was one of the players that
they exercised the option on. Connie Mack gave them twenty
thousand dollars for my contract and I went to the majors. At
the same time the war was on and everybody was getting

drafted. I was registered for the draft and I was called up one time and turned down, and by the time that I was called up again the war was winding down. I still don't understand why I wasn't drafted, but I didn't complain because I wanted to play ball. I just kept playing ball and I played right on through the war—lucky me.

I don't really remember if there was some particular point when I realized that my dream had come true. I don't really remember having a dream that I was going to make it; I just always wanted to play ball and everywhere that I played I felt like I belonged, whether it was the American Legion, Class D, or Class B league. Even when I was called up to the majors I looked around and I thought, "I can play as well as these guys . . . and better then some of them."

When Philadelphia bought my contract, they still had about three weeks to go in the 1943 season. My wife was teaching school in Swifton and we'd been married only a couple of years. During the war they were looking for schoolteachers and anybody in Arkansas who had at least one year of college work could get an emergency certificate and teach. So they called me and asked if I would teach too, with the understanding that I would have to leave for spring training. So I told Mr. Connie Mack, "I need to go home; school has started and they want me to teach." He told me to come up and play one day. Just one game and then I would be on the major league roster. That way if I was drafted into the service I'd have all of that time behind me as a major league player. So I went up and played one ball game in Philadelphia. I was awed walking into the clubhouse, being with a big-league ball club and big-league players. I played in that one ball game, then got into my car that night and took off for Arkansas.

I remember Mr. Mack gave me a hundred-dollar bill and some money for expenses because Lancaster is only fifty miles from Philadelphia. He gave me a hundred dollars to play in that one game, which seemed like a ton of money since I was playing then for three hundred a month. When he bought me for twenty thousand, I went to the Lancaster club and said, "Hey, wait a minute. You signed me as a free agent and two years later you've sold me for twenty thousand dollars. I'm entitled to something." In those days they'd usually tell you to take a hike, but they were very nice and asked me what I wanted. We had been traveling in cars during the war, not even a bus. We had three automobiles, and I had been driving one of them. So I asked them to give me that car and five hundred dollars. I just threw that out, and they said, "You've got it."

I drove away from Philadelphia in that car with five hundred dollars in my pocket and another hundred from Mr. Mack. I was rich. I had more money than I'd ever seen before.

The following year I was to leave for spring training in March and my wife wanted to go too. I said, "Well, we don't have any money, but I'll ask Mr. Mack if he will loan me the money."

So I called Mr. Mack and told him the situation and asked if he'd send her a ticket too and let her stay in the hotel with me and sign meal checks. I told him to keep a tab on it and that I would pay him back during the summer out of my check. Mr. Mack was one of the finest men I've ever known. He encouraged families to stick together, so she went with me on the train.

My wife stayed in the hotel and signed for everything, and then when the season opened Mr. Mack didn't take any money out of my check, and he didn't take any out of the next check. So I went in to see him and he said, "That's on me. You just play as hard as you can." That was a big item—we must have owed him five hundred dollars which was a lot of money to us in those days.

My first full year in the major leagues was 1944. I had always been one of the better players and sure of myself whenever I played, but when I got to the big leagues I was not at all sure of myself. It was a struggle and Mr. Mack was very kind. He told me I was going to be his third baseman now, so I should play as hard as I could, do as well as I could, that I was going to get better every day, and not to worry about it. That helped a whole lot. But I was not totally at ease for a long time. Maybe not even the first two years.

By the time everybody began to come back after the war, I'd already been there two years and was fairly established. But I don't think anybody ever gets totally at ease in the big leagues. Even at the end of my career there were times when I'd begin to doubt myself a little bit.

Baseball is a very competitive game, a tough game, and

everybody stands on his own. It's not like football or basketball or other sports where one guy can cover up for another.
You are all alone out there and if somebody hits a ground ball
to you and the bases are loaded, you don't get any help from
anybody else. You catch it and throw him out or you don't.
And standing at home plate you don't get any help. There is a
certain lonely feeling about it and you have to develop the
mental toughness to handle it. I found that out early, because
it's day after day after day. You can play well five days in a
row, five days out of the week, but they expect you to play
well seven. Every time you have an off day, people will be
pointing their fingers at you. When I was with Boston, I rode
back and forth to the ball park with Jimmy Piersall because
we lived out in the same neighborhood. Jimmy was just getting started and always on the edge, hyper like he always was,
and worried about what was going to happen. Every day in the
car I would tell him, "Jimmy, one game at a time, just like
going to work every day. One game at a time, play as hard as
you can, be as good as you can that day." You know you are
supposed to be good every day, but if you get to thinking about
it, then you can't do it. Just go to work, play as hard as you
can, go home, and come back tomorrow and do the same thing.

Baseball can be a very, very tough sport for a player who is
on the fringe. He might play in the major leagues or he might
be sent back to the minors. I was never sent back but I know
from actual experience the terrible agony that wives and children suffer when a player comes home from spring training
and says, "We've been sent to Denver, or wherever; Now we've
got to pack up and go there." It is very hard on the families. I
was traded four times; I've been there. And my wife followed
me everywhere. For spring training, she'd have to pack the
station wagon, put the kids in the car, and drive all the way by
herself. And then after spring training she'd pack it all up again
and head for wherever I was playing. In those days when we
broke from spring training the team got on a train in Florida
and played all of the way north and slept on the train. One
year we went all the way to Denver: We started in Knoxville,
Tennessee, then Nashville, Memphis, Little Rock, Oklahoma
City, Denver, back to Chicago, and then on to Detroit.

Every town we played it was turn-'em-away crowds. When

the Tigers came into Denver for a weekend we drew one of
the biggest crowds ever drawn in that town. And we'd always
play in Atlanta, which was a great minor league town. It was
absolutely standing-room-only crowds.

It happened by accident that I got into broadcasting. I made
above the average salary the last ten years that I played in the
major leagues and we had saved some money, built a house in
Swifton, and bought farmland in Swifton. I knew that I was
going back to Swifton after I stopped playing. The broadcasting just came up out of the blue and I got into it. The last year
that I played, I had made up my mind that I was going to quit.
I was only thirty-five, but I had been playing in the major
leagues fifteen years. My children were growing up and they
didn't want to move from one school to the other; they wanted
to stay in Swifton. That was understandable and my wife said,
"You go ahead and play as long as you want to, we'll be here."
At that point I really decided to quit. Paul Richards was my
manager and I told him that I was quitting and he said, "Why,
you can play two or three more years." When I finally convinced him that I was going to quit he told me that CBS's *Game
of the Week* had an opening with Dizzy Dean and Buddy
Blattner. So he called New York, and CBS called and asked
me to audition.

Whenever Dizzy Dean had a day off, then I'd work with
Blattner. It sounded good because I could leave home on Friday night and I was back on Sunday night. I don't know how
I did it because I'd never done any broadcasting and I was
scared to death. It was much worse than walking into a big-
league clubhouse. Everything was live—they didn't do things
on tape like they do today. My first interview show was with
Casey Stengel in Florida before a Yankee game. I was scared
to death. I met Casey that morning for breakfast and he was
really gruff. I said to him, "I'm supposed to do an interview
with you for *Game of the Week* today and I want to know what
I am going to ask you." His answer was "I don't see any pur-
pose in it, we're just going to talk for ten minutes, aren't we?"
But he did agree to it and he set up the whole thing. He said,
"Just ask me a question and I'll talk, ask me another one and
I'll talk. You can do that, can't you?"

That's the way it happened—Stengel just talked his head

off. I opened the show and asked him a question and he talked two or three minutes, then I asked him another one and by the time he got through with that they were signaling for me to break for a commercial. We did that and came back and I asked him a couple more questions. At the end of the show I went up into the booth and I got a call from the guy in New York who had hired me and he said, "It was great, absolutely great!" All I could think was "My God, I didn't do anything."

I knew that they were not all going to be that easy, and they weren't because the next weekend it was Willie Mays, and it was more or less yes and no. I had to talk a lot just to get anything out of Willie. But I fell in love with broadcasting.

It's the ideal job. It's a great deal. When I get tired I go back to Swifton and I'm with my people there. I can't imagine anybody who has a better life than I have.

Nothing can top being inducted into the Hall of Fame. I wanted to be selected so badly that when they notified me, my wife and I cried. I will never forget that weekend. I had worked on my speech and gotten it ready. I've made a thousand or more speeches in my life, but I got up the morning of the induction and I was so nervous that I told my wife, "I don't know if I can deliver my speech. I'm about to come unglued." I really was, thinking about the great honor, plus all of my peers were going to be there and the big crowd and national television. But once I sat down on the platform, everything fell into place. It was very overwhelming. I kept thinking, "I don't know whether I belong here or not." When they took us through the museum with all of the great ballplayers, I wasn't sure if I belonged there or not. But I am very proud to be one of them.

Like I said in my speech that day at Cooperstown, "I have taken far more from the game of baseball than I will ever be able to put back in," and I believe that.

Ted Williams, Johnny Pesky, 1946

JOHNNY PESKY

Johnny Pesky, born John Michael Paveskovich, played from 1942 to 1954 for the Red Sox, Tigers, and Senators. He played shortstop, second base, and third base and was an All-Star in 1946. Pesky has managed and coached since his playing career ended in 1954.

I THINK THAT EVERY kid who ever plays ball as a youngster aspires to be a big leaguer. Years ago there were a lot of people who were good minor league ballplayers who never got to the big leagues and never realized their life's ambition or their dream. Some were more successful than others but some fellows worked just as hard as anybody and never got there. They played because they had a love for the game.

I've been in baseball all of my life. I started as a youngster just hanging around the ball park, then I went away to play ball and had a little bit of success—I got to the big leagues. I've done just about everything in baseball that there is to do.

Being a little guy, I am always impressed by size. But I didn't have that kind of a body. I was always a little guy. I hit a ball here and there, and I played hard and went out and worked every day. Some fellows have different work habits. I was very fortunate in that I had good coaching starting out as a kid. The first thing that our coach made us do was some stretching and then he'd let us warm up. We'd just play catch. We'd throw so many balls and then he'd lengthen us out a little bit to strengthen our arms. That was the program that this coach had.

That was in Portland, Oregon. I was a clubhouse boy out there in the summertime. After a couple of years in the club-

house, I played semi-pro ball in the late thirties and early forties and that was big-time baseball. We went to towns like Bend,
Oregon. In those years there were traveling teams like the
House of David, the Kansas City Monarchs, the Memphis Blues,
the Birmingham Barons. There were tournaments and leagues,
and baseball took up all the summer.

We were lucky that in high school we got to play seventy
to seventy-five games all summer long. When we had a local
tournament, if we won we went to Wichita for the national
tournament, and people came from all over the country to play
in that. There were players there who had some experience.

My father thought I was going to be a bum if I played ball,
but he got used to the idea. My parents were immigrants and
their only thing with us was *school, school, school.* My parents
were from Yugoslavia, which was Austria-Hungary at that time.
My father was in the Austria-Hungarian Navy before World
War I. He was just a nice man and a great parent. He insisted
on school for all of us. My mother was a very clean woman.
We wore clean clothes every day. We had rules and regulations, like 5:30 or 6:00 P.M. was suppertime and you had to be
there. Otherwise you got left out. None of us missed very many
meals. What I'm talking about here is getting away a little bit
from baseball, but we gained a sense of discipline from our
parents.

When we went to school we always responded to some
teacher or coach. In those days we had coaches who were really
concerned about the kids. The atmosphere and the programs
set up by these people taught us how to get along in life. They
always recommended that we be decent people. As children
growing up, we never even had a misdemeanor. None of us
went to jail—we all turned out to be nice kids.

It was a tough time, after the Depression, yet we managed
to play ball every summer. I signed with the Red Sox; the Yankees made overtures, as did Cleveland, Detroit, the Cardinals,
and the Browns.

The scouts had heard about me from high school games and
the American Legion games. Then when I got too old to play
American Legion, I played semi-pro ball and the scouts would
always come there to see us, four or five of them in the stands.
They had their likes and dislikes. The Red Sox were my folks'

choice because the man was so nice. So I signed with the Red Sox.

Eventually my parents got to understand baseball because my sisters and my brother would explain to them what I was doing. At suppertime, my brother would come home from work and get the paper and he'd look at the box scores (we had a friend who worked on the Union Pacific and when the streamliner from Chicago would come in he'd bring a Chicago paper) and my brother would read it to my mother.

My mother came out to Boston in the late forties and she saw me play. In Fenway Park she had never been around that many people before in her whole life. My father never saw me play in the big leagues, but he saw me play as a kid. He didn't understand baseball; all he knew was boccie because he and his cronies played that in the fall when they were making their wine. The first time he ever saw me hit a triple, he didn't understand why I was running so far.

In those years you had to get your parents' okay to sign. I was nineteen years old when I signed with the Red Sox and just out of high school. I didn't go to college, I went to the Red Sox. They sent me to North Carolina to Rocky Mount, and I did fairly well there. Then I went to Louisville, Kentucky, and then the next year I was in Boston. That was 1942.

We opened the 1942 season against the Philadelphia Athletics and the first time up I got a base hit. My first time up in the big leagues. It wasn't a home run like a lot of guys claim they had.

I really wasn't sure that I had arrived because in those years you had to show some consistency. I did that and the more that I played the better I liked it. I played almost every game. I was a regular player and I had a fine year. Then the war was on and Ted Williams talked me into going into the flight program with him. I didn't become a flier, but I did become an operations officer.

Since I was from the West Coast, my draft board was sending my stuff to me in Boston. I had a high number and I didn't get called until late in June or early July 1942. I joined the flight program in Boston and they said that we wouldn't have to go until November. Then two weeks after the season was over, we were in. Ted Williams, myself, Joe Coleman from the

A's, and a lot of guys. In 1943–45 we were in the service. I got a commission in Atlanta, and Bob Kennedy was there for his instrument flight training. The war took a lot of years from all of us, but the game was still there when we came back.

I have no regrets about my life and no regrets about my baseball life. I do wish things would have been better in some areas. I was hoping that we'd be in more World Series and win a few Series because no one ever remembers a loser. But baseball has been good to a lot of us and I am very grateful to have come to the Boston Red Sox. Mr. Yawkey had this great affection for people. He wasn't a flamboyant person. He was very quiet and reserved and he took care of people. Mr. Yawkey was a wonderful man to work for, he loved his team, and he loved the men that made his team.

In those years we seemed to have a little bit more respect. I think baseball is tougher to play today than when we played it. Back then, there were only eight teams in each league. We traveled on trains, and the farthest west we went was St. Louis and Chicago.

When you are on a train you have a chance to move around. We had a Pullman car for the writers, a dining car and a Pullman car for the players. We got to know one another because we were together. We worried about one another. If your children or someone else's youngsters got sick, everyone was concerned, and genuinely so. There was just more affection and togetherness.

Now you have a different kind of ownership, you don't have single ownership anymore. In Boston, we had Mr. Yawkey; in Detroit, Mr. Briggs; in Chicago, Mr. Comiskey; in St. Louis, the Dewitts; in Washington, Mr. Griffith; and in Philadelphia, Connie Mack. It was really a whole different atmosphere.

If you are a decent person you can make a living in the game. I never made a big salary, and that's why I'm still working. I say that I would like to retire but I'm not going to. I'm going to go as long as the Red Sox want me. That's just how I feel about this game and I am seventy-two years old. I was the oldest manager in baseball last year.

Pressure is an overused word, I think. If you can play, then you can play and if you can't, then you can't. It's as simple as that. People always ask what's wrong when you have a bad day, and nowadays some players will answer with things like, "Oh, I'm having trouble with the position of the bat," or something about the physics of it all. There are too many excuses. They should just go ahead and say that they were playing lousy. No one's perfect in this game. The game is very difficult to play.

It's a simple game, but it is tough to play. I've seen guys six four who couldn't hit a ball three hundred feet and you see little guys five eight and 160 pounds hit balls almost four hundred feet. Like Campaneris, Rizzuto, Pee Wee Reese, and others down through the history of the game.

Either you can play or you can't. God gives you a talent, but you go out and develop it. There is an old thing that they say about hitting—God takes you to the plate but he leaves you there all by yourself.

When you're twenty-one you think this is going to last forever, but you've got to realize when the end comes. Sometimes guys don't realize when the end is in sight. In fact, I thought I could still play. I went down and no one really wanted me, so I went with Ralph Houk to Denver in the American Association and I played 90 games for him and I hit .340. I thought that I could still play in the majors, but I couldn't, so I started managing.

I had no idea that I wanted to be a manager, but Ralph Houk talked me into it. I worked for Detroit five years and then I came back to the Red Sox. I was throwing batting practice every day, hitting for the infielders, and working the guys out. It was just something that I had to do. I had enough energy and I always associated myself with the game. There are a lot of people like me who just wanted to stay in the game. Like Bill Fisher—he's one of the best pitching coaches in baseball. I've got to put him in Harvey Haddix's class, and Rube Walker.

Playing baseball was a job. We brought home a week's pay. Years ago, people came to this country to feed their children. My goal was to raise a family too. I've been married for forty-seven years and I've got no complaints. I still think my gal is twenty-two. She's got a few wrinkles in the kisser, but I still love her.

Baseball can build you up to the sky one day and the next

day you have to climb a stepladder to look up to a snake. That's the beauty of baseball. The great players always had a little extra of the God-given talent and they knew how to handle it.

I have so many great memories. Being a little guy and hitting a home run to win a ball game was a big thing. That happened right after the war when I was twenty-five years old. It was Opening Day in 1946 against the A's and we had a one-hitter going into the bottom of the eighth with the score tied, 1–1. I hit a home run just inside the pole down the right field line. I still have the picture. In the top of the ninth the A's filled the bases and the ball was hit to Bobby Doerr at second base. The ball hit him and went toward the bag at second and I reached out like a first baseman and threw to first. Double play. That was the way the game ended.

I also remember one time when I let a ball go through my legs that cost us a ball game. I wanted to dig a hole, but those things happen. It has happened to everybody.

I think if you play the game any length of time you are going to have ups and downs. It's always going to be that way because no one can ever know what that little white rat is going to do.

The beauty of baseball is that the older you get, the better you were. Pretty soon you think that you are Hall of Fame material. By God, there are a lot of us who were decent players, but we weren't Hall of Fame.

TERRY MOORE

Terry Moore played outfield from 1935 to 1948 for the St. Louis Cardinals. He played in two World Series, in 1942 and 1946, and was an All-Star from 1939 to 1942. Moore managed Philadelphia in 1954 and coached for the Cardinals from 1949 to 1952.

EVEN AS A KID, I never even dreamed of playing big-league baseball. The only thing I wanted to do was play the kids on the lot, and eventually we grew up and played in a league. There was a semi-pro league here in Collinsville, Illinois, and there were also a lot of professional players who came back to Illinois because they weren't making much money. That was the time of the Depression. I got to learn a lot about baseball from those pros and they told me I could make it in professional baseball.

Our team's coach, Bill Walsh, was a Cardinal scout, and he said he thought he could get me on the Cardinals if I wanted. I tried out and they sent me to play for the Columbus Redbirds at the very end of the season and I didn't do too well. I had been working at the time as a pressman for the Bemis Bag Company, and Mr. Rickey had called me in before I went to Columbus and called my boss and asked, "If I send Terry away, will you still give him back his job?" My boss agreed, so when I came back I worked in this printing place, and it was a horrible place to work. I had to oil the drums and it was really a terrible spot. Finally it occurred to me that I'd like to play baseball if I could get out of that work.

Well, the Cardinals sent me a contract for $75 a month and I had been making more money than that in the printing business! So I stayed out of baseball that year and the next year they sent me a contract for $150 a month with the Columbus Redbirds and I went with the club. We won the pennant and the little World Series and that was the year I came up to the Cardinals, 1935. The Cardinals had just won the last year's pennant and I came into a club that was really all "hepped up," me, just a rookie. The only stuff we got from the team was the uniform, a hat, a shirt, a pair of pants, a belt, and socks. We had to pay for our sweat socks, we had to pay for our sweatshirts, we had to buy our gloves, and we had to pay for our own sunglasses. Now they get all that free. They should be much better ballplayers today because they get more rest, and they've got everybody pampering them.

I didn't get much recognition and I couldn't even get a chance to hit with them. All of us "scrubbinis"—that's what we called ourselves—would get out really early in the morning and get our batting practice, and then late at night, when they'd finished, we'd get more batting practice and work out. I was lucky enough to have a good spring training and I got a chance to start the season.

It wasn't easy to break into the club, 'cause all the other players were old friends. I think I had one of the toughest managers on earth: Frankie Frisch didn't like rookies, and every time I'd make a mistake he'd always yell, "Who was your manager? I wish he'd taught you better than that!" He was tough on you!

There was an incident that same year with Joe Medwick. I was playing with Medwick and there was a ball hit over Durocher's head. I could have caught the ball and Joe called me off of it. Joe came running, just flying, and hollering he was going for the ball and missed it and it cost us a run. So after the game, Frisch really started to eat me up, but Durocher was the captain of the club and he took my side. He said, "Don't blame the kid, it was Medwick's fault. He called for the ball and the kid stayed away from it." After I got dressed, Frisch called me in and said, "Kid, any ball that you can catch out there, you catch. I don't care if you run over the damn Hungarian [Medwick] at shortstop or not."

When I broke in with the Gashouse Gang, they were really rough. They were a tough bunch. There was always a battle going on, always a fight. That was the way that club played. They didn't give an inch, and everything was thrown at them. They took it and then they'd give it back and that's the way they played. You had to be part of that or you didn't play.

I had a big family but my brothers and sisters were all scattered. I had one sister that lived here when I played and we lived with my mother. They were really great about me playing ball. My mother and dad didn't live together; he was in another part of the country. So I was supporting my mother until I went into the service. But, oh, my mother was crazy about baseball. She'd go to a game and when somebody'd criticize me, she'd have an umbrella, and boy, she'd whack them with it! She figured they'd better not say anything about me. She was an Irish gal, a *big* Irish woman. She got in trouble a couple times out there and they put her down in back of Sam Breadon's box so that when she'd come to the game she'd stay out of trouble. She was funny though, and she was really a pistol.

After I came back from the service I wasn't a good ballplayer at all. I was just fooling the crowd; I had spent better than three years in the service, and I had gone in when I was twenty-eight years old. When I came out it was tough, really tough. I was married and had a child at the time. It was hard trying to come back and play.

Slaughter was five years younger. Musial was eight years younger than me and they didn't have trouble. They were young enough to come back. They brought back all of us players who had been away in the war ahead of time to train. It was nice that they did that but it was still tough. That was just when the money began to get better. I was the highest-paid player before the war and I only made thirteen thousand dollars.

The conditions that we played under were terrible, riding those darn "iron horses" like we did, trying to get some sleep in them, and then staying in hotels with no air-conditioning before playing another day game. Coming off of those trains, especially in Pittsburgh, was always tough. We'd finish a doubleheader in St. Louis and it would be about 110° in the shade, then we'd get on the train, and it'd be so darn hot we'd have to go into the dining car because that was the only one that they'd cool off with ice. Then we'd try to go to bed and we'd roll and toss and sweat and everything else. We'd get into Pittsburgh in the morning around eight o'clock, and we'd grab a cab, go to the hotel, and jump in bed and try to sleep. We played about three o'clock in the afternoon and we'd get up in time to eat and go out and play.

We were the originators of the pension plan, the Cardinals and the Boston club in the 1946 World Series. We donated our radio rights, which wasn't a whole lot, to get the pension plan started. We won, and we got thirty-two hundred dollars for winning, and the Red Sox got nineteen hundred for the losing end of it (and Williams, I heard, gave his share to the clubhouse boy). The umpires made more money than we did in that series, so after that the commissioner and all the owners said the winning share would have to be at least five thousand dollars.

When you're a ballplayer you're under pressure all the time. I don't care what anybody says—because you've got the people watching you, you can't afford to make many mistakes and you've got to try to play the game as hard as you can to stay there. The way I looked at it, it never was easy and I didn't call it fun. We were under strain all the time and you played hurt. Only the manager could give you any rest. If he thought you were getting tired and the bat was getting slow, he'd give you a couple of days' rest. I could never say that I thought that it was an easy game because I never did. It was fun after you won and were in the clubhouse to celebrate, but the next day you knew that you still had that pressure coming back at you again.

Every once in a while I hear a player today say, "Boy, I go out and have fun." I guess if they're making two or three million, they could have what you call fun 'cause they have no pressure. If I had been paid a million or two a year, would I have been the type of player that I was? I don't know, but maybe I would have had fun. If I made an error, so what? If I didn't get a base hit, so what? If we lose, so what? I'm gonna get paid, I've got this money. Knowing my own self, I had pride—I had a desire to play the game and I don't think it would have affected me.

St. Louis was a great baseball town. And part of our job then was to promote baseball. For instance, at the World's Fair in 1939, we had a place where we talked baseball and practiced with kids. It was fun for them, and to be honest, it was good for us too because it reminded us that without the fans we wouldn't even have a job. My wife, Patty, was a professional singer. She sang in Detroit and she was asked to join a band but she was taking care of her mother at the time. So she worked at a lot of the big hotels.

I would say that my biggest memory was playing in All-Star games and getting to be with all the really great players in the league at that time. And also playing in the World Series, especially when we were playing against a club that was great like the Yankees. I loved it when we played the Yankees in 1942. We were the underdogs and we went into their territory and beat them three straight in their own ball park. That was really great.

And in the 1946 World Series against the Red Sox we were the underdogs again and we came out and had to play seven games to win that. Those are the things that have stuck mostly in my mind. Other than that, all the other things were just routine baseball—you know, you got your hits.

I always thought you could win more ball games by being a good fielder rather than a good hitter. I worked on fielding more in my career because everybody else was willing to hit and have you run 'em down in the field. I didn't really worry too much about hitting. I just went up and looked for the ball over the plate and hit it.

One thing I remember well was that night ball really ruined your eating. We had to eat really early in the afternoon and we didn't really eat. We just had something light, but after the game we were hungry and we had to stay up a couple of hours or so before we could even wind down.

In Cincinnati, we used to enjoy the Netherland Plaza. It had the only hotel lobby that was air-conditioned in the city. After the ball game they had a place where we could eat and we'd stay there sometimes until four or five in the morning. Slaughter and I roomed together, and if we had a doubleheader on Sunday, we'd order up a lot of ice, throw it in the tub, take our sheets and throw them in the tub, then wring them out and throw them on the bed and lie there until they'd get hot again. Then we'd jump up and take our sheets and

throw them back in the tub. We'd sleep maybe an hour at a time that way. Then we'd have to play the doubleheader the next day. Boy, down in that hole there in Cincinnati it was hot and we had those darn old wool uniforms on in those days. By the time the doubleheader was over that deck felt like an iron. You didn't care about getting on base or not because you were so tired. The pitchers didn't have much to throw, so you didn't have much to swing at. And everybody was stinking, just wringing wet. When you'd come into the dugout your shoes would squish. The sweat, just squish, squish, squish. I'd lose as many as fifteen pounds at doubleheaders.

I used to go into the clubhouse to see old friends when I went to the ball park because I know Herzog and Schoendienst. I'd go out to the game, but I haven't been for the past five years. I suppose it was the attitude of the players. A lot of those guys couldn't carry my glove the way they play ball. They don't hit as much as I did but they really think they're the greatest.

It is a funny thing, but people are always trying to make comparisons. They always talk about Marty Marion and Ozzie Smith and then they ask me what I think of Ozzie in comparison to Marty. I tell 'em I'd give Ozzie the nod; he's the best shortstop I've ever seen on AstroTurf. But if you put Ozzie on the fields that Marion played on and put Marion on the fields that Ozzie played on, then I think that you could compare them. I don't think Ozzie would have been the shortstop that Marion was in Marion's conditions. And that's the way that I look at it.

AL
LOPEZ

Hall of Fame catcher Al Lopez played from 1930 to 1947 for the Dodgers, Braves, Pirates, and Indians and managed from 1951 to 1969 for the White Sox and Indians.

I FIRST GOT ENTHUSED with baseball when I followed the World Series between Cleveland and Brooklyn in 1920. We used to play it in the Tampa sandlots when I was twelve or thirteen years old. It's amazing how well we played, and I'm not bragging, because we never practiced at all during the week. We only played on Sundays. We used to go out there and play, with no practice at all.

I trained with the Washington club here in Tampa in 1925. In those days the major league clubs would bring just the players that were on the roster to spring training. They already had three catchers but they had a lot of hitting practice. They needed somebody else to catch batting practice for them, so they asked me if I'd come over. And for me just to wear the Washington uniform was a big thing—being among major league players in 1925 when I was just sixteen years old! I was always the first one on the field because I liked it and I'd be the last one to leave.

By the time that they were about ready to head north, the trainer, a fellow by the name of Mike Martin, told the owner, Mr. Griffith, "We ought to take that kid with us—he likes to play baseball." Mr. Griffith said, "Doesn't he belong to his folks? Tell them I'll give them a thousand dollars for him." My folks turned him down; they wanted five thousand and Mr. Griffith said, "No way." I only weighed about 150 or 155 pounds and I was just a kid sixteen years old.

Years later I was in Brooklyn and Mr. Griffith was talking to the manager, Max Carey, and said, "You know, I could have had that kid when we were in Tampa, but they wanted five thousand dollars and I turned them down."

In 1925 someone asked me if I'd go and try out for the Tampa Smokers, which was a local professional team in the Florida State League. I said that I would try it. I was sixteen years old at the time. I went out and played and they offered me a contract for $150 a month, which I thought was great. They were paying me to play baseball and from there it seems like everything just fell into a pattern. The following year I was a regular catcher, and from there I went to Jacksonville. They bought me, so I played at Jacksonville; it was as simple as that.

In those days there were very few chain operations; most every club was independent. Jacksonville was independent and we had a pitcher that was outstanding. There must have been six or eight scouts up in the stands every day watching this pitcher. By the first of August he had 25 wins and 5 losses. Finally, the New York Giants (at that time the Giants and the Yankees were the powerhouses in baseball), needing a pitcher, made a deal for this fellow. Ben Cantwell was his name and he went to the major leagues and stayed for about ten years. He was a good pitcher, and McGraw, the manager of the Giants, bought him for twenty-five thousand dollars.

The scout for the Brooklyn club, Nap Rucker, an old southpaw from the Dodgers, was scouting at that same time and he wrote back to Brooklyn that he liked the catcher better than he did the pitcher. Their answer was "Well, if you like the catcher better than you do the pitcher, and McGraw paid twenty-five thousand for Cantwell, then buy him."

That's how the Brooklyn club bought me in 1927 and I reported to them in the spring of 1928. I was sent to Macon to play for the Macon Peaches in the South Atlantic League. The following year they sent me to Atlanta, which was the Southern League, and in 1930 I went up and stayed up with the Brooklyn club.

It was like a dream to me because I had never had any idea that I was going to be a professional baseball player. I was just playing sandlot ball and even when I was playing in Tampa I didn't realize that I was going to be good enough to go any higher.

When Brooklyn bought me I thought, "Well, they'll just look at me and send me back to the minors." But I went to Macon and had a pretty good year. Then I had a pretty good year at Atlanta and I was lucky enough that I had a good start at the beginning when I went to Brooklyn. I was a regular catcher after that.

I sure was nervous that first time I walked in a clubhouse. It was in Clearwater, where they were training at the time. I had a little old glove that I'd had for about two or three years. In the big leagues, you know, you change gloves every year. You break them in during spring training and catch with them all year.

At that time there was a company from Massachusetts by the name of Draper and Maynard [called by many "drop 'em and moan"] and they used to give everybody that was on the major league club a glove for nothing. One day, the clubhouse man, a man by the name of Dan Comerford, said, "Hey, kid, why don't you get Draper and Maynard to give you a catcher's mitt?" I said, "They won't give me a catcher's mitt, I'm just a rookie." But he told me they would because I was on the Brooklyn roster.

There was one fellow there, Hank DeBerry, who was a catcher and he must have had about six brand-new gloves in his locker. So this fellow Comerford asked him if he would give the kid (that was me) one of those new gloves and let him break it in. DeBerry answered, "Let him get his own glove, I'm not going to give him no glove." They were tough on young kids in those days and I sure knew I was the rookie that day. But it all worked out because after he was let go I became the regular catcher.

The first game that I caught here in Tampa in front of my friends and my father was a big thrill. But then, when I got to the big leagues, that was really it. The first game I played in the big leagues was in 1928 against Pittsburgh. They had a pitcher by the name of Burleigh Grimes who was a spitball pitcher. I didn't even know what a spitball was in those days! I went up to hit against Burleigh Grimes, one of the outstanding pitchers of all baseball, and thought I'd just try to do the best that I could. I hit the ball every time. He didn't strike me out.

At that time I was just strictly a pull hitter and Pittsburgh had two of the best infielders in baseball then at shortstop and at third base, Pie Traynor and Glenn "Buckshot" Wright. All I did was pull the ball to them and they would throw me out by six or eight feet easy! I hit some pretty good shots, but those guys were terrific, just outstanding. Glenn Wright is not in the Hall of Fame, but he should be.

That first game for me was really the big moment, a real thrill. But I went home and said, "Well, I've got to do something. I've got to start hitting the ball all over instead of pulling."

The first game in 1930 that I actually caught was against the New York Giants, and McGraw was the manager. I was 4 for 5 that first game against the Giants. We were scoring a lot of runs that day and it was a big thrill for me to play in the Polo Grounds.

I was playing against people that I had idolized. When I was a youngster, Rogers Hornsby was my idol. He was a great hitter. First thing in the morning I would go and pick up the paper and see what Rogers Hornsby had done the day before. If he had had a bad day then I would feel bad all that day. Then there I was in the big leagues catching behind him when he was up at the plate hitting.

I met my heroes. I met the Babe and I had some pictures taken with him. We used to play the Yankees every year. They trained in St. Petersburg and we trained in Clearwater, and we used to travel with the Yankees all the way up north. We'd stop in Jacksonville, Atlanta, North Carolina somewhere, then go on to New York, where we'd play one game in Yankee Stadium and one game in Brooklyn in Ebbets Field.

They had a tremendous club, with exceptional power. I think that the 1927 Yankee club was the best team ever. They'd just kill us, especially after they got in pretty good shape. At the beginning of spring training we could maybe get close, but after they got into shape they used to murder us.

There have been a couple of big changes in baseball and I think the biggest change as far as hitting goes is that we were more concerned with simply making contact with the ball. We did that to keep from striking out because that was the period just after they had barred the spitball and the emery ball and all those kinds of tricks. There were maybe three pitchers who were still allowed to throw the spitball because they were spitballers before the rules were passed. In those days there were so many tricky pitches that people concentrated more on making contact with the ball.

Now everybody swings as hard as he can for the fences and there are more strikeouts than ever. Striking out 150 times today is a lot. But in our day the only one who really struck out quite a few times was Babe Ruth. I think he struck out 90 or 100 times at bat and that was a lot.

There are more home runs now than there used to be, but personally I'd rather see contact made with the ball. If you hit the ball you are liable to make a beautiful play or something that the fans can enjoy. With the home run, naturally it's a thrill, but all you do is run around the bases. There is no action in the field.

If you have speed on the club, it's a great advantage. That's the kind of club that I had at Chicago and we won the pennant. We had Aparicio, Minoso, Landis, and those guys could really run. That was 1959, and I followed Marty Marion managing that club. I was at Cleveland and had told Hank Greenberg that I was going to resign. He asked if I had another job and I told him no, that I was going to take my time.

That was a Saturday and I was going to quit officially on Sunday. I went out to dinner at Cavolli's, a ballplayers' hangout on the way out of Cleveland toward Toledo, and while I was there they paged me in the lobby for a phone call. It was Hollis "Sloppy" Thurston, who was scouting for the White Sox at the time, and he asked me about this rumor that I was going to quit.

He said that the owners of the White Sox, Comiskey and Rigney, had called him and asked if this was true and he said that they wanted to talk to me before anybody else—if I'd talk to them.

I asked why they wanted me because I thought that Marty Marion had another year to go with his contract. Thurston told me that Marty was going to be let go. I think what happened was that Marty got so mad because they were playing so badly that he went into the clubhouse and left the dugout, and the bosses saw it from upstairs. That's the story they told me, and I don't know if it's true or not.

When I managed, all my players did in spring training was get in shape to play baseball. They did a lot of hitting and throwing and a lot of running. We used to really run them; we'd sprint them back and forth for forty minutes after the workout and then we'd have them sprint right into the clubhouse. They'd come in there puffing and sweating.

I learned that from training with the Washington club way back in 1925. Walter Johnson was on that team, and I was a great admirer of his. Walter was a great man, a great pitcher, and I used to watch him and the way that he trained. We used to train at what they called Plant Field, which was a half-mile horse track, and he would get on that track and run around five times without stopping. He threw a lot, he threw batting practice, and he hit and he ran a lot. That is an essential thing for playing baseball, to get your legs in really good shape and to get your arms in really good shape. I don't think you have to do any other thing.

These boys today are bigger and stronger. They have gymnasiums in the clubhouse so that they can work out. Why is it that they get hurt as much as they do? Why? I played with broken fingers! Every time you look, so-and-so is on the inactive list or the disabled list. Most of the clubs have got maybe five or six guys on the list. If we had four guys in the whole league in those days it was a lot.

This is only my theory, but these kids come up lame because they exercise and develop muscles that they don't need to use in baseball.

Another thing that I don't approve of today is that they are always worrying about how many pitches a pitcher throws. We never kept count. It was up to the manager or the pitching coach to watch if the guy was losing his stuff. If he had his stuff, if his arm was in shape, then he could pitch. He'd rest the following day, then pitch a little batting practice and he was ready to go again. Someone like Early Wynn must have thrown 130 or 140 pitches during a game because he was always 3 and 2 on most everybody! I think that counting pitches is just kind of an affectation.

In the old days, on a hot day, a pitcher might warm up for maybe five or six minutes, because he saved himself for the game. I've seen Dizzy Dean walk up to the mound from the dugout, toss the ball to the catcher, and say, "Let's go."

I think that one thing that was better was that we used to play day games. We'd get through with our game and we'd go eat dinner. It was more homey and friendly. We used to stay around the hotel at night and talk about baseball or we'd go to a movie once in a while.

We traveled by train. We could sleep overnight, and we'd play cards. We'd sit around and talk to each other and we were a lot closer. We used to have to eat at the hotel, because when they started giving real money for meals the players scattered every which way.

This money thing is out of hand. I remember when Babe Ruth got eighty thousand dollars from the Yankees there were a lot of write-ups in the paper criticizing him for making more than the President of the United States. My God, a .260 hitter today is making three times more than the president of the United States.

DEL WILBER

Del Wilber, a catcher, played major league baseball from 1946 to 1956 for St. Louis, Philadelphia, Boston, and Chicago. Wilber had a "perfect day" with 3 home runs on just 3 pitches in 1951 and is major league baseball's only undefeated manager. In 1987 he retired after fifty years in professional baseball—a career that included playing, coaching, managing, scouting, and broadcasting.

WE WERE ALWAYS PLAYING neighborhood baseball in my little town of Lincoln Park, Michigan. We had a couple of teams and we had one ball. When the cover came off we would fix it up with black tape. That was in the Depression years, so we had to do that. We'd nail the bats back together too, and we'd play. We had a couple of good semi-pro teams in the area that had pretty good baseball diamonds. The diamonds were well taken care of and we kids could use them. I played one year in grade school, but that was all because we didn't have any real team to speak of and the weather is not always that good in Michigan. And then I played in high school; even as a high school freshman I got to play in a few games. As I went through high school I played more and more. We had a little interest in our team. A couple of us kids were pretty good and the scouts would talk to us.

One of my teammates, George Hill, was a pitcher who lived in River Rouge, Michigan, and he had an automobile. Well, he saw one of those little fillers at the bottom of the sports page that the St. Louis Browns were holding a tryout camp in Springfield, Illinois, on a certain date in July and he said, "Let's go," and I said, "Okay, we'll go." It was just that simple.

We drove from the Detroit area to Springfield in his car.

Del Wilber tagging out Yogi Berra, 1952

That was about four hundred miles, I think, and we slept out-side the ball park in his car that first night. Then the next day when the tryout camp started they took one look at us—we were both pretty big guys—and they had us start.

Anyway, George pitched and I caught the first three in-nings that morning and they told us to come back the second day. George was a little older than I and more savvy, so he said to them that we'd like to have a place to sleep. They got us a room at the Farmer's Hotel which was kind of like a big boardinghouse. The next day we went back and played again, and after the tryouts were over, they took us up to the hotel in Springfield where the two scouts were staying and gave us contracts to report the next spring, in 1938. Later we got to work out with the Browns when they came into Detroit. George pitched batting practice and I caught and that was the biggest thrill yet! Then I went to spring training in Belleville, Illinois. I went on the Greyhound bus to Belleville, and that was the first time that I ever saw St. Louis.

I was supposed to go play in what they call the Kitty League—that was Kentucky, Indiana, and Tennessee—at Mayfield, Kentucky. But the fellow who was the manager of the Mayfield team was an old big-league catcher himself and he was still playing. So they sent me to Findlay, Ohio. In Findlay, an old New York Giants catcher named Grover Hartley was the manager. I played at Findlay and did pretty well. Then in 1939, the St. Louis Browns decided not to give Grover the working agreement, so he bought the club. He bought the team personally from the St. Louis Browns. With the buying of the team he also got to keep a couple of the players and I was one of them. So I played there again in 1939 and had a tremendous year. At the end of that season he was supposed to sell me to Toledo in the higher minor leagues. It was in the American Association which was then like a Double A team and now is what they call Triple A. But he didn't sell me, so I was eligible to be drafted. In the meantime the St. Louis Cardinals had a team in the league at Fostoria, Ohio, and their scouts and managers had been coming through town. They drafted me for their team in Springfield, Missouri. I went to spring training with the Columbus, Ohio, team in Hollywood, Florida, and then played the year at Springfield and did really well, although I was slowed down a little bit by a broken thumb from a foul ball. Then the next year, 1941, I went to spring training with the St. Louis Cardinals, just to catch batting practice more than anything else. I wasn't on the roster or anything. I played that season at Columbus, Georgia. I caught some games, and I also played right field and third base.

The South Atlantic League was a bus league. Columbus was an outside town in the league because it was on the westernmost edge of the area, right on the Chattahoochee River. We had a 1936 red school bus with straight-backed, wooden chairs in it. It had the "Columbus Redbirds" written on the side of it. A guy named Chick was our bus driver and also our trainer. We'd all pile in that red bus and away we'd go. We'd travel all night and, lo and behold, when we'd come back, dog-tired, we'd see the sunrise over the Chattahoochee. That was something else all right. And when we'd travel all night like that, the very next night we'd have a game. No off days back then. The only off days you'd have back then were rainouts and then you'd have to make them up with a doubleheader the next day. We had a 140-game schedule in 140 days. We made the playoffs with Columbus, but by that time things were getting really confused. The war was coming and everyone was leaving for the service.

I spent the next four years in the service with a lot of other ballplayers. That was 1942 through 1945. I didn't officially get out until April 1946. I went from a private to a sergeant at Jefferson Barracks in Missouri and then from sergeant to Officers Training School, without a college education. I managed to graduate. They graduated 4,000 of us and I was 2,999. I was right in the middle of the pack and I was kind of proud of that. I then went to San Antonio, Texas, as a second lieutenant and a physical training officer. I stayed there the rest of the war. We were a preflight school for pilots, the aviation cadets. That is where I met my wife, Taffy, and, well, one thing led to another.

I stayed right there until the war was over and by that time the Cardinals had moved me up. We played baseball in the Army and we had a pretty good team. We got quite a bit of publicity about it. The air bases around San Antonio each had a team and there were quite a few big-league players involved. We had Howard Pollet and Enos Slaughter on our team. Then after 1946, well, that's all in the record books from then on in.

Playing baseball was a dream and it came true. Even after I had played in the big leagues for a while and was playing in Boston with the Red Sox, it still seemed like a dream. When we played in Detroit, which was home for me, our manager, Lou Boudreau, would always see to it that I would get to play because my folks and all of my relatives and friends were there. There I was, a big leaguer, playing in my old hometown, and a guy from Lincoln Park came up to me on the street after a game. He looked at me, realized that he hadn't seen me for a long time, and said, "You know, I've often wondered about you. Boy, in high school you were some kind of athlete. What ever became of you? What do you do for a living?" Well, that kind of took the wind out of my sails. So much for being a famous big leaguer.

My dad was a pretty good athlete and my mother was a great athlete. She was an outstanding bowler in the 1930s. In fact, she was such a good bowler, my dad quit. He wouldn't go bowling with her because she beat him all the time. They were both all for me playing ball. Also I was just getting out of high school—you know, what was I going to do? I could have been going to work at the Ford Motor Company like the rest of the guys. There weren't too many guys going to college in 1937 because there weren't too many scholarships being handed out. But what it boiled down to was that I was lucky enough to make it. When I got out of the service and by the time I got to the big leagues I was already twenty-seven years old, with a wife and a young son. When I got to the St. Louis Cardinals I was twenty-seven years old and Joe Garagiola was only nineteen years old. That automatically made me a second- and third-string catcher. But major league teams had to have more than one catcher. That year I played fifty or so games. I did well enough to stick around. I'm kinda proud of it.

I would say that the 1953 Boston Red Sox were the greatest bunch of ballplayers that I played with. Ted Williams was just coming back from his second tour of duty in the Air Force. Dom DiMaggio was just an outstanding person. And then of course George Kell was on that team with Milton Bolling, Johnny Lipon, Billy Goodman, Mel Parnell, Mickey McDermott, Sid Hudson, and Sammy White and I were the catchers. Lou Boudreau was a fine man and a fine manager.

The 1947 Cardinals were a fine bunch of guys as well. I was proud just to be there. Just to know them. Just to walk on the same field with Stan Musial. We all wore the same uniform. That was a thrill in itself.

One of the best road trips with the St. Louis Cardinals was playing in Chicago, playing day games at Wrigley Field. When the ball game was over we'd get on the bus and go to the Dearborn Street Station and we'd catch the Wabash Cannonball. It was classy, there was a big domed lounge car that we'd use and the fans would be there to meet us at the Delmar Street Station in St. Louis.

Then there would be the off day traveling to New York. We would play a day game here in St. Louis and about six o'clock we'd be on the New York Central as it pulled out. We'd leave St. Louis, go across the river, head back to the dining car and get something to eat. Then first thing you know you'd be in Indianapolis and you'd wake up the next morning and be in Albany, New York; then down the Hudson River to New York City—now that was an off day because the trip took a whole day.

When we went to New York City we stayed a whole week because we played four against the Giants and four against Brooklyn. Then we'd go to Boston or Philadelphia and then stop in Pittsburgh or Cincinnati on the way back to St. Louis. The road trips were twenty-one days long, with no day off when you came back. Didn't look forward to one either—we'd get off the train and say, "Lets go play!" Sometimes the train would get into a town, say, into Pittsburgh, about three o'clock in the morning and they'd just pull our cars off and put 'em on the side and when you woke up the next morning you'd grab your bag and get off. You'd wait for somebody else to get off too and catch a cab to the hotel. It was time to go to work.

Sometimes guys would miss the train. The manager would be hotter than could be and that train would simply pull away. They didn't wait for anybody. Nobody was that important! If you missed that train it was up to you to find some other way to that town and, boy oh boy, you'd better be there when that train pulled in.

There was one fellow who played for the St. Louis Browns, an outfielder who had played for me in the service. His name was Paul Lehner, he was from Dolomite, Alabama, and he was a real rowdy. One time he had some things that I guess were more important to do than catching the train. I guess he'd been drinking some beers or something and he missed the train as the Browns were heading out for the East Coast. The players all knew he missed the train. But when they pulled into Grand Central Station the next day, there he was standing there. He had his suitcase with him and was standing there so the manager would never know that he missed the train!

It turned out that he had flown all night in little one-stop airplanes. He got there in time to get from the airport to Grand

Central so that it looked like he'd been on the train all along.

Eddie Dyer was our Cardinal manager and he was a real pinochle fanatic. He liked his players to play cards in the clubhouse and when we were on the train, but he only wanted us to play pinochle because it was a game where you had to think. You had to be able to remember which cards had been played. If you couldn't play pinochle, well, Eddie Dyer wouldn't talk to you. And if you did play but you didn't play well, he'd get mad. He'd say, "How can you play ball if you can't even play pinochle?" Lots of hours went by on those trains playing cards and trading lies, but those days are gone.

I sat many a night in those train roomettes. That was a luxury when we graduated to roomettes 'cause after the war we traveled in Pullman cars with uppers and lowers. The regulars got the lowers and the rookies got the uppers. Except that the pitcher who was to start the next day always got a lower regardless. Then, when we got roomettes I'd go into mine and prop my feet up. Not pull the bed down, just prop my feet up and sit there in the dark looking out the window. Watching the towns go by, you'd hear the rails clicking and the first thing you'd know it would put you right to sleep. Watching those little country towns go by, every once in a while you'd see a fire out on some farm. Occasionally you'd pull into some little backwater somewhere to collect the mail or drop off the milk. You'd get up in the morning and have a big breakfast: ham and eggs, hash browns, toast, coffee. Those were the days, they really were, but they're gone.

Just walking into Ebbets Field was a real thrill. We didn't take any team bus to get there. You had to get to the ball park any way that you could, usually by subway. But just to walk into Ebbets Field in Brooklyn and to be part of it all, the aura of it, the atmosphere, the Brooklyn fans. They really were the beautiful bums. To see Pee Wee Reese and Jackie Robinson and be right up there with them. It's hard to explain but that was really something. It was something you used to dream at night about and suddenly it belonged to you.

There are two ways of looking at why certain athletes are great. Some think it's all in the work ethic and hustling to improve, and some think you either have it or you don't.

For example, there have always been guys who were natural hitters. They were just born that way, and were actually very poor defensive players. And they would never work on their defense. They'd always be at the ball park taking batting practice. But what they were practicing is what they already had a gift for.

And there have been ballplayers who were so gifted that nothing they did or didn't do would affect their greatness. There were even great drunk ballplayers. One of them is even in the Hall of Fame. As the stories go, even old Babe Ruth was no teetotaler, and a womanizer to boot, but he could really hit.

I have a record that is called baseball's perfect day. It was August 27, 1951, when I was with the Phillies, and I was sicker than a mule that day. I had a bad, bad cold. I sat in the dugout between innings with a big jacket on and that was August! I never took my chest protector off, I just slipped a jacket on over it and stood there like a guy with malaria or pneumonia or something. I was loose—in other words, I had no tension that night. I was too sick. I didn't really realize what had happened until the ball game was over. It was the second game of a doubleheader and we had won the first game, 2–1.

Andy Seminick had caught the first game and I caught the second game. I was catching a left-handed pitcher from Wichita, Kansas, who was also an ex-Cardinal named Ken Johnson. He had a tendency to be wild, but in this game he had everything under control. He even struck out seven or eight guys. Anyway, when my turn came up to bat, I just swung at it and hit a home run. I did that three times that night. Three swings—three home runs. I didn't really think anything about it until I got back to the house and Taffy, my wife, said she had heard all about it on the radio.

There was an Irish tavern across the street from the house we were living in. I used to go in there when games were over and get great big sandwiches. So I went over and got us some sandwiches and they had written the line score on the mirror on the back of the bar: WILBER 3– CINCINNATI 0. And the sandwiches were free! It wasn't really until then that I realized what I had done. Three times at bat, three swings, and three home runs.

When I got back to the ball park the next day I only needed to hit one more to tie Lou Gehrig and an outfielder from the turn of the century named Bobby Lowe to hit 4 consecutive home runs. And I wasn't in the lineup! Andy Seminick, who was in the starting lineup, told me to go on out and take infield practice, even though our manager, Eddie Sawyer, had written Andy's name down as the catcher. So I went out and took infield practice and when I came back in the clubhouse the trainer came up to me and said, "Hey, you're catching, Seminick is sick."

So, I went out and started the game against St. Louis because Cincinnati had left town. The fellow who was renting our house in St. Louis, Gerry Staley, was pitching against us. What a coincidence! The first time I went to bat, he threw me a curveball and I hit a fly to deep left field. I think Erv Dusak caught it and I was out. When I came back into the dugout, there was Seminick sitting there with a smile on his face. He gave me a big wink and said, "Well, I got you up to bat, didn't I?"

In 1956, I was a player-coach with the White Sox with Marty Marion. He was the manager and I was a coach. They could have made me eligible to play. I did everything a player would do as far as working out, except that I was the fourth coach. So that made me the fourth coach and the third catcher. Sherman Lollar was catching every day. I stayed in pretty good shape up until about the Fourth of July. But, boy, after the Fourth of July, Lollar was catching every day and I made good and sure that he did catch every day. I was up in my middle thirties by then and when a half a season had gone by, I'd started getting out of shape. I brought Sherman towels and wiped him down. I'd say, "Get right in there, Sherm buddy, you're doing fine." I was in Chicago for two years. We stayed at the Picadilly Hotel there on the South Side of old Chicago and we played at Comiskey Park.

Then came scouting and coaching and of course the instructional league. I have another record to go along with the perfect-day record. I am baseball's only undefeated major league manager. In 1973 my Spokane team had just won the Pacific Coast League playoff in Tucson, Arizona. We were the Triple A team for the Texas Rangers and we had just won the playoff against my old friend Sherman Lollar. The next day we flew to Dallas for various reasons to the main offices of the Texas

Rangers. We got off the plane in Dallas, and I headed over to the ball park to go down in the clubhouse and shave, take a shower, and maybe sit in the Jacuzzi for a while. As I walked in the ball park at about five minutes to seven, the head usher came running out and grabbed me. He put me in the elevator and said, "Up to the office."

When I walked in, Joe Berg said, "Whitey Herzog has just been fired and you're the manager." I wasn't any more ready to manage than anyone. I didn't even have a uniform. I was just going in to report on the Pacific Coast League championship and the playoff and what do you know if I'm not suddenly the manager! I was just stopping in on my way home.

As I was walking into the clubhouse, and there were TV cameras and whatnot, Whitey Herzog yelled over to me, "Chuck Hiller's got the lineup. Use it if you want to." So I went down and the clubhouse guy gave me a uniform. We were playing the Oakland Athletics, and I had just got through beating their farm club. Hell if we didn't beat 'em! It was 9–6 or something like that! I didn't change the lineup or anything. I just changed the pitchers a couple of times. I put guys in to pitch that really hadn't pitched much for Texas, but that was because I knew them, they had played for me. I had to change pitchers in the ninth inning because we had a two-run lead and two men on base with Reggie Jackson hitting. So I brought Jim Merritt in and he threw Reggie a pretty good curveball. He hit a ground ball to third base for the third out.

I went into the clubhouse after the game and I kind of expected the press to show up, but nobody came in. The players all autographed a ball and gave it to me—you know the game ball and all that kind of stuff. I waited and waited and finally the clubhouse guy came in and said, "Hell, we might as well get dressed and get out of here. They're having some kind of a press conference upstairs."

They called me the next morning and said, "First of all, we're glad you won the game, we couldn't have won it without you. And second, in the seventh inning of last night's game, we finally got a hold of Billy Martin and we hired him. He's the new manager." Billy Martin took over the next day. So I only managed one game in the big leagues. But I won! And I'm the only undefeated major league manager. I'm at the point now where I don't want the opportunity to ruin my own record. I could ruin my tombstone.

The most outstanding athletes that I ever had the opportunity to play with were Musial, Williams, Marion, and George Kell. You'd have to turn over a lot of rocks to find anything equal to George Kell. The best natural hitter I ever saw was Tony Oliva. Absolutely the best natural hitter I ever saw. I once told the late Joe Haynes during instructional league as we watched Tony hit, "Anybody who ever attempts to tell Tony O. how to hit ought to be fired on the spot!" He didn't know how to play the game, he had two left feet, and he couldn't do side-straddle hops. But he had this natural ability. In his book he mentions that I had told him, "When you get to the big leagues, Tony, and you're playing Detroit, watch the Detroit right fielder and do everything that he does. Then you'll be a Hall of Fame ballplayer." That right fielder was Al Kaline. He and Joe DiMaggio and Dom DiMaggio were on the other end of the graph when it came to ability. They could do no wrong.

Of course Garagiola and I always got along fine. We became really close buddies. In his book he referred to me as the "bullpen philosopher." That's because we could sit out there forever and just talk. We'd see who could out-lie the next guy.

We all used to have jobs in the off-season and Joe Garagiola and I worked together a lot in St. Louis. We sold Christmas trees together. Dick Sisler was the head of this thing and it was for some charity but we got paid too. People would come in and Joe would be talking to somebody and I would be talking to somebody else. They would be looking at this and that, and we didn't have prices on anything. So we gave signals to each other about the prices. Garagiola would be scratching his head, and that would mean go top price for this guy, or he would be scratching his belly, which would mean go bottom dollar for this one. We laughed like crazy and we made a lot of money too sometimes! Just two old catchers who couldn't stop giving signals! We'd sell that first tree for eight dollars or so and pay for the whole bundle and everything else was just profit. It was snowing and it was cold and we were laughing like hell selling those Christmas trees with Joe scratching his head. And we got a free Christmas tree.

And then there was my friend Sid Hudson, a pitcher whom

I was very close to through the years. We were both finishing up our careers about the same time. We knew our playing days were numbered—our legs were beginning to go and his arm was bad and getting worse. He was starting to throw practically underhand. Near the end, that last year, we'd come out of the bullpen and the game would be over and we'd be walking toward the dugout. We'd take a look around, you know, our last days in each town. We'd look around at the stadiums, getting our last look. Mr. Yawkey would be sitting up in his box in Boston and we'd wave at him, "Good-bye."

Mel Parnell after pitching a no-hitter against the White Sox, 1956

MEL PARNELL

"Marvelous Mel" Parnell pitched from 1947 to 1956 for the Boston Red Sox. He led the league in wins and ERAs in 1949 and was an All-Star in 1949 and 1951. On July 14, 1956, his last year in the majors, Parnell threw a no-hitter, the first for the Red Sox in thirty-three years.

WHEN I WAS VERY small, I played with boys much older than I was and everybody kept telling me that I had a future in the game. In high school I was a first baseman and an outfielder. I loved to play first base and take my chances getting up to the plate and swinging that bat—that was the big thrill for me. Finally one time we were short on pitching and the coach asked me if I'd pitch, so naturally I agreed. I was willing to do anything just to be playing.

I pitched and on that day a Red Sox scout, a Yankee scout, and a Detroit scout were there watching and I had a pretty good day. I struck out seventeen and pitched a shutout. From then on, the professional clubs became interested. I made my choice to go with the Boston Red Sox and to this day I'm very happy that I did because it all turned out really well for me.

The St. Louis Cardinals were also interested in me. I used to go out to the local ball club, which was a Cardinal farm club, and pitch batting practice to them. Ray Blades, who was very highly regarded in the Cardinal organization, was the manager and he got Branch Rickey to come down and look me over. As I was pitching batting practice Rickey became very interested. He came out to the house and talked with my dad, and he said the Cardinals were interested in signing me. The only problem for Mr. Rickey was that I wasn't interested in signing with the Cardinals. At that time the Cardinals had a very big farm operation, they had three Triple A ball clubs, and you were known as a number in the organization rather than by name. That didn't interest me and I had been told by Howard Pollet, who was one of their top pitchers, that it was very hard to get anywhere in the Cardinal organization.

Howard and I grew up together; we were next-door neighbors and played a lot of ball in the neighborhood. Howard was the reason that I played so much first base, since he was a very capable pitcher even as a youngster. Howie Pollet and I were very close and shared a lot of things, including our love of baseball.

We also had in our neighborhood an outfielder who drew a lot of attention, a fellow by the name of Ed Levine who signed with the Cardinals. As a matter of fact, seven of the nine players on our high school ball club signed to play professionally and of the seven, six of them signed with the Cardinals. I was the only one that didn't. I was really fortunate in signing with the Red Sox. Mr. Yawkey was a fine owner—you couldn't have asked for a man to treat you any better than he did. We all appreciated that and gave everything that we had to try and make a winner out of our ball club. It was a great experience, something that I enjoyed tremendously, and I just wish that I was young enough to do it over again—especially at today's salaries.

When I signed, I went first to Owensburg, Kentucky. They had four left-handed pitchers on their pitching staff already and when I got there the manager told me, "What I don't need is another left-handed pitcher."

So then they sent me to Centerville, Maryland. I weighed only 130 pounds at the time. I was all bones. The Red Sox sent word down to the manager in Centerville, "Pitch the little skinny kid just once a week." So on Sundays I was the pitcher. I had a pretty good year and from there I progressed to Canton, Ohio, in the Middle Atlantic League. To this day I still hold the ERA record in that league.

From there I went to Scranton, Pennsylvania, and I also hold the ERA record for the Eastern League. And from there I went up to the Red Sox in 1947, right after they had won the pennant in 1946. I lost four good years to the service between

1943 and 1947, but at least I played ball in the service. It was because of baseball that I didn't go overseas. The post commanders wanted to keep me on the base to play ball. We had a very good ball club at Maxwell Field in Alabama. We were in the flight training command and we'd win the championship each year because our post commander was keeping most of us there rather than sending us overseas.

We had four major league pitchers on our ball club at Maxwell Field. We had Bill McCahan, who pitched for the Philadelphia Athletics; George Turbeville, who also pitched for the Philadelphia Athletics; Cy Blanton, who pitched for the Pittsburgh Pirates; and myself. We beat just about everybody. We played a lot of Southern League teams at the time and we beat them with such ease that we played an 85-game schedule and won 78 of those 85 games. Hugh Mulcahy, a great pitcher with the Philadelphia Phillies, was with one of the teams in Memphis, Tennessee, and we played them. While I was pitching against them, Mulcahy approached me and asked me if I could get a release from the Red Sox. He said to me, "If you can, I guarantee you seventy-five thousand dollars right off the bat to sign with the Phillies." That, of course, sounded tremendous, so I tried to get a release from the Red Sox but Joe Cronin said there was absolutely no way and that I should forget that idea. I kept at him, trying to get him to the point where maybe he'd say yes, but he never did. I got out of the service in 1947 and I was twenty-five years old. I lost four good ones, but we all did; we were in the prime of our careers when we went to the service.

The Red Sox were a good paying ball club; I never got a cut from the Red Sox. I played for the same salary just one year and all the rest of the years were increases for me. That was Mr. Yawkey's method. The day I pitched my no-hitter the first man to greet me when I walked into the clubhouse was Tom Yawkey with a new contract in his hand.

I told him, "Mr. Yawkey, you don't have to do this, you've paid me already for this kind of stuff." He said, "Yeah, but I want you to have this new contract." I said that I'd be glad to sign it, which I did in a hurry. He didn't have to do that. We had signed a contract to play ball and that was that.

Mr. Yawkey was a great individual—if you couldn't play for

him you couldn't play for anybody. He was a real plus to the game of baseball and it's just too bad that they didn't have more Tom Yawkeys in the game. If they had, then I think that the game could have been as lucrative then as it is now.

It's true that we used to throw at the batters, but we didn't throw at a batter to hurt him, just to try and push him back from the plate, in order to set up a pitch. Sometimes the batter got hurt though and it made you feel just terrible. I hit one of my best friends and broke his hand. I felt bad about it but I was just trying to push him back and the ball sailed in on him and hit him in the hand. Now he's the American League president, Dr. Bobby Brown. Bobby went to school here at Tulane University. We played a lot of ball around town together and became great friends. The time I broke his hand, Bobby was alternating with Bill Johnson at third base for the Yankees. After Bobby got hurt, Johnson had to play every day and he got as hot as could be and helped to win the pennant for the Yankees.

Then I got hit; I had my arm broken by a pitched ball from my ex-roommate, Mickey McDermott. It was an accident; he pitched to me and I was starting into the pitch, swinging to hit it, and all of a sudden the ball took off and came sailing toward me. In defense, I threw my left arm up and the ball hit it and broke it. At the end of the inning he came into the clubhouse and wanted to see how badly I was hurt; when I told him it was broken he had tears running out of his eyes. That was one of those things, a freak happening, and those things sometimes happen.

Those things happen in the game; I guess you don't want to see it happen but you expect it to some time or another. It's almost as bad as guys hitting balls back through the box at the pitchers—you can't move fast enough to do anything. The ball is moving faster than you can react and you just see the blurred object coming back at you. If you don't react fast enough, then you're going to get hit with it. It's happened to just about every pitcher in the game. I know I got hit with a couple of them and I got a broken finger out of one. That's part of the game and it's just a matter of being ready to do the best that you can.

Years ago we had so many minor leagues that baseball was much more competitive. We had to play every day, with or without injuries—you didn't want to get out of the ball game and let someone else get a chance because they could be wearing your uniform. We played, injured or not. I know that I pitched many games when my arm was hurting but I was hired to do just that, so I did it to the best of my ability. The same goes for a lot of other fellows.

Ted Williams without a doubt brings to mind the word "respect." Ted is the most perfect self-made man I have ever seen. Anything that he encountered, he worked at until it was 100 percent. Fishing was his love really, I think Ted loves fishing even more than baseball, and at one point he felt that the fishing lures he was buying weren't as good as the ones that he could make, so he made his own. There he was the greatest hitter of all times and he would sit home making his own fishing lures so they would be perfect.

He *worked* at hitting, everybody says it was a God-given talent that he had, but it was much more. He had talent—more talent than a lot of people had—but he worked and developed that talent. I for one worked along with him and I think it was an asset to me. Ted felt that because of the short left field wall in Fenway Park he saw very little left-handed pitching when the teams came to Boston. So Ted liked to get out and hit some batting practice against left-handed pitchers. We had Mickey McDermott, Chuck Stout, and myself, and we'd pitch batting practice to him. We'd pitch to him under game conditions and we tried to figure him out because if we could figure him out, it was certainly going to be an asset when we faced other left-handed hitters. I have to give Ted credit for some of my success too, having had the opportunity to pitch to him.

Another extraordinary fellow was Bobby Doerr. Bobby was one of the finest that you'd ever meet. A class individual all the way and a great fellow to have behind you in the infield. Bobby could make the plays and of course he was a pretty good hitter all along. But Bobby was a fellow I admired most because of his mild-mannered attitude. His disposition. He wore uniform number 1 and he was number one.

Boo Ferriss was another fellow that I had a lot of respect for. Boo was a very quiet individual who never used a profane word. I think the strongest word out of his mouth was "shuckins"—whenever he'd get really mad he'd say, "Aw shuckins!"

That used to tickle the life out of us. Mickey Harris was the real character on the pitching staff and Mickey used to say, "Go ahead and say what you want to say, Boo!" But Boo would never dream of it. That was his way, that was his makeup, he was just a good clean liver and a good guy.

Boo was the coach at Delta State College in Mississippi and two years ago when he retired they named the ball park after him. We got an invitation and decided not to tell him we were coming. We showed up and surprised him, and Boo when he saw us had tears running down his face. He was crying. We were as happy as he was to share that with him. We had some really good fellows on our ball club and some really good friendships.

The press used to call us the "country club," but that wasn't so. That was a misnomer by the Boston press. They were perturbed because we didn't win the pennant, but the main reason for that was the New York Yankees. They were just about a step ahead of us. I think if there hadn't have been a mistake on the part of Joe Cronin we probably could have won the pennant a couple of times from the Yankees. He had a chance to pick up Max Surkont as a relief pitcher and he failed to do it, so our bullpen wasn't giving us the results that we should have been getting. I know in 1949 between Ellis Kinder and myself we won forty-eight games. Had the rest of the pitching staff duplicated that forty-eight we would have had ninety-six wins and that would have been enough to win the pennant. If we had had Max Surkont, he could have saved enough games for us to make the difference between us and the Yankees. He could have been the big difference—we were just one good relief pitcher short. But that's water under the bridge now.

My most exciting moment was the no-hitter. A no-hitter is something that all pitchers dream of but never expect to happen. When it does happen, you're living on cloud nine. In the seventh inning, Jackie Jensen, our right fielder, came over to me on the bench. Everybody on the bench was pretty quiet, and Jackie said, "Look, fellow, you got a no-hitter going here now. Don't let them hit the ball to right field because I don't want to be the guy that messes it up." I told him, "Jackie, forget it, if it happens it happens, I'm worried about getting a win, and that's all I am interested in."

But when I got down to the last inning and the last out, things started to prey on me a little bit. Even so, I was probably the most relaxed guy on the whole ball club because I just wanted to win. As it turned out, the last batter was a former teammate, Walt Dropo. This was against the Chicago White Sox and Dropo hit a ground ball back toward the mound, just on the first base side. I came down off the mound, retrieved the ball, and continued running to first base to make the out unassisted.

To this day I can't tell you why I ran. I guess I feared throwing the ball to first base. Mickey Vernon was our first baseman and when I got to first base, Mickey said, "What's the matter fellow, you don't trust me?" I said no, I didn't trust myself to throw it. Also I figured I could beat Dropo because he wasn't the fastest one afoot that I'd ever seen.

Pitchers have often said that they didn't know they were going for a no-hitter. I can't believe that because as you get late into the game the fans remind you. They are constantly up and yelling with each out. If you're in the game, you are paying attention to the scoreboard and if you see that big zero up there you have to know it. I can't believe these fellows when they say that they didn't know they were going for it. It's impossible not to know.

The other big moment for me was starting the 1949 All-Star Game. I was more nervous in that game than any game I had ever pitched, partly because of the fact that I was representing our league against the best from the other league. Warren Spahn was the opposing pitcher for the National League and at that time the American League was in command of the All-Star Game.

Baseball was really a family sport at that time. The admissions were much lower than for other sports and a family of four could go to a game cheaply. Baseball is really a disease too, like a virus. It gets in your system, you can't get rid of it, and then you are a fan. When we'd go to New York to play the Yankees we'd go through Connecticut and Rhode Island. We traveled by train and when we went through small towns we'd see people clustered around in the station there waiting to wave to us as we went by. We didn't get a chance to speak to them or anything because we were on a moving train, but they were

just out there to see us and wave to us as we went by.

When we would go into New York the applause was so tremendous for us that sometimes we'd feel we were the home team, and when the Yankees would come to Boston, sometimes it sounded as if they were the home team. It was a great rivalry during a terrific era.

Years ago we were like a family. We traveled by train, and we were constantly together. We used to get on the train and have dinner, after that we'd lounge around and play cards or whatever, but most of all we'd get into discussions about baseball. We'd sit there and talk situations, we'd talk opposition, we'd talk certain pitching, and so forth. I think we bettered our game by doing that. Today they don't do that. One guy couldn't care less about the next guy. I think a twenty-one-day road trip would kill some of these guys today.

When I first got to the big leagues I was living on cloud nine. It was the dream that came true and I wanted to do everything that I could possibly do to stay there. It was such an enjoyable life playing a little kid's game. I certainly didn't want it to slip away from neglect, so I worked hard at it.

DON
LENHARDT

Don "Footsie" Lenhardt played from 1950 to 1954 for the Browns, White Sox, Tigers, and Orioles. When a broken ankle in 1954 forced the end of his playing career, Lenhardt began a new career as a scout.

WE PLAYED SOME FORM of ball all the time when I was a little kid. It seemed it was the only thing that we did. There wasn't really organized ball, but there was a playground in my home-town of Alton, Illinois, that was close by, so during the summer we would play softball and baseball. If I didn't have anyone to play with, then I would hit rocks, but I was always swinging at something. Like many others I developed my skills without knowing what was going to come from it. We were training all of the time, not knowing it was training, but that was what it was.

When I got into high school we didn't have a baseball team but there was a league sponsored by the local paper, the *Alton Evening Telegraph*. So we got up our own team and got into that league. We played without uniforms, but we played. I also played on Sundays in the semi-pro leagues. There were a lot of older men playing and I was only about seventeen. I had it so that I was playing almost every day of the week.

I started working then at the glass company in Alton and at Western Cartridge, which was an ammunition plant. The glass company had a team. They had a lot of industrial softball leagues at that time, and a scout from the Browns came up to watch me. He didn't really make any decisions then because it was a softball game, but then on a Sunday he saw me play baseball and liked me.

They wanted me to go to some backwater somewhere to play and I said, "No, a gentleman in Alton has gotten me a partial scholarship to Illinois University." I thought I was going to eliminate all of those low minor leagues by going to college. Well, I went to college, but I didn't eliminate any minor leagues!

World War II came along and I missed about five summers because of the war. But I had been contacted in the meantime by the Browns. When I got out of the service my dad and I went down to St. Louis. I worked out with them one day and they signed me and I went to spring training with one of the Browns' minor league teams in Farmington, Missouri.

They sent me to Aberdeen, South Dakota, and I didn't make the Aberdeen club, which was Class C, so they sent me down to Pittsburgh, Kansas, which was Class D. By the time I arrived there I had nothing, not a penny in my pocket. Jimmy Crandell, our manager, loaned me enough money to eat and that same night I hit a home run and they passed a hat around the stands and I made a hundred dollars. That was a lot of money! More than I was making in salary in a month. I figured the key to success in that town was hitting home runs, because then they'd pass the hat! That was 1946, and I was twenty-three years old.

I had a good year in Pittsburgh and in 1947 they sent me back to Aberdeen. Great place, Aberdeen! We had bus rides you would not believe. After a game we'd ride all night and all day and get there just in time to play. We'd play in places like Fargo, North Dakota, and Duluth. The league was spread out all over.

In 1949 I played in San Antonio and I had an excellent season with twenty-six home runs and was asked by Mike Gonzales to play winter ball in Havana, Cuba.

I went down there and had a great year. I set a record with sixteen home runs and got lots of publicity. When I came back I went to spring training with the Browns and supposedly I was going to go play Triple A ball. But I was in good shape from playing all winter and we played a lot of teams that had little left-handed pitchers, so I had a great spring training and they kept me with the Browns. By that time I was twenty-seven years old.

So you see I was getting old already. The war took so many

years from a lot of us. But we can't really complain because we don't know what we would have done if we had played those years.

The Browns changed my position from left field to first base, which I had never played until I got to the big leagues. I think they probably just needed a first baseman more than they needed an outfielder. There I was suddenly with the Browns, on first base and not very good, although I did very well—I hit 22 home runs and hit .278. I almost got to be Rookie of the Year, but Walt Dropo happened to have a very good year that same year.

I always thought of the pros as superstars. What changed my mind was one day in Class D ball when we played our Triple A ball club and they were not the supermen that I thought they were. That helped me a lot as far as thinking that I could get there. But it is a thrill of a lifetime.

When I walked in the clubhouse I sure felt like a rookie, although being older (twenty-seven) may have helped the situation and maybe playing with the Browns, who were losers constantly, made it easier to feel like I belonged. I think people were closer at that time on ball clubs than they are now. After a game six or seven guys would always go out together and have dinner and today I don't think they do that. I don't think they even associate with each other. It was a lot of fun. To be honest, I think we had more fun than they have now.

My nickname, Footsie, I got from Buddy Blattner. I can't lie and say that it was because I was so fast. It's because I have a very narrow foot and I had a lot of trouble getting shoes to fit. My foot isn't really exceptionally big for my size or anything but it was very narrow and I'd have shoes made and half of them wouldn't fit. Buddy had a nickname for everybody.

My strongest memory, other than getting to the big leagues, is the fact that I participated against players who really were superstars. Like Ted Williams, DiMaggio, Feller. There I was competing against those people and playing with them. I look back now and I think of all those names of guys who played when I did. And I can say, "Well, I played also."

I always worked in the off-season, always. I did everything from unloading boxcars, digging ditches, and cutting carpets to selling clothes. I worked every winter from then on, even after

I quit playing ball. It was a necessity. The minimum baseball salary when I started was just five thousand and it just wasn't enough to live on all year. My first year, that good year I had with the twenty-two home runs, I couldn't get a twenty-five-hundred-dollar raise! And I was scared to death that somebody was going to take my place if I didn't sign the contract. It was not then who you were or how much money you got, it was simply that you had to be better than the other guy. If you weren't you got released.

I played five years in the big leagues, then I went down to the minor leagues and played two more years. First with Louisville and then with San Francisco. In San Francisco I broke the other ankle, only this time I broke it badly enough that I had to think about not playing anymore. There I was sitting around feeling sorry for myself and saying stuff like, "I'm really not qualified to do anything else." Then Johnny Murphy from the Red Sox organization called me up and asked me what I wanted to do. So I told him, "Well, whatever you want me to do, I'll do." He said, "I'll tell you this, I think you'll be better off scouting because you don't have to be away from home as much."

A lot of ballplayers pursued their dream because it was the only skill they felt that they had. I could have worked at Owens, Illinois glass company the rest of my life . . . or I could have taken the risk to play ball. I'm glad, really glad that I took the risk.

BOB KENNEDY

Bob Kennedy, an outfielder and third baseman, played from 1939 to 1957 for the White Sox, Indians, Orioles, Tigers, and Dodgers. Kennedy's baseball career spans more than fifty years and just about every job in baseball from popcorn vendor to general manager. His son, Terry Kennedy, is a major league catcher.

AS FAR BACK AS I can remember, I never thought that I wouldn't make it. I never thought that I'd fail. I knew that I was going to be a big leaguer.

I used to sell Blue Valley popcorn at Comiskey Park when I was a kid fifteen years old. Then when I was sixteen, I sold popcorn for the big fight when Joe Louis won the championship by beating Braddock, and the next day I went away to play ball in Dallas, Texas, for seventy-five dollars a month.

My parents were very supportive. They were also extremely strict and I had to be in the house when the streetlights came on. I had to obey. The amazing thing was that they let me go. I had never been away from home and they let me go play ball at age sixteen. Even after I was in the big leagues and I would have a date, my parents would always ask what time I was going to be back. I'd say ten-thirty or eleven and my dad would say, "Nope, nine-thirty," and that was the way that it was.

The first year I stayed in Dallas for about a month and a half, went over to Vicksburg and played a month there in the Cotton States League, then went back to Dallas and finished the season. The following season, I went to Longview, Texas, in Class C, the East Texas League, and I stayed there all year.

The next year I asked if I could go to Shreveport in the Texas League, just to see if I could make the club. It turned out I made the team, which was equivalent to Triple A in those days. I stayed there until I was called to the big leagues.

I joined the White Sox in Philadelphia in 1939. This is an unusual coincidence, but I got my first base hit and made my first out in Shibe Park in Philadelphia and I got my last base hit and made my last out also in Shibe Park in 1957. The last out that I made as a player was the last out for the Brooklyn Dodgers ever; it ended the regime.

I was a Marine pilot; Ted Williams and I were both Marine pilots and we were both pulled out twice to serve. I lost 1943 to 1946, and then again 1952 and 1953 for Korea, but I was fortunate that I had that time playing before 1942, and I got to play the full year in 1942. I had enlisted in the Navy D5 program and asked them if I could stay till the end of the season. "I may never get another one," I told them. They asked when I wanted to go and I said I didn't care so long as it was after the season.

During the Korean War, I buzzed the Ponce ball park in Puerto Rico just to say hello. It was right after Opening Day and they were working out. None of them had ever seen a jet and I came down and flew right through the lights about five or six hundred miles per hour. Scared the daylights out of everybody around. They didn't know what happened because I was already gone by the time the sound got there.

One particular game stands out in my memory. We had a game in Washington in the pennant battle of 1948 and Larry Doby and I weren't in the lineup. It was the bottom of the ninth and the score was tied, the bases were loaded with one out, and Boudreau put Doby in center and me in right field. In those days, when you came in as a substitute in the middle of an inning you didn't get a chance to warm up; they wouldn't take the time. So I waved my arm and Lou asked if I was all right. I said I was okay and we played.

Right away somebody hit a ball back over my head to right center field, quite deep, and I went back, caught the ball, and threw the guy out at the plate. That ended the inning and then in the tenth inning I got a base hit to win it. It was in a pennant drive and it was a fantastic finish.

Another big moment was the one-game play-off we won in 1948. We went into Boston and packed 154 games into one game. Winner take all right there. That was it.

Sometimes I think that I must have been a dummy because I never thought about failing. It never entered my mind that I wasn't going to get to the majors. And in those days it was a very select group of people. I wanted to play in the big leagues and then I got a chance. I played in one game and said, "Well, I made the big leagues." That was all I had asked for. I didn't know what would happen with the war, but I thought I'd like to get a year in. I got a year in and then I thought I'd like to get five. Then I got five and thought well I'd *love* to get ten.

I'll never forget being in Boston in 1948 in my tenth year in baseball. I went to Boudreau and I said, "Louie, I'm going to celebrate ten years in the big leagues tonight. I'm not coming in; I'm going to stay out all night." Johnny Berardino and I went out (I didn't know anything at all about alcohol) and we were drinking. I think he drank ginger ale and Seagram's, something like that, so I drank the same thing. We got in at daylight, went out to the ballpark, and I got 4 for 4 that day! But the next day I was beat.

In 1940 we trained in Pasadena, and Pittsburgh trained in San Bernadino. That was the year they talked Paul Waner into stopping his drinking. They said that he would hit .400, so he stopped drinking; he didn't touch a drop until about the first part of June when he was only hitting .278 or something and they said, "Paul, go ahead and drink, please," and he ended up hitting .318 or .320. It worked for him, but I sure don't think it could work for everybody. The old-timers are like that, they didn't care, I knew some guys that wouldn't be part of anything. They were really feisty and when they walked on to the field it was a war. It was a war because everybody was trying to scratch and save his job and be able to play again next year.

My wife, Claire, and the kids would come to the city where I was playing, and when I went to play in Cleveland for seven years, we moved there. Later we moved to Salt Lake City because we thought that was it. We thought that I was going to stay there for the next twenty years. I had no intentions of managing in the major leagues. In fact, I turned down the Cubs

job, but Herman Franks, who owned the Salt Lake club at that
time, jumped all over me. "You *can't* turn down a major league
manager's job. How many chances are you going to get?" I
said, "I've only managed one year, and I don't know whether
I'm ready or not." He said, "Get a good coach and you'll be
all right."

So I managed the Cubs in 1963–65. In 1966 I went back
with the Dodgers as a manager in Double A, and the following
year I was a coach at third base for Atlanta. Then in 1968, I
was the first manager at Oakland, when the A's moved out there.

In 1969 I went with the Cardinals. I was the farm director
and head of player development. That was where the term
"player development" started—Bing Devine came up with that.
I was with the Cardinals from 1969 through 1975. Those were
great years with great people.

Toward the end of the year in 1976, the Chicago Cubs' general manager's job became available, and I made a call. On
December 1, 1976, I met with Mr. Wrigley in Scottsdale and
we were talking about different things and he said something
like, "Well, we ought to do this when we get started . . ." I
looked at him and said, "Are you telling me I've got the job?"
When he said yes, I about jumped off the porch.

I stayed there until they sold the club. Then I went to
Houston with Al Rosen. I happened to be in the hospital in
1985, in August, and Al called and asked how I was feeling. I
told him that I felt good and I was just ready to get out. Al
said, "Good, because I've got some news for you, we're going
to San Francisco."

That was a lot of moving around and that's what a life in
baseball is about. I have a cliché that I tell to all of the young
players: "The two hardest things that you will ever do being a
ballplayer are to learn how to eat right and marry the right girl,
someone who will put up with this vagabond life." I always
tell them, "You'd better be a super scout when you look for
the girl that you are going to marry." All the guys laugh at the
start, but then after they've played a couple of years they come
back and tell me I was right.

When I think of all of the guys I played with during those
years, many of them are in the Hall of Fame and a lot of others
should be, there is one man who stands out. Marty Marion is

a guy who absolutely should be in the Hall of Fame. People don't understand how great he was, playing on the fields that he played on, like that skinned infield in St. Louis—the first of June there was no grass on the blooming place. Marty was a good manager too, and a fabulous guy for the game.

Jimmy Dykes, my first big-league manager, was a great influence on me when I was just a kid. Another person who was really important to me was Mike McNally, the old farm director of the Cleveland Indians. He got me started in the administrative part of baseball and he was a stickler for dates, time, paperwork, and everything. And Bill Wrigley was very important to me for giving me a salary that I had never had before. He made living a little more comfortable.

My first year in the big leagues, I came up in the month of September in 1939 and I got $235 to finish the season. I played every game in 1940 for $400 a month and then I jumped to $5,000 a year. After the war, I went to the minimum, which was $6,500, and the most I ever made was $17,500. I really never made any money until I became a manager and I got $20,000 managing the Cubs.

My first game was my biggest thrill, finally being able to get into a ball game. I was so excited I couldn't even pick up the bat. Somebody had to hand me one. Another big thing was to see my son, Terry, play. Then there was a thing called payday. I said that one time and my mother heard me. Somebody asked me, "What was your greatest day in baseball?" and I answered, "Payday," and, boy, she got all upset. I can say from start to finish up to this point, I never missed a payday.

It's been a wonderful life; there have been a lot of disappointments, but then when something good came along we just enjoyed it twice as much. The funny thing about baseball is if you are only right three out of ten times you're in the Hall of Fame—it's the most inexact science that there is. It has been great, there is no question about that, but I am getting toward the end and I'm getting tired. I'm tired of packing.

ALEX GRAMMAS

Alex "the Candy Man" Grammas played second, third, and shortstop from 1954 to 1963 for the Cardinals, Reds, and Cubs. Grammas managed the Pirates and Brewers and coached for Sparky Anderson in Cincinnati and Detroit.

LIKE MOST KIDS WHO eventually play in the major leagues, baseball was something I had always done. As a kid, I would go with my brother and a couple of friends to the park and we'd throw to one another and play catch all day long. We didn't have much in the way of organized baseball like the little leagues that they have today. But we went out by the hours, literally by the hours, and we loved it.

I don't think my dad was all for it because he was an immigrant, and being from the Old Country, he was used to the work ethic more than playing baseball. My dad was born in Greece, in Sparta; my mother was born here, but her parents were born in the Old Country. We didn't speak much Greek in the house, but we went to Greek school for eight years. For as long as we went to grammar school, from first through eighth, we went to Greek school in the afternoon. We'd leave school at three, get on the streetcar and go from the north side to the south side, and attend Greek school from 3:30 to 6:00 every day, including Saturdays. So even though we went to school all of the time, whenever we had a free minute, we ran off to play baseball.

I was playing down at Mississippi State and a scout by the name of Doug Minor, who was with the White Sox at the time,

approached me and he asked, "Are you interested in playing pro ball?" I said, "Absolutely," and it all got started that way. He continued to watch me and at the end of the season he contacted me and made me an offer. That was how I started playing.

I went to Muskegon, Michigan, my first year, which was 1949. I didn't go until after graduation from college, so it was mid-season. I finished there and then the next year I went to the White Sox team in Memphis, Tennessee, which is Double A in the Southern League. I played there for part of the next year and was traded to the Cincinnati organization in Tulsa, Oklahoma. The next year I played at Kansas City, Triple A, and from there I went to the Cardinals, because Cincinnati had traded me during the winter for my first year in the big leagues, 1954.

My dad never watched me play a baseball game. But when I went to the major leagues, my opening day he came with the camera and sat up in the stands. He liked baseball after I got involved in it because he saw how much I liked it. He was supportive then, but in the beginning he didn't know baseball. Baseball was the furthest thing from his mind.

I wish he could have lived a little longer. He's been gone since 1969 and I wish he could have stayed around a few more years and seen a few World Series and seen how big the pension plan got. That would have pleased him.

When you first arrive as a rookie, you don't know if you belong or not and it takes a little while. I was a kid just looking around the clubhouse and really thinking, "Do I belong here?" And then Stan Musial, who was the biggest man in baseball, befriended me. I was sitting by my locker and he walked in, a guy I had read about and never seen in my life, and said, "Come with me, let's go to dinner." Stan Musial, who was the very best there was, extended himself to me, the rookie. You just don't forget these things.

Stan probably doesn't realize that meant that much to me and if you asked him today he probably wouldn't remember it that way, if he remembers it at all. He was the first person that I really respected, and it was because of that. He made me feel like a part of the team and he knew that I didn't know what the heck I was doing. He knew that I didn't even know what restaurant to go to. I was all by myself and he said, "Come on, let's go." That made me feel like a million dollars and I'll always love him.

I told Pee Wee Reese one time after Pee Wee was through playing and was working for the Louisville Slugger Bat Company (I was coaching Cincinnati at the time), "Pee Wee, I don't want to embarrass you, but you were always my idol." We all have idols, we all have people that we look up to and admire, and Pee Wee was my idol. If you're going to emulate somebody you might as well pick the best you know. These guys were stars in the world of major league baseball, but they didn't make you feel that way. They played as if they were just another ballplayer on the team. When you watched them play, you knew that that wasn't so. Everyone knew that they were way above the rest of us mortals, but at the same time they made you feel like you belonged there too.

Why did America rely upon or idolize the ballplayers so much? That's *the* question and I don't have the answer. I know it was true but I can't answer why. The guys were bigger sports in those days and they enjoyed playing and being part of the team. It's a different deal today. Loyalty is a thing of the past. It no longer exists. Baseball is different in that respect. It's also drudgery to some of these guys today. For the amount of money they get you'd think they would enjoy it, or at least pretend to.

I don't know how far they can go with these four- and five-million-dollar salaries. There has to be a breaking point somewhere because I don't see how television can keep footing the bill for all of this. Somewhere along the line something has got to happen. I don't know what kind of plans they are going to come up with to alleviate the problem, but it's got to be done. How can you run your payroll up to forty million dollars? You can't do it. When I first started playing for the Cardinals our whole payroll wasn't a million dollars and Musial had a hundred thousand of that.

There isn't any question about the biggest moment for me. It happened during one of the playoff games that I was coaching at Cincinnati. We were playing Pittsburgh, in the final game. I think it was 1972, and it was the year that Johnny Bench's mother got involved. We were down a run going into the bottom of the ninth inning and John was leading off the bottom of the ninth. His mother came down from her seat to the railing and told him, "Johnny, this is it." In other words, if we don't score, we lose. He got up and hit a home run. I have never in my life seen fans react the way that they reacted to that. When he hit that ball and it left the ball park—they knew it was gone as soon as he hit it—they started screaming and not one person sat down until that inning was over and we won the game. Tony Perez came up next and got a base hit, then we got another base hit, and we finally won the ball game on a wild pitch or something. It was the most exciting thing that could ever happen to a baseball player. I'll never forget it. I get chills just thinking about it.

I've never had too many great moments myself; I wasn't that kind of a player, but I've been fortunate enough to watch great moments that other people had in the game. Like Henry Aaron tying Babe Ruth's record against us in Cincinnati or guys getting their three thousandth hits. I've been a part of so many of those things, things that are all just great memories. If you stay around as long as I have, you're going to see a lot of those things. You can't avoid it. It's fun, it really is. You can get excited for the other person's success. I just love to watch baseball, a baseball game is a thrill to me. I think when I quit working, I'll go out and watch these minor leaguers play.

Baseball was something that my parents didn't understand. But once I decided to give it a shot, they gave me all the support that a guy could want. It made me feel that I could give it the best shot I had and try to make it. I decided to give myself four or five years to make it, and fortunately I made it after the fifth year in the minor leagues. Since that time, it's been fun. I have a job that I really and truly enjoy doing—and every day I walk around and see people in jobs that they hate. They hate to get up and go to work and I get to work at something that I love. Next year [1991] will be my forty-second year in baseball and my thirty-seventh year in the major leagues. What else could you ask of a job?

To be with young kids all the time is a great thing. They keep me young. If you asked me to sit down and pick something I'd rather do, I couldn't, because there wouldn't be anything I'd rather do.

I try to stay away from thinking about the past because I've had older guys tell me how it was in their day and I'd always say, "It couldn't have been that way." But you know, you find yourself doing it. I do think that we appreciated the game a lot more than they do today. At least that is the way it appears.

I worked every off-season, and temporary employment is tough to find. I was fortunate because my dad at the time was in the wholesale candy business. He manufactured candy and stuff like that and that's where I got my nickname, the "Candy Man." I worked in the candy business and I had some uncles who were in the produce business and I worked there for years. I'd get up at three or three-thirty in the morning and be down there at four o'clock. It was hard work, but I never complained; I needed the money.

I think scouting is probably the hardest job in baseball, and people outside of baseball hardly know it exists. It's a rough life and lonely. The only time that you see anybody that you know is when you get to the ball park. Maybe you'll be sitting up with some other old scouts in the stands, but otherwise you're pretty much alone. These advance scouts that we have today are out there scouting the club that we're going to play next. Those guys get tired; they're just out there, lonely, watching ball games.

I think if I were scouting there'd be a lot of things that I just couldn't watch. They do things nowadays that make me just shudder, all of these actions and gyrations, the high-fives and the low-fives. I'm telling you, anyone who did that back when we played would have been in serious danger! He'd have to ask the pitcher's forgiveness because the next time that show-off came to the plate, he'd get drilled. I admit there is really no place for trying to kill somebody at the plate, but sometimes some of them need a little lesson or two. A little humility wouldn't hurt a bit. If I were a pitcher and the batters did some of the things that they do nowadays, I don't know if I could contain myself.

I was lucky to be able to stay in baseball. My last year I played with the Cubs in 1963 and John Holland was the general manager. I was thirty-seven years old and I felt I didn't know if I still could play. I was sitting in his office in the middle of August, we had another month and a half to go in the season, and I told him, "John, I think I'm at the end of my rope

as far as a major league baseball player goes. I haven't played this year and I really think it's about the end, but I want to stay in the game. That's what I'm here for, to ask you if I can stay in the game."

Before I left his office that day he had told me that I could manage in the Cubs system the next year, either in Fort Worth in Double A or Salt Lake City in Triple A ball. By the end of the year I had the job managing at Fort Worth.

I managed the Fort Worth ball club in 1964, and the very next year when Harry Walker got the Pittsburgh job he called me and asked me to coach for him. I was anxious to get back to the major leagues, so I started coaching and I've been coaching ever since, except for two years managing Milwaukee.

After I left Pittsburgh I went with Sparky Anderson and he was just a kid then too. He didn't know how long he would be around, but it turned out to be the best thing that ever happened to both of us. If there is one thing that I could identify as the single best that ever happened to me, it was to have been around Sparky for that many years. He is such a wonderful guy. He makes your job so easy and he's just fun to be around. We've never even come close to getting mad at one another and it's been close to twenty years that we've been together. He is like a brother to me. I love him and I don't know how he put up with me all of these years.

FRANK ROBINSON

Frank Robinson, Hall of Fame outfielder and first baseman, played for the Reds, Orioles, Dodgers, Angels, and Indians. Robinson has been Rookie of the Year, MVP, Gold Glove, and All-Star. His twenty-one years in the big leagues is legend.

ALL I CAN REMEMBER is that I played. I played from a very young age. I always loved baseball and I knew that baseball was my best sport. So I played it and the other sports to pass the time.

When I was about eleven years old, a wonderful man named George Powles came into my life. He would take on kids from the time they were ten or eleven years old and he had some kids as old as seventeen or eighteen. He started shaping my life when I was eleven years old.

That was in Oakland, California. George had a big influence on me, there is no doubt about that. Once he came into my life he was the *biggest* influence. He felt I had a career in baseball and a life in baseball, and the things that he taught me and the way that he taught me—I still draw from those things today.

In high school I told everybody that I was going to be a major league baseball player. I knew exactly what I was going to sign for. I told everybody that I was going to sign for seventy-five thousand dollars. I had a tendency to reach and to put things a little out of reach to make me strive harder and maybe that's why I said seventy-five thousand. I was sure I would make it. I fell short of my bonus though—when I signed, I was averaging four hundred dollars a month!

I signed right out of high school. I was aware very late of being scouted. I played on an American Legion team at fifteen; I was the youngest kid to play on that team. We had won the championship the year before and we were the first team to win back-to-back championships. I knew that at the time they were scouting a player on our team, but I didn't know that they were scouting me.

Then, when I was in high school, I knew that the players in the area were signed by a particular scout, but I didn't think too much about it until my senior year when he started coming around and checking me out. He'd take me out on Saturdays and hit me ground balls. I didn't realize what he was doing at the time, watching me or whatever, but my senior year in high school I was finally aware that I was being scouted.

He considered me his prospect and I had become kind of attached to him because he had showed a lot of interest in me and in my family. He made me feel like a human being and not just somebody that he was going to sign as a piece of merchandise. That was Bobby Mattick.

Not too many people scouted me. I was really hurt that Oakland, which had a Triple A club (Pacific Coast League) didn't even give me an offer or anything. They had no interest in me. The year before, a good friend of mine and a player on my high school team, a pitcher, signed with Oakland and I had gone out to the ball park with him when he went for preliminary talks with the ball club and I was really impressed. I was really looking forward to Oakland signing me when I came out of high school because that was baseball to us, the West Coast and the Pacific Coast leagues. When I was getting ready to graduate my senior year and Oakland didn't even make me an offer, I was really crushed.

The difference in the offers I had (Cincinnati, St. Louis, and Chicago) was the level. The money was the same but the White Sox wanted me to sign for Class D, which was the lowest classification, and Cincinnati wanted to send me to Class C. Class D? I'd played with better high school teams than that. So I took Cincinnati's offer, which also had a lot to do with Bobby Mattick.

My mother was the one who had the decision to make and she had put away money for me to go to college. She *expected* me to go to college. But she also knew I loved baseball, how crazy I was about it. I told her that it would be a waste of time for me to go to college. I wanted to play baseball and I had an opportunity to do it and if I went to college it would just be a waste of money. So she didn't pressure me, I signed for thirty-five hundred dollars, and my career got started.

I was seventeen years old and I was off and running. They took me to Ogden, Utah. I didn't even rate a bus ticket, they drove me. I was there in Mormon country, but I didn't even realize what it was about at the time. I realized all that later.

That was June 1953 and I was just happy to be there. I had no thoughts about when I'd get to the big leagues or how long it would take. I just wanted to play baseball. There was one other black player on the team in Ogden, a Cuban and he spoke no English. Between the two of us, me seventeen years old and the first time away from home, and a non–English-speaking Cuban, we made a great pair.

I found out early about the racism and it was very shocking. It was tough and it knocked me for a loop. I went down to go to the movies and they said no. I didn't understand and said, "What?" "We can't let you in here." So we just stayed in our little area and went to the ball park.

I led the team in home runs and RBIs and I was just there half a year. They were a good ball club before I got there, and they were on their way to winning the championship. But I helped and they appreciated it.

In 1954 I went to Double A in Tulsa, Oklahoma, but after 8 games they sent me to Class A in Columbia, South Carolina. I stayed in Columbia in 1954 and it was tough, but that was when I decided that I was going to have a good year and get out of there. It wasn't like, "This bothers me and I can't play baseball here." I was simply determined to have a good year and get out. I was still just eighteen years old, and I did have a very good year until I came up with a sore arm at the end of the season.

I went to spring training in 1955, but I couldn't throw. I would have made the ball club if I had been able to throw. At the end of spring training they wanted to know where I wanted to go. They said that Tulsa wanted me back but I said, "No, they didn't want me last year, how do you think they're going

to treat me now with a sore arm? They won't care about me."
So they asked again where I wanted to go and I went back to
Columbia.

In 1956 I came up to the big team. I went to spring training
with the big team and I knew before the end of spring training
that I was going to stay with them. Birdie Tebbetts, the manager, had told the reporters that if I could throw the ball from
the outfield back to the infield I would be in Cincinnati on
Opening Day. I could barely get the ball back into the infield.
It hurt, but I did it.

I wasn't the type of individual who was overwhelmed by
situations or surroundings and being in spring training with
the guys had helped. Birdie made it very easy because he took
a lot of the pressure off of me. He had talked a lot about me in
spring training to the press and I just walked into the clubhouse and got ready. I wasn't overwhelmed on Opening Day
or anything like that. I took it like it was just another ball game.
At that time the black players didn't stay with the ball club
downtown at the hotel. We had to stay in private homes and I
think that also gave me a sense of belonging because we were
close together. We did things together, and we were together
on and off of the field.

As Americans, we felt like baseball was our sport, like we
invented it. We played it the best and ballplayers were the
elite. We dreamed about wanting to be ballplayers, but everybody couldn't make it, so we admired and respected the people who were able to do it and performed at that level.

If kids didn't play baseball on the field, then they played
on the streets, pretending to be Babe Ruth or Lou Gehrig. It
was our game and we all had a dream of playing. Even if you
never played it on a real field or in an organized game, you
still were someone living out some role.

The desire to change your life or get something a little bit
better was part of it too. That was the part that pushed you. To
get out of the ghetto, to get off the farm, and not to have to go
to work in some tough job.

I think we all knew and felt deeply about our responsibility
as heroes, our responsibilities to the fans. Whether we wanted
it or not, we knew we had to accept it because we were there.
We weren't saints in our day—I hope people don't think that's

what I'm trying to portray—but what we did I think we did more discreetly. We thought about the consequences and what it would do to some kid or fan and what it would even do to our own individual careers. I think we accepted more readily the responsibility of being a major league ballplayer.

It really bothers me when I read that a player today says, "I'm not responsible, I don't have to be an idol, that's not my thing. I just have to play baseball. I'm a major league baseball player and I am a human being, I don't have to do this or that." I hate to read that. Players don't feel that they have to interact with the fans today as much as they used to. They just don't feel they have that responsibility; they think that the only responsibility they have is to go out and play the game.

When we got traded, with our low incomes, we packed up and went to the other place. We rented a room or an apartment and that was it until the season was over. It was hard on baseball families but we endured. Families made do. There wasn't a lot of pressure put on individuals because that was the way it was. We were away from our families, our kids, and our wives for long periods of time. If you were very fortunate and one of the better players at the time, maybe you could get them to come to where you were during the summer and spend some time with you. The entire summer sometimes, if you were at the top in the game, but other than that you were away from your family for six or seven months every year.

I didn't take my family to spring training. I just didn't feel I was going to take my family and be part of the South: When I got married and had a family it wasn't segregated to the point where the players were living apart, but still the South was the South and my kids didn't need that.

The life of a baseball wife was hard but it was a part of her life and it was something that the women didn't complain about. They knew that they would have to be the mother, the father, and whatever else at that time because their husbands had to be away earning a living.

You don't ever lose your kids—but you do lose some of the closeness because of those years when they needed you or you weren't there to enforce or help shape their lives. When my kids were younger at least they were with me during the season. The toughest thing that I remember was when they finally got to the point where they had their own priorities in the summer. They got out of school and they asked to stay in California. That was kind of tough.

I think that a lot of people only see the glamour side of it. The worst thing that I used to hear was "Well, you guys only work two and a half hours a day," and that type of thing. That's ridiculous, we go to the ball park for a night game—as a player you get there at three-thirty or four o'clock in the afternoon and you don't start the game until eight o'clock. After you're there four hours before you even start to play the game, you play the game for two and a half or three hours. You're talking about seven or eight hours a day plus the travel and all of the other stuff. The pressure, the stress, the strain, and the sacrifices that you have to make—it's not all that glamorous.

You go to the ball park and come back and it's eleven or twelve o'clock at night. You don't see your kids, they're asleep and they have to go to school. When you wake up in the morning they're gone and when they get back then you're gone.

But I wouldn't trade it for anything in the world. I think every job or every position has its hardships and every position has its bonuses and its rewards. I don't know of anything else that I would want to do.

One of the things that has really changed with the players is how they feel about the game. They don't stay in the game. When we were coming along it was our life, it was our livelihood from one year to the next; you were judged by what you did any one year and that's the way that you were paid for the following year. Today players don't really understand that. Not only do they have the multiyear contracts and the security of them, they have all these rules and regulations that protect them. You can't threaten anyone anymore. Not even a rookie. You can't even say something like, "Produce or I'll ship you out of here." You just can't say a thing.

I never really made an exit from baseball. I never cut the tie. I wanted to stay and I started preparing myself. I went from a player to a player-manager and then a manager. I realized it was coming to an end and I started preparing myself. I had standards I had set over my career and I just didn't want to drag it on.

People ask me why I didn't stay around to hit 14 more home

runs for .600, or 43 more hits for .3000 and my patent answer is "Well, no one wanted to pay me." But numbers at that time weren't that big of a deal. I played twenty-one years and if I didn't get those hits or home runs in twenty-one years, then I was not going to hang around two or three more years just to acquire numbers.

It was sort of a nice easy transition because I prepared myself for it. Now I am looking forward to one day in the very near future getting out of uniform and putting in a few years in the front office.

That's my thinking right now. That's the way I have always been. I've tried to look ahead a little bit and prepare myself for what the next step will be so it won't be a complete shock to my system when it happens. And it is going to happen. Someday, somewhere, someone is not going to want to give me a job in baseball. I think it would be better to look forward and be able to call the shots myself.

What really stands out the most in my memory is my induction into the Hall of Fame. That's everything wrapped up into one. To be honored as one of the best who ever played the game and to be inducted on the first ballot, there is no feeling like that. It just kind of overwhelms everything else you've done in baseball. There are a lot of great memories that I have but that one overshadows all of them.

RED SCHOENDIENST

Red Schoendienst played for the Cardinals, Giants, and Braves from 1945 to 1963. Primarily a second baseman, Schoendienst also played the outfield, shortstop, and third base. As manager of the St. Louis Cardinals from 1965 to 1976, he led the Cards to win two pennants (1967 and 1978) and the World Series in 1968.

WHEN I FIRST GOT started, baseball was everything. Now you have so much, football, basketball, hockey, and other sports. Back in the late thirties and early forties, you didn't see much other than baseball. When I was a kid I followed the Cardinals and all of the other National League clubs as well as the American League clubs. The time just came when I said, "I'd like to be a big-league ballplayer."

I saw in the paper one morning that they were having a tryout camp in St. Louis. At that time St. Louis had a lot of baseball players; in fact, there were so many of them at the tryout camp that they separated the out-of-town kids and the kids from St. Louis, and they sent all of the guys from St. Louis home that day. I got to stay and they kept me the next day and again the third day. Then they sent me home.

Joe Mathes and Walter Shannon, the scouts who were running the camp, went to Peoria or some place for another camp and when they came back they wanted to know what had happened to me because they had me down in their book. They called me back up, and I signed a contract for seventy-five dollars a month. They sent me to Union City, Tennessee. That was Class D ball—as low as you could go. If you went any lower then you were back home.

Red Schoendienst completing a double play over Johnny Pesky in the
1946 World Series

But it was better than getting up early in the morning and doing what I had been doing. I was still going to school, but I'd work if some farmer needed help. In those days they didn't have combines like they have today. We shucked wheat and corn and everything. We kept busy and I thought baseball would be a little easier—which it is.

I finally said, "Well, I'm going to give it a shot. If I can't make it to the big leagues in three years, then I'll go home, go to school, and do something else."

I was pretty fortunate. I played well my first year. I was eighteen years old. I spent that half of 1942 playing for Union City; then the Kitty League broke up and they sent me to Albany, Georgia, for the rest of that year. The next year they signed me to a B-league contract and I thought that was pretty good. I spent spring training there and then I went all the way from B to Triple A when they sent me to Rochester.

Pepper Martin was the manager at Rochester. I was pretty frail and skinny, and he noticed that and took care of me. I played that year and I led the league in hitting. I was named MVP in the International League, so I guess I caught their attention. Then I went into the service for a year. I came out of the Army early in 1945 because of some health problems and I went with the Cardinals. I didn't go back to the minor leagues again.

So, actually, I only spent a year and a half in the minor leagues before going to the Cardinals. I got back in time for the 1945 season, right before spring training.

At that time just a year and a half in the minor leagues was pretty good. Lots of the guys would spend four and five years or more down in the minor leagues. They'd hit .300 every year down there and never get a chance to come up because there were so many ballplayers. They still have a lot of good ballplayers in the minors, but they don't have as many as there were years ago. Everybody played ball; that was the big thing in this country.

I appreciate the time that Joe Mathes and Walter Shannon gave to look at me. I've got to thank the Cardinals for giving me the opportunity. I see Walter Shannon every once in a while; he's in a retirement home now. I was with him one day and he got to talking about the days when they had those tryout camps. He said, "You weren't too tough to scout. We figured you could play ball; we could pick you out." That was a nice compliment from Walter.

When I finally got to the big leagues, I knew it was just as hard to stay up as it was to come up. If somebody gives you the opportunity, you had better take advantage of it and do everything possible to help yourself. You get help from scouts and coaches, but you have to do a lot on your own.

You get nervous at the start of every year no matter how long you've played, and I played for eighteen years. You're nervous up until the first pitch is thrown and then after that you're pretty well relaxed.

I played with some great guys. There were only eight teams in the National League and eight in the American League. It was a big thing to be there, a big thing to come up when I did. The Cardinals had great ballplayers like Marty Marion and George Kurowski, Terry Moore and Musial, Slaughter and the Cooper boys.

Everybody had roommmates in those days, and Leo Ward, our traveling secretary, put me with Stan Musial, and we've been close friends ever since. And to be around Marty Marion, and learn how to play the infield from him was a fantastic experience. Those guys had been in World Series before and that made it a lot easier for me.

I learned what I had to do from them. They went out and when they put that uniform on it was all business. We played guys who were all business against us, too. When we played the Giants or when we played the Dodgers, nobody talked to one another on the field. We might have got together later on, after the ball game or something, but not out on the ball field. Out there it was all business.

The travel and the equipment is so much better today than it was years ago. We used to travel by train and it took a long time to get from St. Louis to New York. A lot of times the air-conditioning would go out and we wouldn't have any half of the time. It was hard, but really we didn't know it because there was nothing better. We traveled as well as you could travel in those days.

Everybody's goal is to be in a World Series. I was pretty fortunate in 1946 because we got into the World Series. We

played a great ball club, the Red Sox, with Ted Williams, Bobby Doerr, Johnny Pesky, and the rest of that great team.

Another big thing is when you get a chance to be on an All-Star team. I played ten All-Star games and I managed two of them too, so that was a thrill. I've had some incredible moments in baseball, like my first time coming here to Florida. When the Yankees trained in St. Petersburg, we would play them seven ball games. What a feeling that was to be able to play against Joe DiMaggio and Phil Rizzuto. I really didn't think about it that much at the time, but now I look back in awe at the great ballplayers that I knew and played with. I roomed with Musial for years. When I got traded to the Giants I played with Willie Mays, and I played with Henry Aaron in Milwaukee. Now they are all in the Hall of Fame. I started in the big leagues in 1945 and I'm still here, so that's been quite a little while. I've been on the field for forty five years.

Maybe the forties and the fifties were the golden age, but there was no money at that time, not like there is today. Maybe you'd better say *these* are the golden days. In the forties they had maybe thirty minor league clubs just with the Cardinals; they had *three* Triple A clubs. With all of the minor league clubs that they did have, it made baseball really competitive.

It is an altogether different life today, whether you are looking at baseball or at any business. Everybody has a bigger opportunity to do different things; there are more choices by far. There wasn't that much to do in those days. So we just naturally took to baseball. Maybe it was as simple as that.

PREACHER ROE

Preacher Roe pitched in 1938 and 1944–45 for the Cardinals, Pirates, and Dodgers. He was voted *The Sporting News's* Pitcher of the Year in 1951 with an .880 winning percentage. Roe was an All-Star from 1949 to 1952.

WHEN WE WERE KIDS we lived in a very small town and there wasn't very much entertainment. In fact, there were only 160 people in Viola, Arkansas. Viola's grown since we left it; it's up to 300 now. My dad was a country doctor—I even remember when he rode horseback to see his patients. He owned the first car in the county.

There were six boys in my family and my dad always promoted the local baseball team in the summer. We'd listen to Cardinal games on the radio and naturally we wanted to be major leaguers. I wanted to be a Cardinal back then and when I did sign with the Cardinals, it was the first of my dreams to come true.

We didn't have any high school baseball teams, we just had the team with my dad in the summer. When I graduated from high school there was a fellow in our town who went down to Harding College at Searcy, Arkansas. They had a pretty good baseball team but they needed pitching, so I went down for a tryout and got a full scholarship to college.

The scouts had just begun to follow college teams, and Branch Rickey sent his brother Frank there between my junior and senior years in college. We'd go to bed at night and wake up the next morning and Mr. Rickey'd be in one of the beds asleep. He knew us that well and he just wouldn't let me go.

Branch Rickey with Preacher Roe after shutting out the Yankees in the
1949 World Series

My college baseball was just the aftermath of my dad's help. My dad was an ex-professional player and a good teacher. I had good coaching in college too. I played one year with an amateur team out of Russelville, Arkansas, when they put on a drive to recruit some players. I pitched over there and had good luck in a really good amateur league.

The next summer I went to Kansas City to a state tournament and I had good luck again there. After that, with my college team, I had as many as eight or ten scouts at the games.

I finally made it, but it was a long haul—I was twenty-eight years old before I got to the majors because I went to college and had five years in the minors.

The St. Louis Cardinals signed me in 1938 and kept me from July 28 to September 1 as a bonus for signing. I was on the regular team, got credit as a regular player, and was supposed to pitch batting practice and exhibition games. Frankie Frisch was the manager and he could pull some spur-of-the-moment things that were deuces.

We were playing Cincinnati and they were beating the Cardinals dead when Frisch hollered, "Where's the kid at?" Lon Warneke was trying to teach me to chew tobacco at the time and when Frisch hollered I swallowed my tobacco!

I pitched three innings without warming up. He put me out there, I pitched three innings, and that was the highlight of my Cardinal career right there. I gave up nine runs and that made my earned run average 27. Just three innings and I gave up nine runs! All my life I had to battle to get that darn thing down. As long as I pitched that still counted on my career earned run average.

I only had one dream that I didn't fulfill and that was to be in a winning World Series. I was in three World Series but we didn't win. I never did dream of a no-hitter; of course I'd have liked to have had one, but that wasn't really at the top of my list. Top of my list was to be in a World Series and win it.

There was never any time when I realized that I belonged in the major leagues. Even through my minor league career I was working pretty hard at it and I wasn't sure, so I went ahead and prepared an alternate career—I had hopes of being a high school basketball coach if I didn't play baseball. In fact, in the minor leagues I did coach during the wintertime.

The first time that I realized that I might really make it was when Pittsburgh bought me from Columbus (Triple A). I'd been with the Cardinal organization for five years then and Pittsburgh only had one left-hander in their whole system. I thought, "Well, I've got a real chance. Now this is it, I'm gonna be a major leaguer." That was 1944.

I was with Pittsburgh four years and Frankie Frisch was the manager there also. We had a really good team and took second place when the Cardinals beat us by half a game. But then Mr. Frisch was moved on and we kinda deteriorated. Then my third and fourth years in Pittsburgh I had very bad years. I only won three ball games the last year there and that was when Mr. Rickey brought me to Brooklyn. I've always wondered why he brought me. I was in the Billy Cox–Gene Mauch trade and we were traded to Brooklyn for Dixie Walker and Hal Gregg and Vic Lombardi. I always wondered if he was trying to buy me or if they just threw me in to get the trade. Mr. Rickey, in fact, said to me, "I bet you wonder why I bought you," and I told him frankly I did. He said he figured I had had tough luck the last three years and I was gonna have a lot of good luck now and he wanted it to be with Brooklyn. He hit the nail right on the head. We just started right out.

Leo Durocher was the manager and since I had a really good spring training, Durocher kept me on the main team—I didn't have to go to Montreal. The first two games I pitched that year were shutouts, and I was pretty well set up by then.

I loved working for Leo. He was a very controversial, to say the least, manager. But if you hustled for Leo, boy, he'd fight for you—he'd do anything. I never saw Leo get on a person who didn't have it coming. If any of his players disobeyed orders, it would cost 'em, man, he'd get rid of them. But, as long as you hustled he stood by you. I saw players make mistakes, really serious boners, but they were really hustling and Leo'd stand by them.

When I first went off to the big city I could hardly see how in the world I could do it. I was so used to being out in the country. When I signed with the Cardinals in 1938 I joined the team in New York, and they said to go to the Hotel Lincoln, they were expecting me. So I thought I should take a taxi. I got out of the train station and got a cab and it charged nine dollars to take me to the hotel.

We played the series there and when we started back to leave, Lon Warneke said, "Come on, Preach, let's go to the train." So I started to the cabstand. He said, "Where you going?" "Well, to take a cab." He said, "It's right across the street, Grand Central Station." That guy charged me nine dollars to take me across the street. So that shows you about how well they had seen me coming!

I had no idea and of course I was bewildered. I think it's quite an accomplishment really, because people in that part of the country have a tendency to think we can't compete with the big-city boys. My dad always taught me that it didn't matter. He also taught me not to get overconfident and I think that's the reason I made it.

To be a ballplayer was to be a hero. First thing I knew when I'd come home, everywhere I went everybody'd want to see me and talk to me. I realized the responsibility and I always tried to meet that head-on so I could look the person in the eye and know I'd done what I thought was right. I always treated everybody right, especially the kids. We thought that was the best thing in the United States of America—to be a major league ball player.

When I did make it I realized there were thousands of youngsters that would like to be in my shoes and when they'd come by to visit with me I always took the time with them.

The fan is what makes baseball. The fan pays the way. If the ballplayers didn't draw any fans they wouldn't have jobs. Billy Southworth was one of the greatest teachers in the Cardinal organization. He was the best teacher I ever had in baseball and he always taught me never to get too big for the game because when you do, you're out. Baseball is bigger than you. It's making you, you're not making the game. He told us that time and time again and that's what I still believe.

We had a wonderful time earning our living by playing ball. We were all friends but when we went out on the field it was serious. I went out there to beat the other guy. I'd beat him any way I could, but I didn't have to be mad or fight over it. We had a wonderful time at it. I always talked to the other team when I was pitching. I always talked to Musial. He would come to bat and of course the fans didn't know this, but I'd say, "Stan, pop up." Course he'd say something back like, "I can't afford it, Preach." And then I'd say, "Well, you already had two hits." And he'd say, "I gotta hit a respectful .340, Preach."

I know one time I told Campanella that Stan's father was sick, and I told Campy to ask Stan how his father was. When the inning was over I said, "Well, did you ask Stan?" and Campy said, "Yeah, but before he could answer he was on third."

We associated with our teammates and we were friendly with our opposition off the field. We were very close to each other because we were together all the time. When you travel on a twenty-day road trip, you're on the train at night and you're at a hotel and you go to the park and back and *that's* your family.

I roomed with Frank Gustine three years in Pittsburgh and then the last year I roomed with Lloyd "Little Poison" Waner. Old Lloyd is really a legend in his own right. He was an old-timer then—and I was just a kid—and he'd talk to me for hours about baseball and life or whatever. Then I roomed with Billy Cox for seven years in Brooklyn. He was in the trade with me from Pittsburgh and I suppose they thought we were on a team together and we'd like to stay together, so they put us in a room together. And seven years we stayed there. That got to be quite a thing. We'd get up a little late, and whichever one'd get up first would dress and hurry down and order breakfast for both of us so when the other got there we'd have our break-fast. We knew each other like a book.

The other guys used to kid us. Billy was a small fellow and I was six one and only weighed 165 lbs. We'd eat breakfast with Carl Furillo and Gil Hodges, and Billy and I would have a small orange juice, a scrambled egg and coffee, and an order of toast. They'd have double orange juice, a quart of milk, four scrambled eggs, a double order of ham, and then they'd finish off with a double order of toast and another glass of milk. Billy and I would eat our little helpings and those guys'd eat like horses, and they were just as thin as we were.

When my youngest son was three, four, five years old, he knew every man and woman on our street in Brooklyn because he'd play and they knew who he was. They'd all say, "Hi, Tommy," and he'd come by and say hi back. But you know, if he and I walked to the store for milk, Tommy would speak to them sitting on the stoop and they'd say, "Hi, Tommy," but if I spoke to 'em, they wouldn't answer because I wasn't supposed to do that. That would be too friendly I guess for those city people. I never could get over that. Tommy and I would be going along and he'd be holding my hand and they'd know I was Tommy's father but they wouldn't say hi to me. They didn't care if I spoke to them or not, but it was "Hi, Tommy." I never could understand that, and then they'd come out and root for me like crazy when I was pitching.

Lots of people ask me how I got my name and then they proceed to tell me how I got it. Afterward they say, "Isn't that how you got it?" and since it's easier I just say, "Yeah."

But the truth of it is that when I was three years old, before we moved to Viola, we lived in a little town with about eighty people, called Wild Cherry, Arkansas. I had an uncle who had been off in the First World War; he was wounded pretty badly and he didn't get back for a few years. I was three years old when he got back and he had never seen me. He came up to me and said, "Young man, what's your name?" I was very bashful as a kid and still am, but I said, "I'm not gonna tell you." He pulled out a nickel from his pocket and he said, "I'll give ya a nickel if you tell me your name," and I said, "Preacher."

I remember my brother, older than me, (we lived out about a half mile from a couple of little stores) he took me by the hand and we went down to the store with that nickel and bought a big striped piece of candy. I remember my mother laid it down, took a case knife, turned the handle out, hit it, and broke it into pieces and we all ate candy.

Now, the reason I said Preacher, my mother told me, was because of the Methodist minister in our town. We had a little church and he'd come there twice a month and preach and then he'd have another town about four miles over that he'd preach at. But he lived by us and he had a one-horse buggy. He and his wife didn't have any children and everywhere they went they took me with them in that buggy. My mother thought I associated liking the preacher with what I'd like to be called.

And she thought that was why I said Preacher Roe. Anyway, it stuck. And that's the true story. That's really the way that I got it.

My biggest thrill in baseball was really just being a Brooklyn Dodger. There was something about being in the biggest city in the country with the best fans in the world and being a Dodger. We had a great team then, not the best team, but it was a great team. I can still feel it all these years later. If I had to pick out one thing it would probably be the 1949 World Series game that I won, 1–0. But it's hard to think of that as the highlight when the whole time was just outstanding.

After I got out of baseball, I just enjoyed myself. I thought I had to do something to get away from baseball. One day about a year after I quit, my wife and I went to buy our groceries, on January 1 in fact. While my wife was shopping the guy who owned the store came in and was talking to me, and when she came back around I said, "Just push 'em on out, they're ours. I bought the store!" She didn't know anything about it. Right here in West Plains, Missouri. We'd come here in 1951, I believe, and this was in 1955 that I bought the store, and I thought that in three or four years I could maybe do something else. It was nineteen years later when I finally decided I'd do something else. We stayed there nineteen and a half years exactly.

When we grew up there was no television where we were down there in the sticks. But my daddy had a big old high-powered battery set and he'd get maybe four or five stations on the radio. He'd get a baseball game and people would come to listen. For no other sport could you get ten or twelve kids, men, and women, sittin' around and listening to the radio and knowing what was going on. We all knew baseball from the school yard and we could follow it.

I remember listening to the World Series on that old radio one time and this kid named Goose Goslin was the star at Detroit. I always liked Goose Goslin, if for no other reason I just liked the name Goose. He was about as big an idol of mine as Stan Musial, except of course it was different. I had to put up with Stan.

It's funny, but I beat the Cardinals a lot. They hit me pretty well but I was lucky. I knew them all. One time Harry Brecheen called me early the morning when we came into town

and said, "Hey, Preach, Vera said to call you to come over and
have dinner with us tonight after the game." So I'm pitching,
he's pitching. Old Harry was mean and after anybody hit a
home run off him, the next guy would go down. Well, Billy
Cox hit a home run and he was hitting eighth. When I walked

For the Love of the Game

up I thought, "Old Harry isn't going to throw at *me*," and, boy, he stuck one under my chin, wouldn't you know it! I said, "Harry what's wrong with you?" Harry said, "You know how it is, Preach, you ought to have been ready."

I beat him in that game. He finally hung one to Snider and Duke got a home run off him and I beat him. And I said to myself, there goes my dinner. But when I came out of the locker room, old Harry was waiting for me and we never mentioned the game. And that's the way it was. Off the field, we were great friends, but, boy, when we were on that field, we'd beat each other if we could.

I never threw at anybody. Back in those days, you'd throw it inside to get a batter back, to knock him down. The secret was to know how to back the man up without hitting him because that'd just put him on first.

Don Drysdale was so good at brushing the batter back that somebody told him, "Don, I hear you'd throw at your own mother." And he said, "Yeah, but my mother's a good hitter."

I can remember just about every home run that was ever hit off of me. I can remember the gates, I can see where it was, and I just can't believe that so many things can keep coming back. I really think it was because back in those days we lived it, we breathed it, we really concentrated on the game. There were only eight teams in each league and no reserve clause or anything. If we didn't produce, somebody else was gonna take our place. So we studied it and paid attention to what was going on. My wife says I can remember too many things; she gets tired of me talking about it. She says when you reminisce you're getting old, and I say, "Well, I'm getting pretty old then 'cause I just love to talk baseball." I don't know when to quit.

I never really lost the dream, but I never thought that I had it made until I went to Pittsburgh. I worked hard but I never did know whether I was gonna do it or not. And then when I went to Brooklyn, I changed my attitude and I said, "I think I'm gonna quit trying to find that dream. I'm a better player now and I'll try to live the best I can and do the best I can." I relaxed and then I was a better pitcher. I realized I had my dream, and when I was at Brooklyn I lived the dream for seven years. Now I've been living it ever since, and it's great.

ROBIN ROBERTS

Robin Roberts pitched from 1948 to 1966 for the Phillies, Orioles, Astros, and Cubs. Roberts led the league in wins from 1952 to 1955, was an All-Star from 1950 to 1956, and was inducted into the Hall of Fame in 1976.

I WOULD GO OUT in the summer, take a sandwich in a bag, and play ball from nine in the morning until four in the afternoon. There would be six on a team and that's all we would do.

When I was fourteen or so, we worked occasionally for farmers, picking potatoes, peas, or whatever, but most of the time we were off during the summer playing ball five days a week. We might ride our bikes three miles to play and then play all day long. But I had no dream of being a ball player—I just played ball. It was the thing to do and I enjoyed it.

By riding our bikes all over and playing, we developed strengths that we didn't even know about; we were just trying to get from here to there. We walked and rode and we did an awful lot of exercising just by living.

Though I had been a pretty good hitter as a kid, once I started pitching I never could control my emotions at bat—I always was lunging. You have to wait to be a good hitter and you've got to keep from moving your head, but I was always so excited about hitting that I'd leap at the ball.

After I started playing baseball in college, I still wasn't all that driven to be a major league ballplayer. I just knew it really beat working. My father was a coal miner. I didn't want to be a coal miner; I knew I didn't want any part of that.

303

In fact, I didn't particularly want to work at all. I loved competing in sports, and it never occurred to me that I was going to end up having to work. It was the competition that I liked, and getting paid for it was the perfect life for a young guy like me.

I was at Michigan State on a basketball scholarship and at the end of a basketball season, I went out for baseball, practicing indoors, of course, because Lansing, Michigan, was cold. The baseball coach recognized me because of basketball and I asked him what he needed. When he told me pitchers, I said I'd do it.

I was basically a third baseman in high school, but I did pitch because I could throw strikes. I didn't enjoy pitching as much because I liked the fielding and the batting. But the coach needed pitchers, so I threw strikes for him. About twelve games into the season I became one of his regular starters and the next year I did very well for them.

I went up to Vermont and played in a summer league and that's where the Phillies saw me. I worked out that September with the Phillies in Wrigley Field when they came to Chicago. (I was from Springfield, Illinois.) I worked out for three days and they offered me ten thousand dollars, fifteen thousand dollars and twenty-five thousand dollars after each of the three days. I didn't have an agent but I should have known enough to hold out a little bit longer. If they had a seven-game series in Chicago I would have been rich as could be! That was in 1947.

I signed in September, then I went back to school. In those days you couldn't play another sport, so I wasn't eligible for basketball. I didn't get to play my senior year at Michigan State but I didn't feel that I could turn the money down for the baseball contract. I stayed in school and watched my basketball team play and that was the longest year in my life because I couldn't play. But I did get my degree before I started baseball.

I went to spring training with the Phillies the following February. They almost kept me on the team without any minor league experience, but then they decided to send me to Wilmington, Delaware. I went to Wilmington for two months and then they called me up. I stayed eighteen years.

I had two occasions on the mound when I was nervous to the point where I couldn't perform, and one of them was the first game. They called me up June 17, 1948, and I got to the ball park at 6:00 P.M. The manager was Ben Chapman, and when I walked into his office he asked me, "How do you feel?" I said, "Fine," and he said, "You're starting tonight."

So at 6:00 I found out I was starting at 8:00 and to that first batter I threw four of the wildest pitches you have ever seen. I was really nervous. The next guy was 3 and 2 and he swung on the full count and missed. From then on I was all right. Another time that I had that same feeling was when I had a no-hitter on the opening day in 1955 with one out in the ninth and my knees wouldn't stop shaking. I didn't get the no-hitter, but those two times were the only times I remember being so nervous that it affected my performance. I wasn't one who was starry-eyed about being a big leaguer. I really liked to play and it was a wonderful way to make a living, but it was nerve-racking at times. I learned how to handle so-called big games, but it took a lot out of me. I'd get into kind of a fog, shut the world out, and do my thing.

I came up in 1948, won seven games that year, fifteen the next year, and then twenty the next year. The final game of 1950 was against the Dodgers and we won our pennant at Ebbets Field. That was a big game for the Phillies at the time, because they hadn't won a pennant since 1915.

I knew that we would beat the Dodgers right from Opening Day in 1950. We had come from last place in 1948 to third in 1949. There were a lot of young guys on our club and all of a sudden it just happened for us. We beat Ewell Blackwell in May, 1–0, in a really exciting game. I gave up 3 hits and Blackwell gave up 2 and we won. Somehow that game stands out not for me personally, but for the team. I felt that as a team we knew then that we were good. When we beat a guy like Blackwell—and it was tough because he was a sidearmer who really could whip them—then we could do anything and we went on to win the pennant.

It wasn't easy though. We had a lot of injuries. Bubba Church got hit in the face that season. Bubba was having a big year for us, and that was his first year. He got hit with a line drive and it was an awful scene. I was in the clubhouse and heard the announcer describe it and of course it wasn't a pretty description. We knew he was hurt badly. Then I had to start the second game of that doubleheader. We were playing the Reds and Virgil "Red" Stallcup was the leadoff man. He hit a line drive the first pitch of the game right back at me. I didn't get hit like Bubba—I caught it, but I thought to myself that you really don't realize how close the mound is until they start shooting balls back at you. Of course, if you think about it, then it's really going to detract from your pitching. You can think about it when you're retired and you're not going out there anymore.

It's a wonder that Bubba could ever pitch again after that, and he won 15 games his next year. It may have emotionally bothered him, but he didn't show it. In fact he had his most wins ever that next year, 1951.

Baseball was so meaningful and so special in the fifties because the standard of living wasn't as high as it is now and the expectations of what every guy thought he deserved weren't as high then. We traveled on trains, ate nice meals, and most of us ballplayers would never have done that without baseball.

One day against the Cardinals, my first year up, Gerry Staley was pitching; he threw a pitch and I took a swing at it like Musial. Everything was perfect—boom! There was a scoreboard high out in right center field in Philadelphia, and this ball went right over it like a golf ball. You couldn't believe how I hit that ball. As I was running around the bases, I touched second and I heard Marty Marion at shortstop say, "What the hell is coming off?" I was really impressed that he noticed how hard I hit that ball. I felt a little blessed.

We were the Whiz Kids. We had a traveling secretary, a publicity man whose name was Babe Alexander, and I think Babe was the guy who started calling us that. There were probably twelve guys on our team who were twenty-three and under and that's why they called us kids. There were other older guys who really contributed, like Konstanty and Andy Seminick, but Ennis, Ashburn, Jones, Hamner, Goliat, Simmons, Bubba Church, Bob Miller, and I were all young. If we go around the country now people still call us the Whiz Kids. We really struck a chord.

What the wives did in baseball then is something that nobody ever has written about. Most of us would drive down to spring training with our families but we would have to return north with the teams. So the wives would have to pile the kids in the car and take off. That was quite an operation then because we didn't have expressways. Old 301 all the way from Clearwater up to Philadelphia was quite a trip. The gals used to get two or three cars as a caravan and stick together.

Team togetherness is a part of the game that has really changed. We used to be stuck with an organization by the reserve clause, so we really grew up together. The trains kept us together too and they were fun. Baseball was meant for trains. From the moment we got on planes, I can't tell you a road trip that I can remember, but up until then I can tell you about almost all of them. We played cards and we laughed. My favorite train memory happened when we were coming north after spring training in 1951. We used to have a diner by ourselves on the train and I was sitting across from Puddin' Head Jones, our third baseman. One of the waiters came up to Puddin' Head, not knowing who I was, and said to him, "Who dat, Robbie Robinson? Boy, dat man could throw the ball right by the pope!" I thought I would die 'cause Puddin' Head said, "There's Robbie Robinson." Of course my name wasn't Robbie Robinson, but it certainly was to that fellow.

I told that story to Maury Wills and old Maury got quite a kick out of it. Then one day we were playing the Dodgers and I was on second base. Maury was playing shortstop and he came sneaking up behind me, holding me on base, and said, "Are you dat man dat throw the ball by the pope?" I thought I would die laughing right there on second base in front of a full ball park. I always liked that story; I didn't know what kind of a hitter the pope was but I took it as a compliment.

My family was thrilled that I made it in baseball. My mother enjoyed watching baseball tremendously, and it didn't bother her, win or lose; she just enjoyed being at the park. My father was different, he was very emotional about it. The second year that I won my twentieth game was in St. Louis, and my parents came to that game. If we were going to stay in St. Louis, after the game I would drive home and stay overnight with them. It's only 105 miles to Springfield and after a game you can't sleep anyhow, so you might as well be driving. We had won 2-1, in ten innings, and as we were driving home my dad said to me, "Bud, do you mind if I don't go next time? I can't stand it." He really was nervous about it and he never saw me pitch again.

I read George Will's book, but it got so technical. Most of what is done on the ball field, and we all knew this when we played, is automatic reaction. You can't and don't think about it. When you play baseball, you know how to play. You don't think about it, you just do it. If you thought about certain things, you would freeze up. You have to kind of flow with the game, and anybody who makes it out to be like a chess match between managers, well, that's just so much bullshit. It doesn't happen very often that you look that smart. My feeling is when you're managing a baseball team, you have to pick the right people to play and then pray a lot.

Baseball brings people together in this country. Everybody has a feeling about how to play it because it's not a very complicated game. People can relate to it from having played when they were kids. And the focus is on individuals. The ball is hit to the outfielder and everybody can see him. The players aren't bunched together like in other sports.

The emotions and the control of your emotions are the complicated part. The guy who can control his emotions on the field is the guy who's great.

One of the advantages of playing for a long time is that you learn what a part of baseball the press is. I had an interesting experience with a writer named Ray Kelly. I was very upset with our manager and I called this writer the day before the season ended and expounded on this guy's shortcomings as a manager and how we weren't going to go anyplace. The writer wrote it all down.

He went home after telling me he was going to put it in the Sunday paper when the season ended. He called me about midnight that same night and said, "I got the story ready and I'll tell you something: It ain't gonna help the manager, it ain't gonna help you, and it ain't gonna help me, so I just threw it away." That was the nicest thing that man ever did for me. He was a writer who could have really used that story and I was a big name in Philadelphia at the time.

After Kelly had died and was being honored at the Hall of

Fame, I went up to his son and said, "You know, a lot of people probably don't know your father, but I know one of the reasons he is here in the Hall of Fame: He saved my ass!"

Bubba Church after being hit in the face by a ball off the bat of Ted Kluszewski, 1950

BUBBA CHURCH

Bubba Church pitched from 1950 to 1955 for the Phillies, Reds, and Cubs. He and Robin Roberts pitched the Phillies' Whiz Kids to a pennant in 1950, but Church's season was cut short when he was hit in the face on September 15 by a line drive from Ted Kluszewski.

BASEBALL NEVER WAS A dream with me; it was something that I knew I was going to do. I had a timetable for myself and I never doubted that I would get there. I was twenty-two years old when I went into Ben Chapman's bowling alley and Ben knew about me because I had been playing on an amateur level. When I got home from World War II in December 1945, I went into the Birmingham Amateur Baseball Federation which consisted of teams sponsored by businesses. They paid us $35 to $50 a game depending on what we could produce. I played with two different ball clubs and made $105 a week, which was not bad in 1946. I pitched and played the outfield.

Two or three clubs offered to sign me but I took a scholarship from Mississippi State University. I went off to school in Starkwell, Mississippi, and they had one traffic light in the town. I had spent twenty-seven months and seventeen days in India and Burma and I'd seen enough places where there were no traffic lights. I took a good look at myself and realized that I was twenty-two years old, and if I was going to get into baseball, then I'd better go. If I were to stay down there and graduate from school, I'd be twenty-six years old and then what was I going to do?

So I came home in December and that's when I went to Ben Chapman's bowling alley. I had been told to wait until

Ben got home from the baseball season and then go talk to him. I did and the rest is history.

The old story goes that he asked me how much I was worth and I told him a million dollars, to which he replied, "Well, you won't get that much money from me." Anyway, we came to an agreement and I signed with Ben and the Phillies. That was 1947.

They sent me to Class C and I pitched and played the outfield in between. Then the word came down that I shouldn't play any more outfield. I pitched the rest of the year and wound up 21 and 9.

In 1947 I went to spring training. I rode with Ben Chapman and we talked baseball all of the way down. There I was, this guy from Birmingham, Alabama, and I was going to a major league baseball camp. I thought that was the absolute top until one day when the Yankees were coming to Clearwater to play the Phillies in an exhibition game and Ben told me I was going to pitch against them.

All of a sudden a hush came over the entire park and somebody whispered, "There he is," and I said, "There who is?" Down the left field line came Mr. Ruth. He had on his cap and his camel hair coat, and all he did was take his left hand and wave a little at the crowd. Then he came over and Ben Chapman said, "Babe, this is Bubba Church, he's going to pitch today." Babe Ruth sat down next to me and said, "Good luck, kid." Talk about feeling blessed!

I think it was 1947 when the motion picture came out about the Babe and we were in some god-awful place, some backwater, like Muskogee, Oklahoma, or St. Joe, Missouri. The whole ball club went to see it and I cried like a baby.

I had a good year in 1947, a bad year in 1948, and a great year in the International League in 1949. In spring training of 1950 I was just another one of the boys. I got to pitch the last three innings of the last game of the exhibition season in Clearwater and we were playing the Red Sox. There was a short porch in Clearwater—it was like 220 feet from home plate—and I had the tying run on base and the winning run at home with two men out and Mr. Ted Williams came up to bat. He spread out and he squeezed that bat so hard that I could see the sawdust leaking out of the end of it. I went to work and I got a strike on him, then I deliberately missed with a pitch that he looked at. Then I threw him what Satchel called the annihilator, which was my down curveball, and he swung through it. I had two strikes and one ball and I came in on his hands, belt high, and he took it. I gave him the best that I had to offer and he swung through it for strike three. He threw his bat straight up in the air fifty feet and stood and glared at me. And I did what I do best of all—I just looked at him and spat right at him. I turned and walked off of that rubber into the dugout and I said, "Bubba, you done made the Phillies."

I had a plan to be in the big leagues by 1950 and I got there in 1950. I was very much aware of being in the big leagues because I never went into a major league baseball park until I got to Philadelphia and I was playing. But what I was most aware of was that once you got there the toughest job was to stay. We were mentally and physically prepared for every game, because if we weren't there was a pink slip and a bus ride waiting for us. We could look back and from Triple A all the way to Class C somebody was coming, coming, coming . . .

During our era we felt it was a compliment for kids and folks to ask us for an autograph, and I still feel that way today. Those people made us. We did the playing, but those people appreciated us and we played for them. How can you ask a child to send you a five-dollar bill for your autograph? How can you do that? Putsy Caballero, my old roommate, and Willie Jones and Richie Ashburn and I used to go to Eastern State Penitentiary in Philadelphia every year. We were called on to go to different places and I considered it a privilege to go to these people. Without the fans we had nothing.

I think in 1950 we had the best baseball team. The Whiz Kids could have played with any of them during any era. And the friends I made during that time *made* my life in baseball. When I think of people who meant the most to me I'd have to start with Eddie Waitkus, our first baseman, because of his demeanor. He was a little older than we were and he was the guy who always called time and came out and said to me on the mound, "Hey, sweets, let's slow that engine down just a bit. Let's get it back together."

There are so many people who had such an influence on me. Guys that I respected not only as baseball players but as men, fathers, and just people. Bill Nicholson was one, Blix Donnelly was one, Del Wilber was one, and Andy Seminick was one. The best of all, though, a man I am very proud to have known, was Satchel Paige.

I coached Satchel Paige. That was the most enlightening education I ever got in baseball. I had never seen him pitch until I got to Miami to coach. We were together from 1957 to 1958 when I was the player-coach with the Miami Marlins. He had thirty-four different pitches, and he could really throw a fastball. So he named them—the midnight special, the annihilator, the spotter, and the hook. The hook was when he threw up and in on someone. His fingers were so long that he couldn't get them to where you're supposed to get them to throw a breaking ball. He could spin a ball and get a little bit of a slider, but I'm telling you, he could surely throw that fastball in through the middle.

The first time I met Satch, I was in the locker room in Miami after a game. He was sitting there in his silk knit underwear and he looked up at me. He knew I was from Alabama and I knew he was from Alabama and that was that delicate time of our lives. We were living in Montgomery and we had gone through a very difficult time there with Miss Rosa Parks and the Montgomery people were all up in arms. I didn't know what I was going to say to Satch, but I looked at him and I finally said, "I have heard a lot about you and this is the first time I've ever seen you pitch. I really enjoyed it." And he looked me straight in the eye and said, "I heard a lot about you too, Hometown." He called me Hometown from then on.

Satchel Paige was the most interesting human being I have ever met in my life. He would go fishing in Miami and when he was fishing he thought he was a commercial fisherman—he was fishing seriously. If we flew from Miami to Toronto somebody would always go by Satchel and say, "Hey Satch, how high are we?" and he would look out the window and say, "Thirty-five thousand feet." Then we'd go up to the cockpit and ask the pilot, "How high are we flying?" and he'd say, "Close to thirty-five thousand feet." Satch was always right.

Whatever he did, he wrote the book. I used to tell him, "The only reason that you know all of these things is because you've lived so long." Satchel was probably fifty-one years old then and he always brought a doctor's medical bag with him. He would never let anybody else touch him. His right arm was something—they threw away the blueprint when they made that, but his left arm was appalling. Satchel had a lot of hair and he looked like he might be only thirty or thirty-five years old; the only way that you could tell he had any age on him was just like you do with a horse—he didn't have any teeth left in his mouth to chew with.

He had more patience than any pitcher I have ever seen in my life because he never made a pitch until in his mind he knew exactly where he wanted it to go, what he wanted to do with it, and what speed he wanted it to go. I saw him one Sunday afternoon in Buffalo, New York, take nine minutes to make four pitches to Luke Easter and pop him up for the third out.

When I was coaching in Miami, our dog Tiger loved to go to the ball park. We always lived in apartments, so at night when we had ball games I took her to the park with me and put her right in the bullpen. Tiger was a really good dog, but when they played the National Anthem, she howled and howled and howled and the people who were regulars at the park would always say, "Well, it's time for Bubba Church's dog to sing."

The biggest thrill of all was the day we won the pennant in 1950. Sisler hit the home run, and Robin Roberts pitched the greatest ninth inning that I can remember. We had lost Simmons, I had been hit in the face on September 15, so the pitching staff was depleted, and Robbie was tired, but he got the three-run bulge and he pitched three outs as great as I have ever seen pitched in my life. That final out was the greatest thrill that I ever had in baseball and nothing will ever top it.

When I left baseball, I guess I died a little bit. I had no profession, so I went into the real estate business, but during 1957 we had a recession. I finally picked up the phone and called Bob Carpenter who owned the Philadelphia Phillies and said, "Hey, I want to get back into baseball."

He made the arrangements and I went to Miami as a player and then wound up coaching. After Miami, I came back and there was no market for real estate at all, so I went into the life insurance business. After that I returned to Birmingham and took a job as the manufacturer's rep for medical surgical supplies, and then we opened a linen service for doctors' offices and worked happily for twelve years. It was very good to us.

When I met Peggy, my wife, she didn't know anything about baseball; she'd never been to a ball game. I used to tease her that she thought the shortstop was a pause that the runner makes between second and third! One time we were out together and someone innocently asked Peggy what she had done during the years when our children were little. She looked at me and pointed and said, "I followed that damn baseball player all over the United States and South America!"

Our daughter Cindy had been to something like thirteen schools by the time she was twelve years old. That was why I stopped, but of course the only skill I had was baseball. I missed baseball terribly and every spring after I quit, I got sick or I got a cold. I needed to head for spring training! I think I finally outgrew that about last year.

Now with Peggy I just enjoy the house and the yard work and the dog. And we enjoy each other most of all. She spoils me and I spoil her—it's a great deal. We're blessed with five grandchildren and two daughters, we've got our dog, we've got our cat, we've got our fish, and we've got each other.

Baseball has been a great part of my life and a part that now I am probably more proud of than when I was playing. I love getting letters from fans. I am getting letters today from the grandchildren of the people who were the fans when we played. I like to think that maybe we were role models, maybe we were the kind of people that somebody wanted to emulate.

WARREN SPAHN

Warren Spahn pitched from 1946 to 1965 for the Braves, Mets, and Giants. He returned from World War II with a Purple Heart at age twenty-five and went on to pitch for nineteen years. Spahn led the league in wins in 1949, 1950, 1953, and 1957–61. He received the Cy Young Award in 1957 and was an All-Star in 1947, 1949–54, 1956–59, and 1961–63. Spahn was inducted into the Hall of Fame in 1973.

I CAN REMEMBER MY DAD taking me to Triple A baseball games in Buffalo as a kid. I idolized those guys that I saw play, and I thought I'd like to play too. It was a love affair.

I played on street teams, and when I got old enough I played American Legion. Buffalo had a great municipal program, and I played in both a twilight league and for my high school. With my high school team, I wanted to play first base—after all, left-handers are limited in what they can play. But the guy who was playing first base was All-City and I thought, "I'm never going to beat him." They needed a pitcher, so I started pitching. At that particular time I was playing with three or four different ball clubs, so I was playing almost every other day. I really loved it. I loved running the bases, I enjoyed hitting, I enjoyed whatever the action was.

When I got a chance to play to play professionally, it was for eighty dollars a month, Class D at Bradford, Pennsylvania, with the Braves. There were no bonuses in those days. I was just happy to earn a living after I got out of high school. The kids I went to high school with worked for Bethlehem Steel or the railroad and they were making seventeen dollars a week. I

317

was making twenty and doing something I loved more than they did being steelworkers.

I got $125 a month the next year pitching at Evansville, Class B. I was successful there and went to Class A. The progress wasn't that hard but there were a lot of other things that factored into it like being away from home. I was really not dry behind the ears before I went away. I'd get a paycheck, pay my rent, and get a meal voucher. I took care of those things and then I waited for the next paycheck and did it again. It was new and it was hard but it was still a love affair. We were doing something that we wanted to do. When I got an opportunity to be in the big leagues I had never seen a big-league ball park. Triple A was the highest that I had ever seen.

The first game that I saw was Opening Day of 1942 and Jim Tobin was the pitcher. Tobin was a knuckleballer and he hit two home runs in that game. I decided that those were things I wanted to accomplish.

Everything builds on everything else and you have to remember the times. We didn't have guaranteed contracts. When I first came up to the big leagues I made five hundred dollars a month and I had to make the ball club. Then I was drafted into the service because of the Second World War and I had to hope that I had a job when I came back.

I received the Purple Heart for my contributions with the Combat Engineers—we got a presidential citation. I fought in the Battle of the Bulge and when my company took the bridge over the Rhine, I got hit by shrapnel. We lost a bunch of people when the bridge collapsed and I wound up with a battlefield commission, which cost me six months of my baseball career. Things like that just happen. I didn't want to be a soldier in the first place but since I was there I wanted to do what I could to get home. I took the commission and I had to spend six months in the Army of Occupation.

I would have been back for the opening of the 1946 season, but I didn't get back until July. I was a replacement for an officer who was killed. I could have rejected it, but I didn't know that we were going to drop the bombs on Japan. I thought we were going to the States for a month and then on to fight the Japanese and that I would have a better chance of coming home alive if I were an officer rather than an enlisted man.

I'm proud of my military career and I am more than delighted that I was able to come back and accomplish what I did afterward. I won my first ball game when I was twenty-five and I won more games than any living pitcher in history. I was pretty lucky and I played until I was forty-four.

When I came back three and a half years after being drafted, the government said that we were guaranteed our jobs back. Billy Southworth was our manager and he remembered me pitching against the Cardinals in St. Louis. He gave me a chance to start and I won.

Soon I was 5 and 0 and, boy, I was on top of the world. My girlfriend and I wanted to get married. Southworth wanted us to wait until the end of the year and I said, "No, we've been through a lot and we want to get married." He even offered to be my best man at my wedding if I waited until the end of the year! But we got married on August 10 in Boston and I had pitched on Friday to the Giants and I beat them. I got off on Saturday to get married and the game was rained out. On Sunday we played a double header to make up that Saturday game and I was in the bullpen. Sid Gordon hit a home run off me when I came in as relief and I was the losing pitcher as a wedding present.

My dream was survival. When I came out of the service I was twenty-five years old. We won the pennant in 1948 and I was twenty-seven. I was the senior citizen of the ball club every year after that and the ball club had four or five young left-handers who were trying to get my job. I resigned myself to one thing—if any of those guys were going to get my job, they were going to have to be better than me. I made myself rise to higher levels. I never dreamed that I would accomplish what I did, but hunger accomplishes a great many things.

There was always someone right there to take our jobs. I think that's the thing that is missing today. The players have guaranteed contracts and the farm system isn't as strong.

It was incredibly competitive. We'd go to spring training and there were five hundred people with cardboard numbers on their backs and when we left spring training there were twenty-five players. I didn't want to be just run-of-the-mill, I wanted to be the guy who was chosen to pitch the big game. I loved the challenge. The desire to excel is intangible, but you have got to have it. What made Ted Williams what he was? What made Joe DiMaggio? What made Stan Musial? Or Hank Aaron? How do know what you can be unless you really bust your butt to do it?

I've had some great ideas that were great failures. I've set a hitter up for a pitch that I thought he couldn't hit, and then he hit it out of the ball park. Whoops—back to the drawing board. When I spoke in front of the House of Representatives and the Senate I told them, "Baseball is a game of mistakes and the teams that win the pennant win about sixty to sixty-five percent of the games that they play." I hope in their governmental decision making they have a better percentage of being right than baseball has. Show me somebody who never made a mistake I'll show you somebody who never did anything.

The ugly part of the game is that it's the survival of the fittest. You'd think, if I get this hitter out, I'm taking bread out of his kid's mouth, but by the same token he could be taking bread out of my kid's mouth. I guess it's that way in every walk of life. Survival of the fittest whether it's intellectual or physical.

I am enthralled and pleased when I think of all of the great people who played this game. I happen to think that the forties and fifties was the golden age of baseball, and I played in that era. I feel very proud of my accomplishment in that time.

We had a friend and sometimes an enemy in the media. Who else gets more free publicity than sports people or politicians and movie stars?

The publicity took away our privacy and raised the question of how much we owed the public. I remember my wife and I went out for dinner one night and we drove an hour out of Milwaukee to get a little privacy. But it was the same old story; someone always says, "I hate to bother you, but . . ." There we were and this woman came up to us and said that she wanted an autograph and that she had a bet at their table and was going to lose a hundred dollars if I didn't give it to her. So I said okay, I didn't want her to lose the hundred dollars. Well, she pulled up her skirt and she had a Band-Aid on her butt and my wife looked at me as if to say, "You do that and you're dead." I signed it and my wife wouldn't talk to me for two weeks. Where do you draw the line? Do you sign two hundred autographs and then cut the rest of them off? And how much of your time do you devote to the public? Aren't ballplayers allowed to have private time? We spent half of our time on the road and then when we were at home we were supposed to sign autographs.

I had no choice but to work in the off-season, so I stayed in Boston and worked for Mr. Perrini, the Braves' owner, who was in construction. I worked at Logan Airport doing construction. In fact, there is a runway there with a bump in it that I know that I put there! I had been an engineer in the Army and I liked building things, and I thought maybe I had a future in construction.

After that I went to Oklahoma. My wife was from Oklahoma and she wanted to be near her mother, so we bought sixty acres and I put some cows on it. Then I started buying pieces of property around our land and to make a long story short, I've been in the cattle business for forty some odd years. It all started with sixty acres and that's what I did in the off-season. I stayed in shape over the winter and went to spring training with less weight than I finished the season with, just because I fed those cattle and worked on my ranch. I'm a windshield farmer now; I drive around in a pickup.

I was a shy, unassuming kid when I was growing up. When I came into baseball, I remember getting microphone fright on the radio and now I'm doing television and radio and I'm making a living out of it. Baseball helped me overcome the shyness and educated me. It's kind of nice when you have a name that makes someone want to associate with you, but I've often wondered if people like me for me or for my name. I don't think I want to know the answer either.

Then you have to live up to the name. I think you have to be comfortable with whatever level you put yourself on. Like the Hall of Fame, the great honor of baseball—I remember when I was inducted I felt that I didn't belong there. I was so proud to be on the same dais with Lefty Gomez and all of those great people. But as I have gotten older I've felt that maybe I do belong.

I go back every year for the inductions and I want to reach out to those guys to make them feel more comfortable because

I was once uncomfortable. It becomes a very elite group and I think it would be horrible if someday one guy was inducted and none of the other Hall of Famers showed up to congratulate him.

I managed for five years, then I went to Cleveland for two years as a pitching coach and I didn't like that, so I went to Japan for three different years as a pitching instructor.

Finally one day I said, "What the hell am I doing spinning my wheels?" I got out and when I did I learned a great lesson—when one door closes, two open. You always have choices.

STAN MUSIAL

"Stan the Man" Musial played outfield and first base for the St. Louis Cardinals from 1941 to 1963. Musial was voted Most Valuable Player in 1943, 1946, and 1948. He was an All-Star in 1943–44 and from 1946 to 1963 and was inducted into the Hall of Fame in 1969. Stan Musial's records and accomplishments on and off the field are legend.

I WANTED TO BE a ballplayer ever since I was a youngster and that's all I ever did really. We didn't have much equipment and we couldn't afford to buy balls but my mother made balls for us. She'd make them out of rags and put black tape on the outside. Play ball—that was all I wanted to do.

We had enough boys right in the neighborhood to be able to play games, and I was very fortunate to have for a next-door neighbor the manager of a baseball team in my hometown of Donora, Pennsylvania, who took an interest in me. When he'd come home from work we'd play catch and talk baseball. I was their batboy and water boy and shagged flies with that team for a couple of years when I was thirteen or fourteen.

One day the pitcher didn't show up and they put me in to pitch. I was only fourteen, and those guys were eighteen, nineteen, or twenty years old. I did very well; I pitched five or six innings and struck out a lot of guys, so they voted me into their association as one of their regular members. A regular at fourteen. That was a great experience because I was playing against older fellows. I played with them one year.

About then the American Legion started a team in Donora for the first time, so I played American Legion for a year. And about the same time, our high school decided to have a base-

Stan Musial helping out in his father-in-law's grocery store, 1942

ball team and I played for them for a year. My timing in all
these things was good.

We lived only about thirty miles from Pittsburgh and I used
to always follow the Pittsburgh Pirates, especially Paul "Big
Poison" Waner, who was a great hitter. Waner was one of my
favorites along with Carl Hubbell of the New York Giants. I
was pitching in my early days and Carl was a screwball pitcher—
he was the best. Even as a young boy I was looking to follow
those two guys, Paul Waner and Carl Hubbell. They were my
heroes and I really watched how they worked.

It was a big thrill to become a major league ballplayer and to achieve my ambitions and dreams. The most important part about playing major league baseball was that I enjoyed it. Just putting the uniform on every day—I got a kick out of it. It was exciting, the games, the cities, and the traveling, all that part of it, but I just enjoyed playing. I think I was born to be a ballplayer.

I pitched for a couple of years and at the end of one of them I hurt my arm and couldn't pitch anymore. So I started out with the Cardinal organization in Springfield, Missouri, which was Class C, as an outfielder. I was there a couple of months and led the league in home runs and RBIs, so they sent me to Rochester, which was a Triple A. That was a pretty big jump from C to Triple A.

Then when our minor league season was over in 1941, the Cardinals were in an exciting pennant race with the Dodgers which went down to the last three or four days. The Cards called four of us up at the end of the season: George "Whitey" Kurowski, Erv "Four Sack" Dusak, Howard Pollet, and me. Within one year I went from Class C to the Cardinal outfield. *That* was a pretty big jump and it was a long way from Donora.

Billy Southworth, the manager, put me right in a ball game. We had a doubleheader with the Braves. I watched the first game and he put me in the second game. I was fortunate enough to get a couple of hits, we won the game, and I played regularly ever since that time. I do believe it was a matter of timing and fortunate things, or unfortunate things as the case may be. During that year, 1941, Terry Moore, the Cardinals' center fielder, got hit in the head, so he was out for the season, and Enos Slaughter broke his shoulder. If the Cardinals hadn't been in a pennant race and those guys hadn't been hurt, maybe I wouldn't have had a chance.

I made the best of it. I did well, so I was sort of a flash in the pan in 1941, and by 1942, Moore and Slaughter were back in form again and I had to start from scratch.

That year, 1942, I wasn't sure about making the club because I had a horrible spring training. Everybody there was expecting me to do great things and I didn't do very well because in Florida in those days they didn't have good backgrounds. There were these palm trees waving in the background and it was hard to see the ball coming in to the plate.

Once we got to St. Louis, we had a couple of exhibition games with the St. Louis Browns, and I got several hits in each of those games. Then I was kind of playing regularly, but it's not a one-year thing; it takes two or three years before you finally get your confidence and feel that you belong. It's the same way with hitting. It takes a little time, four or five years, before you feel that you can do what you want with a pitch, pull it a little or hit it the other way. All these things take time.

The amazing thing about the 1941 season was that before I was sent to Springfield the Cardinals were kind of through with me. Down at Columbus, Georgia, they had about three hundred ballplayers and the manager knew I was a pitcher. He asked me to pitch against the Cardinals and I said no. I explained that I didn't want to be a pitcher anymore because I had a sore arm. But he asked me again and he kind of pressured me, so I pitched.

The first inning I did fairly well against them, then Terry Moore hit a long home run off of me, and then Johnny Mize hit a long home run off of me. I thought my future with the Cardinals was over, and it was kind of a surprise to make it all the way up in one year after a start like that.

I was a rookie and the regulars wouldn't talk to the rookies. But I was doing so well that I felt a little bit like I belonged, until one night when we were in a club car traveling somewhere. I was sitting with Terry Moore and Johnny Mize, and Moore said, "Remember that game we played down in Columbus, earlier this year?" Johnny Mize said, "Yeah, I hit a long home run off of some left-hander down there, and Terry Moore said, "I hit a great home run down there too." When I finally got the courage to tell them that pitcher was me they couldn't believe it. They just couldn't believe that at the end of the same season I'd be joining the Cardinals. That was a pretty big challenge.

My favorite team was the 1942 Cardinals, with Enos Slaughter, Terry Moore, Marty Marion, and the Cooper brothers. We had a great team and great spirit. It was my rookie year and we won the Series. That year was the best year for me—doing all those things.

The first four years that I was with the Cardinals we were

in the World Series, and I got to where I thought we were supposed to do that all of the time. Then we didn't get into another one for eighteen years!

In those days, we just barely made ends meet. We couldn't save anything and we had to work in the wintertime. My first year's salary was $65 a month, but only for three months. Then I jumped up at Springfield and I got $150. At Rochester I got $450 and then at St. Louis I got $750 the first year. The Cardinals always said things like, "You know, you're gonna get in a World Series and you're gonna get four or five thousand dollars extra." They'd always use that in their contract negotiations.

Our son Dickie was named for Dick Kerr, because Dick and his wife befriended us when we were young. We were expecting a baby and we were only making a hundred dollars a month. They were lovely to us. Mrs. Kerr was a real maternal type, and she saw that we were just about to be new parents and that we really didn't know what it was all about. They were very warm to us and Dick said to me one day, "Why don't you come live with us and Pep [Mrs. Kerr] will take care of Lil." Lil wasn't having any big problems but she was so little and young and all and Pep was just wonderful to her. We would ride to the ball park together; Dick and I would talk baseball and Pep and Lil would talk about babies the whole time.

Anyway, we named our son Dick after Dick Kerr and it was because of their great kindness to us. A little later on, when we had got into some money, we bought a house for them in Texas. They were having a lot of trouble and baseball didn't give them much. They didn't have any pension. Nothing. He was with the Black Sox and he would tell us stories about the way things were in the 1919 World Series. We knew he was an honest man and yet with the Black Sox scandal he was hurt and they didn't have anything left.

We enjoyed playing, we had a lot of togetherness, and we had a good spirit with the Cards in those days. We socialized quite a bit and we'd go with each other to the ball park, and our wives would get together while we were gone. Those early days were our closest days with our friends. Baseball has changed since those days—I guess they call that progress.

It was a slower pace with the trains. When we traveled we had time to visit and talk, mostly about baseball, and on those three-week road trips we had a lot of togetherness.

Baseball was really a close-knit family and most of us lived in the Fairgrounds Hotel. After the war, I happened to be at a restaurant and I heard this guy who was in the service say, "I'm going to be moving out this week, I'm going home." So I took over the rent on his house right then. This was the same time when the Pascual brothers were trying to get everyone to jump to the Mexican league, and we were moving. I was packing upstairs at the hotel and all the ballplayers and their wives were downstairs in the lobby. They knew about the Pascual brothers being in the hotel and they sent our son Dick who was about six years old then upstairs to ask us, "Are you going or aren't you going?" They were worried that we had jumped to Mexico too, but we were just lucky enough to get a house.

The old parks had a lot of character to them. They were smaller and the field was closer to the fans. We could see who was at the games. The same people sat in the box seats and they were very close, so we knew a lot of them. Some of the seats today in the bigger ball parks are so far away that the fan can't really see the player.

In the fifties we were the focal point in the athletic world. We had a slower pace and we always took care of our fans. After a ball game we'd sign for hours. Even when we were out on the field we'd be signing things.

We would promote baseball. One thing we did was work the "hot-stove league." We'd go to banquets and different functions and talk to the fans, and every ball player did his share of those things promoting baseball.

I had a business manager, but he never got involved in my baseball activities. Today with agents involved there have been strikes. That was unheard of in our day. We just played and did our jobs, and it seemed that we got along in our baseball relationship with the owners. In our day, we *were* underpaid, but today ballplayers are overpaid. That's one extreme to the other. If they could find a happy medium somewhere along the line, that'd be good for the game.

When I was young, my grandmother had a radio and every Saturday night I would tune in to a station in West Virginia.

They had cowboy music on for a couple of hours and I got to listen to it. I also learned to play the harmonica as a kid but when I was with the Cardinals, I never played it in all those years. Later, when I was going to celebrity golf tournaments, I ran into Roy Clark and a lot of other country-and-western guys. Those country-and-western guys love golf and they love baseball. One time up in Iowa somewhere Roy Clark had his guitar out. It was late at night and I just happened to have my harmonica so I played along with him—and I played pretty well. But when he said, "How about coming on *Hee Haw?*" I told him flat out, "Roy, I'm an amateur and you guys are pros, I can't do that." He kept asking and asking until finally I did go on *Hee Haw* about five years ago. Now I never leave home without it—my harmonica, that is!

As much as I love country music, meeting Gene Autry was the greatest thing. Gene was the best, and he was a great Cardinal fan. He loved baseball and he'd come to visit us in Chicago when we'd play there. One thing about Autry, if you were a Cardinal ballplayer and were looking for a job, he would treat you really well. He took care of you. He was fortunate enough to be able to buy a ballclub, and he is still a great baseball fan. I guess he did pretty well singing too.

I loved baseball and I still do. It stays with you.

HARRY WALKER

Harry "the Hat" Walker played from 1940 to 1955 for the Cardinals, Phillies, Cubs, and Reds. He remained in professional baseball for forty-two years in a career that included playing, managing, coaching, and scouting.

I STARTED PLAYING BALL way back when I was in first grade. Teachers would always ask us what we wanted to be and back in those days most kids said, "I want to be a fireman or a policeman." My deal was that I wanted to be a ballplayer. My dad [Ewart "Dixie" Walker] had played in the big leagues, with Washington from 1909 to 1912, and he might have been the first one out of Alabama to make it to the majors. His brother Ernie played with the St. Louis Browns in 1914, 1915, and 1916 and then my brother Dixie came along and played for the Yankees. So I just followed the family. That's all I had ever dreamed about doing when I was a kid growing up.

I played ball all of the time. When school was out and it was summertime I would leave early in the morning and I didn't get in until dark. I played wherever I found other kids to play with. I just liked to play baseball—that was my whole life.

I didn't make any money when I started out. The first three years that I played pro ball I only made fifteen hundred dollars. I had two major operations because of a ruptured appendix. The next year I had another problem and played all year and didn't tell anybody. I still have throat trouble from being hit with a ball.

I got released three or four times because I wanted more money. I hit .370 my first year and they cut me $25 a month!

333

They said that I was getting more than I should have in the first place. I was getting a $100 a month in 1937, but they said that $60 was my salary and the other $40 was a bonus. I felt I should have gotten a raise after hitting .370, which was second in the league. They said finally that they'd give me a $15-a-month raise but only on the $60. That got me up to $75, which was really a $25 pay cut. They released me and then I went ahead and signed with an independent club for $150 a month.

Then I was drafted by the Phillies and I got $150 a month in Class B and signed a major league contract in 1939. They sent me a contract for $125—a $25 cut to sign a big-league contract.

I didn't go, I wouldn't go, and they finally sent me to Pensacola. I finished the year there as a free agent and that's when I signed with the Cardinals at the end of 1939 and went with them in 1940. I asked for five thousand dollars, but Mr. Rickey liked to swallow his cigar and said, "Judas Priest, son, we just don't have that kind of money!"

Back in those days the Cardinals were called the chain gang because they had thirty-two or thirty-three ball clubs in the minors. Anyway, I went ahead and finally agreed to play for a twenty-five-hundred-dollar bonus. Then I went to spring training with Rochester in 1940 and at the end of 1940 I went to St. Louis.

Dot and I got married on St. Patrick's Day during spring training. We got married about eight or eight-thirty in the morning—my brother Dixie and his wife and Dot and I went to the justice of the peace in Clearwater. I got pulled over by a policeman while speeding there and I told the officer that I was going to get married. He said, "Boy, I've heard every excuse in the world. For God's sake, it's only eight o'clock in the morning." He let me go, and when we passed him on the way back I waved to him. That was 1941, March 17.

That day was my first chance to start, so when I got back to the ball park, I let Dot have the key to the car and she went back to the hotel on her own. I didn't get back until nine that night! That's how we got started.

Baseball was fun. I've helped some boys get jobs to play and then they go out and they don't like the way that they are treated and quit. When they come back and ask if I can help them again, I say, "Look, your desire is not there. I can't go out and try to sell you to another ball club if you walked off when you didn't like the way that things were going." When I started out it was so easy to quit, but we didn't because we did want to play.

You had to love the game to want to stay in it with as many ups and downs as there were. The one thing that made us fight a little harder was that we got paid the next year on what we accomplished the year before. If we had a bad year, we got cut. I think when you get a little security like the ballplayers have today that you pull back on the throttle a little bit.

Today there aren't the family ties of baseball that we used to have. I felt bad when I left the Cardinals because I was trained to play there and we had won together. When I was traded it really upset me; I didn't want to leave the Cardinals. Today all the players seem to want to go somewhere else. They all want to know "where is the buck at?"

The pension plan was started back in 1946, when I was with the Cardinals. We had a meeting one day and started talking about how we didn't have anything and wondered if we could get a pension plan. Doc Weaver was a pretty smart individual and he knew some folks who were with the Equitable Insurance Company. He suggested that we see what they could come up with. They came up with a plan and then we notified the presidents of the leagues and the commissioner, Happy Chandler. Marty Marion was the number one man and Terry Moore was the number two man from the Cardinals and all the players called it the "Marty Marion Plan" because Marty had been so involved in making it happen. At that time the most that you could get was a hundred dollars a month—a ten-year man got a hundred dollars and a five-year man got fifty. But we didn't have anything from television then.

My brother Dixie was the first rep from the National League and he fought to get television rights as part of the plan. He had a friend in New York who said, "Dixie, don't worry about the radio, fight for TV, that's going to be your big money." Dixie said, "What do you mean? They can't televize a ball game like they do boxing matches." That was in 1946 and Dixie fought to get it. They gave us the TV money and that's where all of the money is coming from today. I just hope the young players today who are getting all of this money understand and appreciate the fact that Dixie is the one who fought to get it for them.

We were in the World Series in 1946 and that was the first time that the money was donated back to the pension fund. Before it had been split up among the first three or four teams. Some of the teams didn't want to do that, but the Cardinals all voted to put the money toward the pension and finally everybody else did.

I played behind some of the great ballplayers of all time. Musial, Moore, Slaughter and those guys were always up at the top of the list, but you had to be the best that *you* could be. You couldn't worry about what Musial was doing—you had to say to yourself, "I got to be the best that I can possibly be." You've got to enjoy the game, you have to love putting the uniform on. You are an entertainer and you have to perform each day because what you did yesterday is history.

Years ago, we'd leave Boston and ride the train all the way back to St. Louis, for twenty-eight hours. After the ball game, we'd eat in the dining car and go in the smoker with about eight or ten guys and sit around talking baseball. We'd discuss the game and so we got to know each other a little better.

We ate in the hotels where we stayed and that was some of the finest food I ever had. In Boston the Kenmore Hotel was great. That was where I ate the first lobster I ever had and the littleneck clams I learned to love. The Bellevue Stratford in Philadelphia had a great dining room with waiters from the Old Country who were really professional. And the Schenly in Pittsburgh was another great hotel. We ate every night together and at breakfast as well. We mingled together. We were a family of sorts.

I don't know any profession that is better than this. I lived such a good life because of baseball, it is hard for me to go back and say what else I could have done. The only thing I never had that I really wanted was a jet airplane. I can't afford that now, but if I could I'd have one. I've had all of the other good things. I've been all over the world. I've had the best of lives.

The war took a lot of time away from a lot of people—it took two years away from me. The Army was hard and I

wouldn't want to have to go through it again, but I'm glad I did it. I'm glad I made the sacrifice.

About two weeks before the war in Europe ended, we were going to try to take a bridge in Germany at night. The lines of communication had gone crazy and we were about sixty miles back of the German line. I shot three men as close as you. They had a gun in my face, and this one guy thought we were Germans. It was cold, rainy, and dark and he wanted to know where the Americans were. When I dropped out the door of my jeep, I hit him and the other two with a .45 revolver that I had carried overseas. I do believe that the only thing that saved me were my reflexes from being in sports.

I got back for spring training for the 1946 season. And I've stayed in baseball ever since. I've had forty-two years in pro ball. I spent 27 years with the Cardinals—minor leagues, major league, coaching, managing, and broadcasting with Jack Buck.

Forty-two years is a long time and now I know just about everybody in baseball; but when I first came up I didn't know anybody. It was all new to me. My first day in 1937 I worked out a whole day with a guy who threw batting practice to me and I didn't know who the devil he was. That was Hank Greenberg! He said, "Kid, you wanna hit?" I said, "Yessir!" And I hit and hit and when I got ready to throw to him the buzzer that signaled the end of your time went off.

So the next day I came out and he said, "Hey, kid, you wanna hit some more?" I said, "Yessir." He said, "You're the one that doesn't want to do anything but hit; you don't want to throw." He just laughed. I didn't know him from Babe Ruth. It's a long road for a rookie!

When I look back, I still think the prestige of a World Series is the biggest thing. I've got two World Series rings. Dixie played in two World Series too, but he never won, and he said, "Harry, the money is fine, but if you don't win, you are not the best. Once you win, you can always say, 'We were the world's champions!'"

CLYDE KING

Clyde King pitched from 1944 to 1953 for the Dodgers and Reds, and he led the National League in relief wins (13) in 1951. King managed three major league teams, the Giants, Braves, and Yankees and worked for George Steinbrenner through the 1980s.

MY PARENTS WERE SUPPORTIVE of sports to a degree. My mother was a wonderful Christian lady who didn't know much about athletics and I'm sorry to say that she never saw me play a game of any kind. We came from a very religious family. We didn't believe in playing baseball on Sunday and my father worked all the time. He had to support seven children and he didn't have a lot of time.

But I don't think that hindered me and I don't think it bothered me. They didn't object to me playing and they were always interested in how I did. If there was ever anything in the paper they would read it and be really pleased. It's great nowadays to see how some youngsters are supported—transported to and from their games and their parents being right there to root them on. It's wonderful. I never enjoyed that. We got to and from the games, my brothers and I, on our own. We either walked or bummed rides. But that didn't hinder us. It didn't take any fun away from it or anything.

Of course it was my dream to play sports, but not especially baseball. I was a better basketball player. I went to the University of North Carolina to play basketball and I went out for baseball kind of casually and made the team. So I ended up playing both baseball and basketball at the University of North

Carolina at Chapel Hill. When I went away to school it was during the early part of the war and I was just eighteen.

There was a guy around Chapel Hill named Howie Haak and he was a scout for the Pirates. Mr. Rickey had called and asked him if there was a boy on any of the college teams down south that could pitch in the big leagues right away, since a lot of the boys had gone away to war. So Howie put me on the train at Raleigh and sent me up to New York City. I had never been to a big city in my life and I went to Brooklyn; I got into Penn Station and took a cab over to Montague Street where the Brooklyn offices were. There I met with Mr. Rickey. He arranged a quick workout in Ebbets Field with Durocher, signed me that afternoon, and put me on the train to Philadelphia.

I ended up pitching in the first big-league game I ever saw! I went straight from college to the big leagues. My dream came true so much quicker than I ever thought it would. I'd grown up as a Yankee fan in Goldsboro, North Carolina, and I ended up managing the Giants and the Yankees, two of the three New York teams. I played for the Brooklyn Dodgers, so I ended up being connected to all three New York teams.

Sometime, somewhere in all of our youths we wanted to be baseball players, and I think it is every boy's dream to play in the major leagues. And I reached my dreams. This is my forty-eighth year in baseball and I've enjoyed every year. My last sixteen years were with the Yankees as George Steinbrenner's assistant and I enjoyed it. It's still not a chore for me to go to a game.

In baseball you are more alone than in any other sport. If you are a lineman in football and a running back comes through and you miss him, the linebacker can get him—he can tackle him for you. In basketball, if your man gets away from you and goes to the basket to shoot, the man on the back line can pick him up and stop him for you. But in baseball you're out there all by yourself. If the ball comes to the shortstop on the ground and goes through his legs, there is nobody behind him to pick it up and throw the man out at first. It's a team game, there's no doubt about that, but it's also a very individual thing.

When you're pitching, you are on that mound before sixty-thousand people and they watch every move. The game can't start until *you* throw the ball. It's a thrill. I've played all kinds of sports and baseball provides a thrill you don't get in any other sport. Batting in the ninth inning with the bases loaded, two outs, one run behind—I don't think there is anything to compare with that.

Baseball has touched every part of our culture. Everyone from the President of the United States to a coal miner uses the vocabulary of baseball to talk about his daily life. Besides baseball itself as a subject, baseball idioms as well are used in literature, in theater, in the movies, everywhere—they have become a way of talking about our lives.

I think there is such a great parallel between baseball and our lives. You don't have to like defeat, but baseball will teach you to live with it. In football, you play on Saturday or Sunday, you lose or win, and you've got six days to lick your wounds and get back in another game. In baseball, we sometimes had only a few hours before we had to come back and play again. When I was managing the Giants, we'd play in San Francisco on Saturday night at eight, then we'd play a noon game on Sunday. That doesn't give you much time. I think it teaches you to prepare, it teaches you to play a lot of times when you are hurt, when you are tired, when you feel that you can't go another step. In baseball you have to do it.

We never ever thought about pitching just one hundred pitches and then going to the locker room and taking a Jacuzzi. Jacuzzi—we thought that was a city in Japan when we were playing.

Players nowadays have outside activities that take them away from baseball. We didn't know what *The Wall Street Journal* was when we were playing baseball. And this is not news, but Nolan Ryan made more pitching in one inning in 1990 than I made in my whole first year in the big leagues for Brooklyn. A lot of people say that is relative, but you can look at it any way that you want. I personally think ballplayers get paid too much. I'm all for players getting paid every cent that they are worth and even more, but not ten times as much.

When we were playing, the salaries we were paid made us a living, but they did not make us rich or fabulously wealthy like some of the ballplayers today. Then again, I'm not sure that all of us did make a living, because when the season was over, I for one had to take another job.

I used to do a lot of different things. I used to take school pictures, the pictures that the kids bring home from grade school. I was a referee for basketball to make ends meet. I worked where I could to make money and pay the bills. We had to do it because our families were starting to grow. We could have left baseball and gone into something else to make more money, but we loved the game, and we were willing to sacrifice. It was not a job, it was not a chore, and I was not a great player. I was just an ordinary player. At times I struggled because of my ability. But it taught me to hang in there.

The specific point when the reality of getting to the big leagues hit me was when somebody asked me for my autograph the first time. I just couldn't believe that. There I was, a little guy from North Carolina, who had never done much traveling and who came from a very modest family, and somebody asked *me* for my autograph. I knew then that I had realized my dream. And that's why I have never refused to accommodate young people or anybody who asked for an autograph. It aggravates me to the nth degree when I see an athlete refuse to give an autograph. It's the fan who makes baseball exist. So I always sign the autographs. I feel obligated and honored.

In the book *Bums*, there is a section where Carl Erskine is talking about riding the trains and he says, "Hearts and Gin were the two games that the players played the most, but when Clyde King joined our team, he taught us to play Bridge." We'd get on a train at Grand Central or Penn Station to travel to St. Louis after a Sunday afternoon game at Ebbets Field to play in St. Louis on Tuesday night. We'd sit and play bridge and talk about the game—how we had got this hitter out or about some situation that had come up in the game.

Deep down, the players' interest and wanting to win and giving 100 percent has not changed that much, even though it might appear to some of the fans that it has. I couldn't say that if I hadn't been in the dugout—in the trenches, as a manager. The majority of the players still want to win, they still want to play hard, and they do play hard. You'll find a few individuals who don't, but the difference now is that the media magnifies the situation when a player doesn't bear down or doesn't hustle. The players themselves used to take care of that. I remember a few cases on our team in Brooklyn in 1944 when somebody didn't hustle to first base and we'd grab him by the jersey and pull him up really close and say, "Hey, we don't permit that on this team, you get with it." Now you don't have that, you *can't* have that. A manager has it so much tougher nowadays than our managers had it.

We all lived in Bay Ridge in Brooklyn. Pee Wee Reese lived around the corner, Duke Snider lived next door, Rube Walker lived upstairs above us (we had rented a big house and there was room upstairs, so he and Millie moved there). Carl Erskine lived nearby, as did Andy Pafko and Preacher Roe, and we'd share rides to and from the ball park because we all lived in the same neighborhood. Pee Wee and I rode together a lot 'cause Dottie Reese and Norma, my wife, were very good friends. As a matter of fact, our first child was born in Brooklyn at Methodist Hospital and she came home to the Reeses'. Dottie took Norma home because we were on the road and for ten days my wife and my first daughter stayed at the Reeses'. We lived together and depended on each other and the Reeses meant the world to us.

When I would drive to the ball park, I'd want to get there early. Pee Wee was a star, he was the captain of the team and a shortstop, and he didn't have to be there early if he didn't want to be. But when he rode with me he knew we got there early. After the game he knew that I got dressed quickly and went on home. So one day he asked me, "Clyde, why do you want to get there so early and why do you want to leave so quick?" I told him, "Pee Wee, you're a star, but somebody could get my job if I didn't get there early. I'm afraid somebody will get my uniform if I don't get there first!" And then he said, "Well then why do you want to leave so early?" and I said, "Because I'm afraid that Leo Durocher will call me into the office and tell me I'm going to Montreal [the Triple A team]." Pee Wee just laughed, but we still left early when I drove.

In Brooklyn we were much closer to the fans. In the ball park the fans were physically closer and they were interested in you. Like Gladys Gooding, who used to play the organ at Ebbets Field. She'd sit up there and watch as we'd arrive to work out. The guys would come out one at a time and when Gladys would see Pee Wee she'd start playing "My Old Ken-

tucky Home" 'cause he was from Louisville and when I'd come out she'd play "Carolina Moon," 'cause I was from North Carolina. The few fans who would be in the ball park then would pick up on it. Those are the kinds of things that I miss the most.

I remember one year Norma drove from Vero Beach, Florida, where we were for spring training, to Montreal, Canada, by herself with our six-year-old daughter because in those days you wouldn't dare ask the manager to let you go with your wife. Walter Alston was our manager and I'm sure he would have let me drive with her, but I was afraid to ask. I was dedicated to staying with my team. Baseball wives are wonderful and tough, they are the greatest. They had the hardest part of the job and I don't think the fans ever realized that part of the baseball life.

Our friendship with Ann and Ralph Branca has lasted for forty-eight years and Ralph has sung at all three of our daughters' weddings. Ann's mother owned a third of the Dodgers and I've known Ann since she was thirteen and I was nineteen. And that's a long time.

Carl Erskine is another good friend. We used to live next door to each other and Carl would make Thousand Island dressing and I would make pimento cheese and we'd swap dishes. Can you imagine these young ballplayers doing that now? Our wives would go to the games together. Tom Lasorda and his wife always teased me and Norma about our three girls. Norma used to dress them up in white gloves and everything and bring them to the park on Sundays and Tom Lasorda and his wife to this day remember that, they always bring up how Norma used to dress those girls. It was something special.

I've met some wonderful people. It's been a wonderful life and I wouldn't change it for anything. It is a wonderful way to provide for your family, and it's still kind of unbelievable to get paid for playing.

Bill Veeck, Larry Doby

LARRY DOBY

Larry Doby played from 1947 to 1959 for the Indians, White Sox, and Tigers. After playing for the Newark Eagles (Negro National League), Doby was signed by Bill Veeck in 1947 to be the first black player in the American League. He led the league in home runs in 1952 and 1954 and was an All-Star from 1949 to 1955. Doby managed the White Sox in 1978.

I CAN'T SAY THAT major league baseball was a dream for me because there were no black players in major league baseball when I grew up. My goal was to graduate from high school, go to college, and come back to my high school as a football, baseball, or basketball coach. I had had some coaches that I thought were great and that was what I wanted to do. I can't put my being involved in major league baseball into the context of dreams. I never thought it would happen and when it did happen I was just dumbfounded. I really didn't know how to react.

I grew up in Patterson, New Jersey. I played all of the sports—baseball, basketball, and football—and I was an All-Metro athlete in high school. I was aware that the only way I could get to college was on an athletic scholarship. My mother and my aunts and uncles who raised me always told me that if you get involved with athletics you can stay out of a great deal of trouble. So when baseball season came around I played baseball, football in football season, basketball in basketball season. That and my schoolwork kept me busy. Part of my dream came true because I did get a scholarship to Long Island University for basketball.

When I was playing for Patterson East Side High School we played a particular football game against Montclair High School and it was my touchdown that won the game. One of the players on the opposing team was Buzz Aldrin, and given the circumstances at the time you could say that I had as much chance then of getting to play in the major leagues as Aldrin did of going to the moon. At that time no black kid thought about major league baseball. But the world changed.

I didn't really have any dream of playing for the Negro Leagues either; I was just on my way to college. But there was a gentleman who lived in our town named Mr. Moore who was an umpire in the Negro Leagues, and he was telling the owners of the Newark Eagles, Mr. and Mrs. Manley, that there was a kid at Patterson East Side who was a pretty good player and that they should come and look at him. So they did come and watch me a couple of times.

When I graduated that June 1942, the Newark Eagles had a game against the New York Black Yankees and Mr. Moore asked me if I wanted to come up and work out with the Eagles. I said yes. I guess he was impressed because he drove me home afterward and asked my mother if I could play the rest of the summer with them. She said that I could but if there was a night game, she'd rather have me stay over than take a bus home late at night. So that's how it happened. I got three hundred dollars a month and I played the latter part of June and July and August.

Then I only had a semester at Long Island University before I was drafted into the service. I was on a little island called Uluthi in the South Pacific when it came on the radio that Mr. Branch Rickey had signed Jackie Robinson to play in Montreal for the Dodger organization. Two former players were physical instructors on that island with me. One was named Mickey Vernon and the other was named Billy Goodman and during the summer we had been going out and throwing balls at each other and pitching batting practice. Mickey was saying to me that I had a good opportunity to make the major leagues and he wrote Mr. Griffith a letter, but I guess at the time they wanted to wait. They weren't ready yet to integrate their teams.

When I got out of the service in 1946, I went to Puerto Rico to play winter ball with the San Juan Senators. In April I returned from San Juan and went to spring training in Jacksonville, Florida, with the Newark Eagles. I had realized by then that I had some future in baseball.

I played that summer with the Newark Eagles and we won the Negro World Series. We played the Kansas City Monarchs with Satchel Paige on the team and Henry Thompson, who finally played for the Giants, and Willard "Home Run" Brown, who played for the St. Louis Browns for a little while. Then in 1947 I went to spring training, and on July 5, 1947, I signed with Cleveland.

Even though I was young I couldn't kid myself or be naïve about what I was up against. I was fortunate enough to have a fine man to work for: Bill Veeck was probably the nicest and the greatest man that I ever met. Even at that particular time he never showed any prejudice or bigotry or racism within himself. He fought for the little man, the underdog. Bill Veeck didn't look at me as a black man but as an individual who could play baseball and who could possibly help his team win some games. That helped me go through whatever I had to go through without negative feelings about it.

It was sort of sudden. I don't think I experienced the same kind of preparational training that the Dodgers put Jackie Robinson through. Gaining acceptance for my playing was not so difficult; what I had to learn was the people. I had to learn how to react to the various levels of acceptance.

I think one of the best things that helped me was the fact that I grew up in a mixed neighborhood. My neighborhood consisted of kids who were as poor as I was. There were Italian kids, there were Irish kids, there were Jewish kids, and there were black kids. We all played together and we had integrated schools in Patterson. I was the only black on the football team, there was one other black on the basketball team for a year, and there was only one other black on the baseball team. I think that because of my success on those teams and living in that neighborhood that I had a pretty good reading of people, of how they would react to certain things, and of their basic reactions to color.

The people I faced in baseball were all grown men and most of them were Southern men. I knew right away how I stood with a lot of those people. I knew what their conception was of black folks. Fortunately, I didn't have any big problems—there were a few individuals who refused to shake my hand and that sort of stuff. I did have some problems, but not to the extent where the majority were against the fact that I was on the team. I knew that with certain guys I could say hello, how are you, and then good-bye, and that with others I could sit and have a conversation.

I look at my situation from the standpoint of when I was a youngster listening to Joe Louis's fights. When he would finish everyone in the neighborhood would come out and have something like a cheerleading rally because we were all so happy about it. The amazing thing was that he appealed to all people, not just blacks. Because of the kind of person that he was out of the ring—a gentleman, with character and discipline and a lot of diplomacy—I think that helped get blacks into baseball. Not only Joe Louis but also Jesse Owens and the situation he faced in Germany at the 1936 Olympics, and people like Paul Robeson who had to go through some things that were not easy. I think they made it possible for me and Mr. Robinson to get an opportunity to play baseball.

After I had been with Cleveland for four or five years and had been successful, I started feeling that I had made it. I don't mean that I felt free to do whatever I wanted or free to challenge another player, because that was a no-no, but I knew that I could play. Then the important thing was to try and play as long as I could and remain the kind of person that I was in the beginning. I still couldn't challenge anyone over name-calling or spitting on me or any of that sort of stuff. From a playing standpoint I knew that I had arrived, but in terms of being a fully and naturally accepted part of the club, I knew that I wasn't there. We hadn't gotten that far.

When people say that baseball is the all-American game, it is true. But baseball started to be an all-American game only in 1947. It wasn't true until then and the two people that made it possible were Mr. Branch Rickey and Mr. Bill Veeck.

I'm not interested in the negative things that happened forty years ago. My interest is in working toward seeing that an equal situation is available. I think that athletes can be a great example for those people who might have other thoughts about

minorities. We need to come together as a group of people and as a country, and everybody has to be involved.

Just because I don't live in a ghetto does not mean I shouldn't try to help. I feel that every player should go back into the community that he came out of and give some suggestions or ideas. Go back into the community from the standpoint of having been successful. The success has not been easy, but by the same token I can tell kids today that the opportunity may be easier now than it was for us in 1947. In 1947 and 1948 there were a lot of players who were capable of playing major league baseball, but there just weren't going to be a lot of black players on the ball teams in that particular era. Now you can have five or six black ballplayers on the same team if they have the ability. These kids have to be told as well that they have to work to get to that point. They can't expect somebody to come along and give them something just because their parents were denied the opportunity.

When young kids today don't know black history I tell them it is their responsibility to find out. They should know and nobody will stop them from finding out. There is no slavery anymore, you don't get whipped if you're caught reading a book. So if the kids don't know who these people in history were, then they are to blame. They *can* find out.

When I think of big moments in my baseball career, I'd say signing the contract was naturally a very big moment, but being part of the 1948 World Series and winning it was the biggest. I hit a home run to win the fourth game and we beat Boston, 2–1. The most important thing about that particular game and that particular situation was the pitcher, Steve Gromek. When the last out had been made and the game was over he ran up and we embraced each other. I think it might have been the first time that a picture like that—a white man embracing a black man—went all over the country.

Steve later told me that he came from a little town called Hamtramck, Michigan, and he said that when he went home a lot of people asked, "Why did you hug the black guy?" and he said, "Well, because he won a game for me and we won a pennant and that's why." I think that picture represents one of the finest moments in my life. I have that picture and I always look at it. I wish we all could embrace each other to that point.

SID HUDSON

Sid Hudson pitched from 1940 to 1954 for the Washington Senators and Boston Red Sox. Hudson was an All-Star in 1941 and 1942. He continued to work in baseball after his playing career ended as a pitching instructor, coach, and scout.

I WAS BORN IN a little town in the eastern Tennessee hills called Coalfield. I lived there until I was eight years old and my father passed away. Then we moved to Chattanooga.

All I ever thought about was playing ball and I wanted to be a major league ballplayer. I used to dream about it every night. When I was really little living in Coalfield, we didn't have little league ball, so we played catch. We started out really early. I read all I could about baseball after I grew up a little, and from the time I was ten years old right on through to when I played American Legion ball, that's all I ever thought about doing.

I was one of those kids who came home only to eat. I was away all day playing ball, and sometimes missed lunch. I didn't even want to eat—I just wanted to play ball. I'm sure you've heard that very same story from a lot of ballplayers, but it was true.

There were eight of us, five boys and three girls. We learned to play bare-handed as soon as we could. We'd play burnout with each other. We'd try and see how hard we could throw the ball so that the other guy had to drop it out of pain. We had such a big family that we had almost a full team right in our own house. There was always someone to play catch with and that made a big difference.

355

When I was a kid, there was a certain point when I knew that if I got the chance I could make it. I had a good arm, and I was a fairly good hitter for a pitcher. My only problem was that I didn't run very fast. But I thought I might never get the chance. Back then there weren't too many scouts around, and if they don't see you they can't sign you.

I didn't play high school ball, but I played American Legion and sandlot. The scouts found out about me because a friend of mine recommended me to Joe Ingalls, who was the president of the Chattanooga baseball team. He said I could go to spring training with them the next year and before that could even happen I got a call from a team in Sanford, Florida. The manager was a fellow who lived in Cleveland, Tennessee, and he wanted me to come down to Sanford in the Florida State League and play for them.

I was a first baseman at that time. Or at least I thought I was. I went down there and played first base for a while and then they changed managers. The new manager brought in a new first baseman. Then I was on the bench in Class D.

One night we were getting beat in the eighth inning and the manager said to me, "You have a good arm, did you ever pitch?" I said, "Yes," and he said, "Go out there and see what you can do." I struck out the side in both innings and from then on I pitched.

When I played in Sanford, I lived with a man and his wife and they had a couple of children. I got a room in their house and a bath for $2.50 a week. I ate at a boardinghouse, lunch and dinner every day, for 25 cents a meal. We never stayed overnight when we played away games, because the cities were close together. When we'd go on the road, we'd get 35 cents a meal from the team and if we added 15 cents to that money we could get a steak. But we could get all the chicken we wanted for the 35 cents. I was making $100 a month my first year and the next year I got $150.

Sanford was an independent team, like a lot of them were back then. I was 24 and 4 my second year, and then I was sold to the Washington Senators. I signed my first big league contract for two hundred dollars a month. I got a little raise or two and I ended up making three thousand dollars the first year and six thousand the second.

It was 1940 when I arrived in Washington and I was with the Senators until 1952, aside from three years in the service. When I first walked into the Washington clubhouse, it was a wonderful feeling. It's hard to describe now, but it was just something that I had looked forward to growing up and I really got a thrill out of it.

I started my first season with Washington with two wins and nine losses. They called me into the office one day and I thought, "This is it, I'm going to Oshkosh or somewhere." Mr. Griffith and the manager, Bucky Harris, talked to me and said they thought that I could pitch there and they were going to leave it up to me. They said they were going to give me some more chances to start and that it was up to me to prove that I could pitch. I ended up winning six in a row after that, with two one-hitters. From then on, it seemed that I was established. They gave me the opportunity, and I took advantage of it.

My biggest thrill of all was just being a major league pitcher. I was on the All-Star team in 1941–42, but one of the biggest thrills I ever had was pitching against Lefty Grove. He was my idol as a kid and I went up against him one day in Washington. Of course he was forty years old at the time, but I beat him, 1–0, in thirteen innings.

I never will forget the first trip that we made to New York. We were staying in a hotel there and I checked in and walked out in front and looked at all of the tall buildings. Bucky Harris happened to be standing there and he said to me, "Don't get a crick in your neck looking at all of these tall buildings; you have to pitch here."

In my days as a youngster you could find a little kid playing ball on an empty lot most anywhere. You can't find that today. The only thing you might see is somebody throwing a football, but that's about it. But back then it was all baseball. I can't put my finger on why things have changed. You'd think that kids would be more interested than ever because of all of the money that players make today.

We were probably stronger overall as kids because we walked or rode our bikes everywhere we went. We didn't have an automobile and we didn't have a television to spend the whole day in front of, so we were outside all of the time. I used to take a broomstick and get a pile of small rocks and pitch 'em up and hit 'em. That was how I learned to make contact. I used to skip rocks across the creek and see how far I could throw one; that's the way we all developed our arms. The kids today, it seems, have never heard of anything like that. They've got Nintendo games instead, so they stay in the house. I guess they get strong fingers and thumbs from pressing those buttons all day.

Del Wilber and I went through the league in our last year in Boston and after the last game in each city we'd stop and look around the stadium and say, "Well, I guess this is it. We must say good-bye to this one." We used to talk about what we were going to do then, after it was all over. Really and truly we didn't know what we were going to do. There was no security and we both had families.

On the day I was released from Boston, Joe Cronin took me up into the bleachers and offered me a job scouting for them. I said, "Well, maybe this is it. I'll try it." You might say it was a whole new ball game.

YOGI BERRA

Yogi Berra, born Lawrence Berra, played from 1946 to 1963 for the
Yankees and Mets. He was voted Most Valuable Player in 1951, 1954,
and 1955 and was an All-Star from 1948 to 1962. Berra was inducted
into the Hall of Fame in 1972.

I GREW UP IN an Italian neighborhood in St. Louis called the
Hill and we were playing sports all of the time. We played
soccer, softball, and baseball. We played a lot of them just in
the street. Growing up in my neighborhood was no different
than in any other neighborhood until I found out that everything we did outside of being with the other guys and going
to school we did in Italian. When we went to the store or our
mothers went to the store, we all spoke Italian. When we went
to church the mass was in Italian. I grew up in a big family, I
had three brothers and one sister and my father worked with
Joe Garagiola's father.

They picked our fathers up in a truck and they brought 'em
back in a truck and we knew that when the 4:30 whistle blew
we had a job to do. That was to stop whatever we were doing,
go inside and get the pail, and head up to Fassi's so that when
Pop came home he would have the beer on the table.

We played on the streets because there weren't that many
cars. I think we only had two cars on the whole block. We
would play games like Indian ball, which was a form of softball. We even played touch football on the street and I used to
switch sides because I could kick the ball straight and I could
kick it pretty far. We never lost our football unless it went into
old man Fahrenkamp's yard—he was the "alien" on the block

The St. Louis Stags, with Joe Garagiola *(front row, first on left)* and Yogi Berra *(middle row, third from left)*

because he wasn't Italian. He had his front yard fenced in and he had this dog in there, so if the football landed there we'd have a tough time getting it out.

My brothers all played ball. My brother Lefty was the best one of all. I think he was a better ballplayer than I was, and anyone who doesn't believe that should ask Joe Garagiola. Lefty couldn't play because my dad wouldn't let him; he needed him to go to work. In fact all three of my other brothers could have gone and played. They were that good, but instead, they gave me the chance to go and play because they were all working. That's why my dad let me go.

Lefty was the hero to most of the guys and especially to me because he was such a good hitter. It was hard to explain to our father what a baseball player was because he had come from the Old Country and had a strong work ethic. It was hard to convince him that playing baseball was a profession or a job because we always said that we went out to *play*. So Lefty didn't get to play.

But Lefty made sure that *I* would get a chance to play. When it came time to play in the city league and American Legion, he was the one who'd sign the releases so that in case I got hurt I couldn't sue. How were we going to sue anybody anyhow? But the city and those people wanted to make sure that they weren't liable, so Lefty signed for me. How could I even explain that to my father? And it was Lefty who convinced my father to let me go out and play professional baseball and sign a contract.

I played American Legion ball and I played for the Stockham Post team. It was that Stockham Post team, I think, that really got the professionals, the big leagues, interested in me.

When Joe signed his contract and he told me that he got five hundred dollars, that's what I wanted. But the Cardinals didn't offer me a contract. None of the guys could understand why because every time we would choose up sides as kids I was always the first one that they chose. When our neighborhood club, the Stags, didn't make it to the city championship, the eventual winner, the Edmonds' Restaurant team, was able to draft one player for the play-offs and championship and they drafted me. So I couldn't understand why the Cardinals didn't at least offer me a contract.

In the meantime, Johnny Schulte of the Yankees came over and offered me a contract with them, which I signed. But I couldn't get the five hundred dollars unless I made the team in Norfolk. I didn't get the bonus right away, but I did get it.

The man who sent Johnny Schulte over there, who deserves a lot of credit, was Leo Browne. Leo Browne was a dedicated man with American Legion baseball and he was the one who told Johnny Schulte to come sign me. On our team in

American Legion, we had guys like Jack Maguire who ended up going to the Giants and Bobby Hofman who also went to the Giants.

In fact, it was Bobby Hofman who gave me my name Yogi. In a movie we saw there was one of those Indian yogis, and when he got up to walk, Bobby thought he looked and walked like me. He began to call me Yogi and it stuck right away.

It was a long way from a St. Louis neighborhood to the New York Yankees and there were a lot of stops in between. I was seventeen years old. I hadn't gone to high school because I had been working too. My brother talked my parents into letting me go and it was a big change in my family to let one of us just go away.

I went to Norfolk, Virginia, my first year and then I went into the service when I turned eighteen years old. I was in the Navy for two and a half years. I played in New London, Connecticut, at the submarine base during the war and the manager was a former major leaguer named Jim Gleason. I was able to kind of repay him later for his help when I became the Yankee manager and I made him one of my coaches. I played there in New London all during the war.

I don't know how true this story is, but I once heard that Mel Ott went to see the Yankees and tried to make a trade. He said something about, "You got this kid in the Navy now, named Berra, and we'll take him." I think that's the first time the Yankees realized that I was even in their organization. If someone wanted to trade for me, then they figured they had better take a good look at me.

They didn't trade me and they knew then that I was in the organization. After the war I went to Newark and I had a good year there. I came up to the Yankees at the end of 1946 and I guess I did pretty well.

It was all new to me when I first came up. I looked around and I saw all of these great Yankee names. Joe DiMaggio was there, Charlie Keller, and Phil Rizzuto. There is a story that they tell about me. I guess Pete Sheehy, the Yankee clubhouse attendant, told it the best. He said that I asked Charlie Keller, "I'll bet you don't remember the first time that you met me," and Charlie said, "I sure do, you were standing in the doorway of the clubhouse, right over there, in a sailor suit." And I said back to him, "I'll bet you didn't think I was a ballplayer," and Pete Sheehy said, "I saw you and I didn't think you were a sailor!"

The Yankees made me feel at home even though it was such a different experience for me. I remember they kidded me about one time when I was standing in a hotel in the middle of New York City, the Hotel Edison. One of the writers saw me sitting in the lobby and he said, "What are you doing in here?" I told him, "Well, there ain't nothing to do in this city." I was just kind of nervous and homesick. Now I live in New Jersey and I have to laugh myself when I think about that.

When I was young we always played roller hockey, and our favorite hockey team was the St. Louis Flyers. When I was with the Yankees I went back to St. Louis one winter and I got to know Hec Pozzo, a St. Louis Flyer player, and I went with Hec to their workout. I put the skates on and was skating on the ice right with them. I even asked them to check me into the boards like the real guys. I was having all kinds of fun! I really liked that until the Yankees found out about it. They weren't too happy because I had just finished the World Series in 1947 and I was having fun by letting professional hockey players knock me into the second row of the stands.

Joe and I have talked a lot about whether or not our parents knew what it meant to be ballplayers. My brothers knew. I could tell by the way my parents acted that they were proud, but I don't think they really understood. Maybe when my father came for Yogi Berra day in Yankee Stadium, maybe he understood what a big thing it was. For him to walk into Yankee Stadium and see me honored, that made *me* feel good, but I still don't think he really understood how big a thing it was, which makes me kind of sad.

I don't like to make speeches and if it takes some people a sentence to say something, maybe it just takes me a word. Hitting coaches will say things like, "You have to have your arms here, your legs here," and this and that and the other thing. I remember when I struck out once and swung at a bad ball, Bucky Harris, my manager, said to me, "You have to think when you're up there." And I said, "You can't hit and think at the same time."

I think a lot of coaches should tell the hitters, "You've got to be ready to do the job in the batter's box, 'cause if you have to go up and be thinking in the batter's box, it's too late."

Instead of telling me that somebody throws a hundred miles an hour or ninety miles an hour, or he's got a good curveball, or he needs another pitch, or he's got a good move, all I want to know is—*can he play?* When I watch somebody I *know* if somebody can play.

As far as my best memories go, there's more than one. There's the night that they honored me at Yankee Stadium, the night they honored me in St. Louis, and the home run I hit in the 1956 World Series off of Newcombe. I was pinchhitting and that was the first time that ever happened. Of course the Most Valuable Player awards were a big deal too and so was the Hall of Fame. I wear my Hall of Fame ring very proudly, all of the time.

The deepest scar for me was when as a manager I was fired by the Yankees after the World Series in 1964. I took the club to the seventh game of the World Series with the tying run at second base. That's how close we came to winning it. Then I got fired; in fact, when they called me to Yankee Stadium, I thought that they were calling me to renew my contract.

I wasn't ever nervous about playing in the big leagues or playing with guys like DiMaggio. I just went out and played, or at least I tried to play. I was never aware of being famous or being a hero; I just did my job. I was just happy to play ball. I loved it. It beats working!